Many Struggles: New Histories of African and Caribbean People in Britain

Edited by
Hakim Adi

First published 2023 by Pluto Press
New Wing, Somerset House, Strand, London WC2R 1LA
and Pluto Press, Inc.
1930 Village Center Circle, 3-834, Las Vegas, NV 89134

www.plutobooks.com

British Library Cataloguing in Publication Data
A catalogue record for this book is available from the British Library

ISBN 978 0 7453 4765 3 Paperback
ISBN 978 0 7453 4767 7 PDF
ISBN 978 0 7453 4768 4 EPUB

This book is printed on paper suitable for recycling and made from fully managed and sustained forest sources. Logging, pulping and manufacturing processes are expected to conform to the environmental standards of the country of origin.

Typeset by Stanford DTP Services, Northampton, England

Simultaneously printed in the United Kingdom and United States of America

Contents

Introduction

Hakim Adi

The chapters in this book originated in the papers presented to the New Perspectives on the History of African and Caribbean People conference, organised by History Matters and held online in the midst of the pandemic in October 2021. The aim of the conference was to provide a showcase for young and emerging scholars in Britain, especially those of African and Caribbean heritage, and to present new perspectives and research relating to this important field of history.

The aims of the conference reflected those of History Matters, an initiative that brings together academic historians, teachers and students concerned to address the problem that so few young people of African and Caribbean heritage engage with history as a subject, especially at university level. History Matters was launched in 2014 at a time when for Black university students only agriculture and veterinary science were more unpopular subjects than history. Even today, although there is considerable interest in history at community level, there are still too few school history teachers, history students and historians of African and Caribbean heritage. History Matters held its first conference on 'Black British History' in 2017 and has since produced the regular *History Matters Journal*, a 'free and easily accessible digital resource', containing the latest research on the history of African and Caribbean people in Britain, the first edition of which appeared in the autumn of 2020.

Although there are still too few teachers, researchers and students of this history, it is also true to say that there has been an upsurge of interest in the subject in the last few years. The Black Lives Matter protests in the summer of 2020 highlighted a variety of ongoing concerns but one of the key demands articulated was the need to address the neglect throughout the education system of what was often referred to as 'Black History' and particularly 'Black British history'. This was connected with what many considered a reluctance by the powers-that-be to recognise the legacy of Britain's history of colonialism, the exploitation of people of African and Asian heritage in particular, the continuing legacy of that exploitation, the racism and Eurocentrism that still exists throughout society in the twenty-first century, as well as the economic and political system that exploitation created. In regard to the teaching of history in schools, one young woman from Sunderland complained to the *Guardian*: 'The curriculum is ridiculous. They just teach you that there was slavery for a little bit and it was really bad, then the slaves were freed and that was that, Martin Luther King did a speech and racism was over. It's only from reading black authors that I realised how much of my own history I was shielded from.' A young woman from Newmarket reflected on her own experience of history lessons, 'The only thing I was taught about black people in school was that we were slaves, which when you're 12 is very upsetting'. Another commented on the importance of history, 'It really helps people manifest and grasp their identity ... It shouldn't be a young person's task to have to learn these things themselves.'[1]

Such views have often given rise to demands to 'decolonise the curriculum', a phrase which has been variously interpreted but that generally recognised that too often history was taught and presented from 'a colonial perspective', that 'what we learn is the victor's story', and what is required is 'challenging the power structures that we live in'.[2] Some campaigners have even argued that the 'History National Curriculum systematically omits the contribution of Black British history in favour of a dominant White, Eurocentric curriculum, one that fails to reflect our multi-ethnic and broadly diverse society'. Although it must be borne in mind that in the twenty-first century with the emergence of academies, fewer schools are required to follow the National Curriculum.[3]

Such Eurocentrism has resulted in young people of African and Caribbean heritage being alienated from the history studied in schools and even universities. Many of them expressed their concerns at a special History Matters conference held in London in 2015, which led to the creation of Young Historians Project

(YHP), dedicated to encouraging young people of African and Caribbean heritage to discover and research history for themselves and to present it for their peers. One YHP member related her own experience:

> Before joining YHP, I associated studying History with thick textbooks with black and white photographs, boring essays and most importantly, a lack of representation. The YHP project I worked on was about the British Black power movement. This was of particular importance to me as I had only ever studied the Civil Rights Movement before and despite the importance of learning such a subject, it often used to make me feel like I did not have my own history, my own heroes and I longed for that ... The YHP was an experience that greatly differed from my course at University. It was an interactive and creative process of bringing History to life; for the first time in years, I felt a passion for History again ... The main skill I learned from the YHP was inquisitiveness. When approaching History, one must always be curious, it makes you ask the right questions to paint an accurate picture. I also learned the responsibility we have to document our history, to empower ourselves and to never forget the work we have inherited from our elders. All of these things reignited my passion for History and even though I was not always fortunate in having riveting Histories to study in my course.[4]

The YHP is one of the initiatives to emerge from the History Matters conference in 2015 and it is great to see that some of those young historians have continued their research and have been able to contribute to this volume. Another important initiative to emerge from the conference was the creation of the Masters by Research (MRes) Degree programme at the University of Chichester, which aims to train new historians, whether they be young or mature students. It has been particularly successful at encouraging and training students who are interested in researching the history of African and Caribbean people in Britain. Several of its graduates are contributors to this volume.

The University of Chichester is not the only university to specialise in this history. In recent years new courses, or academic posts, have also been established at Goldsmiths University and, after the events of 2020, also at the universities of Oxford, Cambridge, Edinburgh, Durham, Lincoln, Leeds and the Open University.[5] It is to be hoped that such initiatives will lead to many more researching and writing about this history in future years. Certainly, in the period since the 2017 History Matters conference many more post-graduate students of African and Caribbean heritage have begun to research this history and we are delighted to present their work in this volume.

The chapters in this volume focus on history after 1700, a period that many historians might consider constitutes the modern history of Britain. It is therefore interesting to reflect on those time periods most favoured by young and emerging researchers and presented here. We still have a distinct lack of research on the period before 1700 and, even though there have been some important findings relating to the medieval period, there is still much work to be done by historians and archaeologists.[6] Much work has already been undertaken on the eighteenth century but historians have not been so keen to examine the following century, when people of African and Caribbean heritage established important and permanent communities in such cities as London, Cardiff and Liverpool. A great deal of research has been carried out on the twentieth century and the chapters in this volume indicate that it continues to constitute a popular century for research. The 1960s–1970s, often seen as the Black Power era, appears to have become especially popular and several of the chapters included here cover aspects of this period. We still await much more research on the more than 40 years since the conclusion of the 1970s.

The eighteenth century was a time when the empire had already been established in North America and the Caribbean and when Britain became the world's most important human trafficker, transporting millions of Africans to its own colonies in the Americas, as well as to those of its economic rivals. It was therefore also a period when significant numbers of Africans were brought to or travelled to Britain. In the past much attention has been focused on significant African males, such as the abolitionists and writers Olaudah Equiano and Ottobah Cuguano, but Montaz Marché's chapter focuses our attention on Anne Sancho, a significant female figure, and one who was almost certainly born and raised in England, in Whitechapel, east London. Anne's life is presented here through the letters of her well-known husband, the London-based writer and grocer Ignatius Sancho. It may be that her professional life really began after his death when, together with her son, it seems likely that she became one of the first African booksellers and publishers. In the eighteenth century Africans were to be found not just in London but in many towns and cities in Britain, as is evident from the chapter by Annabelle Gilmore, which focuses on their presence in Warwickshire, and the chapter by Kate Bernstock, which focuses on Falmouth and Penryth in Cornwall. The most notable African resident of Cornwall in that period was undoubtedly Joseph Emidy, the violinist, music teacher and composer, but as Bernstock's chapter illustrates there were many other residents, women as well as men.

Britain's colonial relationship with Africa and the Caribbean, as well as the ubiquitous colour bar and the prevalence of various forms of racism provide the context for many of the chapters that focus on the twentieth century in this volume. Christian Høgsbjerg, Rey Bowen and Theo Williams all focus on some of the key British-based activists from Africa and the Caribbean in the period before World War II. Williams's chapter details the role played by female Pan-Africanists, such as Amy Ashwood Garvey, Una Marson and Constance Cummings-John, as well as the significant political relationships established by Black activists and white women in the period. Bowen examines the efforts of the government to monitor the political activities of Dusé Mohamed Ali, a radical journalist and editor of the *African Times and Orient Review*, during and just after World War I. Høgsbjerg details the activities of Algerine Sankoh, a Sierra Leonean Pan-Africanist, one of the founders of the Ethiopian Progressive Association and perhaps the first African to be connected with the revolutionary socialist movement in Britain. In this regard Sankoh was one of many Africans who would become radicalised by the time they spent in Britain and their connections with British political organisations.

The post-1945 period is introduced by A.S. Francis's chapter again reminding us that some British cities, such as Manchester, have had an African population for a very long time before the arrival of ships from the Caribbean in the late 1940s, and that some of the earliest 'Black communities' were comprised of African men and their British wives. The chapter is centred on three remarkable sisters, Kath Locke, Coca Clarke and Ada Phillips, whose father arrived in Britain from Nigeria in 1907, and details the numerous political organisations of which they were a part. Students from both Africa and the Caribbean have played a very crucial role in the political life of Britain, at least since the nineteenth century, if not before. Colonial rule did not generally provide higher education institutions in the colonies, meaning that would-be professionals were forced to study in Britain, as well as in the US and other places. Claudia Tomlinson's chapter highlights the key role played by Caribbean students during the 1950s and 1960s at a time when mass immigration from the Caribbean was also at its height. In particular, she analyses the role of the West Indian Students' Union and the West Indian Student Centre which became an important political and cultural hub in this period.

Women are also the focus of the chapter by Olive Wyatt, which chronicles their activities in Chapeltown, Leeds, during the 1970s, as well as in the chapter by Aleema Gray, that focuses on the influence of the Rastafari movement on 'the lives of everyday Black women' during the 1970s and 1980s. Studies on Rastafari in Britain have often placed great emphasis on Rasta men, an approach that Gray redresses in her research and writing. The emphasis on women throughout this volume reflects a growing concern for gender-sensitive research and a concern to research and present the lives and activities of women. We should expect to see much more research informed by these concerns in the future.

The chapters by Perry Blankson and Elanor Kramer-Taylor both concentrate on the Black Power era of the late 1960s and 1970s, when a plethora of new organisations and publications appeared not only in London but throughout the country. It was a time when new approaches to key political questions, especially those concerned with racism, were being developed in Britain. In presenting this era hitherto there has been much focus on the impact of events, organisations and individuals in the US, but the roots of 'Black Power' in Britain can often be traced to British antecedents as well as connections to Africa and the Caribbean. Blankson focuses on the efforts of the British state's security services to monitor the growing radicalism that developed amongst organisations and individuals in the period. Kramer-Taylor looks at the inter-connections between radical Black Power organisations and politics in Britain and the Caribbean during the same era. One of the organisations that certainly would have come under surveillance by the state's security services was the Black Parents' Movement (BPM) and its allied organisations that is the subject of Hannah Francis's chapter. She highlights the incidents of the state of racism that created the conditions for new organisations of resistance on the street and in the courts and details of the activities of some of the individual involved such as the London-based activists John La Rose and Albertina Sylvester and, in Manchester, Gus John and the Manchester Black Women's Cooperative.

The two final chapters highlight the various sources historians use to present their work. Rebecca Adams details the life of Molly Hunte, an education activists and psychologist, from the standpoint of an archivist, at the same time explaining the importance of the archive for preserving everyday life histories, not just those of celebrated figures. Her chapter demonstrates that the archive should be and must be a place that we can all find accessible and useful. Last, we have a chapter of reminiscences, memoirs from three key activists from the 1970s, Zainab Abbas, Tony Soares and Ansel Wong. Soares has become an almost legendary figure, one of the founders of the Black Liberation Front (BLF), who was imprisoned for his activities, he rarely grants interviews. Abbas and Wong were also early members of the BLF and, as the chapter makes clear, have also much to relate. Abbas for example, was one of the original members of what became known as the Brixton Black Women's Group. Here they give us their own accounts of activism that began more than half a century ago.

NOTES

1. www.theguardian.com/uk-news/2020/jul/30/history-young-black-britons-race-schools-policing (accessed 15 March 2021).
2. www.bbc.co.uk/bitesize/articles/z7g66v4 (accessed 15 March 2021).
3. https://theblackcurriculum.com/report (accessed 15 March 2021).

4. www.younghistoriansproject.org/single-post/2020/05/04/how-yhp-changed-my-relationship-with-my-degree (accessed 15 March 2021).
5. K. John, 'Black History Matters: Then and Now', *History Matters Journal*, 2/1 (Autumn 2021), pp. 75–8.
6. R. Redfern and J. Hefner, '"Officially Absent But Actually Present": Bioarchaeological Evidence for Population Diversity in London during the Black Death, AD 1348–50', in M. Mant and A. Holland (eds), *Bioarchaeology of Marginalised Peoples* (Cambridge: Academic Press, 2019), pp. 69–114.

1
'A Diamond in the Dirt': The Experiences of Anne Sancho in Eighteenth-Century London

Montaz Marché

Ignatius Sancho was an exceptional Black Briton. He was the first African Briton to vote in Parliament, or have an obituary published in the British press and his life and letters testify to Black presence, voice and agency in eighteenth-century Britain. Anne Sancho was married to Ignatius Sancho for 22 years and still, her life and actions are continually underrepresented despite her life being closely intertwined with her husband's. Her presence in the *Letters* offers a rare glimpse into the experiences of a Black middling-class woman in eighteenth-century London, examining themes such as motherhood, pregnancy and marriage, in a source which engages with the Black perspective and experience. By revisiting the *Letters of the Late Ignatius Sancho, an African* I consider the politics of class, race and gender by examining some key elements of Anne's life and representation as they allude to the experience of Black middling-class womanhood.[1]

I draw upon a sample of 158 letters by Ignatius Sancho, published within the first and second volumes of the *Letters of the Late Ignatius Sancho, an African.* This sample utilises the five editions of the *Letters* between 1782 and 1803 alongside modern editions of the *Letters* by Edwards/Newt and Carretta. The sample examines letters dated between 1768 and 1780 and pertains to the letters written by Ignatius to members of his social circle. I chose to focus on these 158 published letters to highlight the known but undervalued commentary on Anne's life present in Ignatius' letters, which has been in the peripheral consciousness of research into the Sanchos since the *Letters*' first publication. However, I precede this analysis by stating that this research refers to references of Anne within this sample of letters and is not a conclusive examination of her life in the historical records.

Anne Sancho née Osborne was born in 1733. The exact location of her birth is unknown, however, in the same year as her birth, she was baptised in St Mary's Church, Whitechapel, on 26 September 1733. As her baptism was in the same year as her birth, it is highly likely that Anne was born in England, in the London area. Her sister, Mary, and brother, John, were all baptised in the same parish in 1735 and 1743, respectively. The familial links to the St Mary's Whitechapel parish indicate that the Osborne family settled in this parish. Anne married Charles Ignatius Sancho in St Margaret's Church, Westminster, on 17 December 1758. St Margaret's Church also holds the baptism records of their eight children: Mary Ann (1759–1805), Frances (Fanny) Joanna (1761–1815), Ann Alice (1763–1766), Elizabeth (Betsy) Bruce (1766–1837), Johnathan William (1768–1770), Lydia (1771–1776), Catherine (Kitty) Margaret (1773–1779) and William (Billy) Leach Osborne (1775–1810).[2] Her husband, Ignatius, died on 14 December 1780 of complications from gout and his letters were published in 1782, where Anne received £500 from 1,200 subscribers, alongside a fee from the booksellers. Recently, Kate Moffatt continued research into Anne's life after Ignatius' death and uncovered a source which lists Anne working alongside her son, William, as a bookseller a few years after Ignatius' death.[3] She died on 25 November 1817, aged 84 and was buried with her husband.

Details of Anne's life are now known thanks to the research of scholars like Paul Edwards, Polly Newt and Vincent Carretta.[4] Yet the consciousness of Anne's presence and involvement in Ignatius' life retains a mythic ambivalence. Firstly, what was known of Anne before this research and what is known outside of this research presently assumes an origin story given to many 'unknown' Black women in this century. Historiographically, Black women born and recorded in British eighteenth-century parish records are often overlooked in Black women's history. The origin histories for Black women in eighteenth-century Britain are instead framed around themes of Black Atlantic migration and employment. Indeed, as Safia Mirza writes 'to be black and British is to be unnamed in official discourse'.[5] Here, the concept of a native or indigenous Black woman or woman of African heritage in Britain is a non-entity.

Still, despite her baptism in the Whitechapel records, Anne is said to be a migrant from the West Indies. Scholars describe Anne as 'a black woman born in the Caribbean in 1733' or as a 'West Indian' woman, with little consideration for her baptism in Whitechapel or the absent evidence of her family's ethnic background.[6] These impressions of Anne's life parallel the historiographic assumptions made about other Black women in the period. For example, until recent research by Joanna Major challenged this perception, it was believed that Dido Elizabeth Belle was not born in London but in the British West Indies. Indeed, Maria Belle, Dido's mother, was pregnant during her time on the *Bien Amie* when it sailed into the Downs in May 1761, meaning that Maria was in Britain when she gave birth to Dido in May 1761.[7]

Nevertheless, Anne is referenced 117 times in 77 of the 158 published letters written by Ignatius. Throughout these letters, Ignatius refers to Anne by different names. Predominantly, Ignatius refers to his wife as 'Mrs Sancho' but he also refers to her as 'Dame Sancho', 'wife', his 'spouse', 'the old duchess' and Anne. Predominantly, Anne is mentioned obliquely, in quick statements of her wellbeing or statements which pass on her sentiments to Sancho's friends. Anne was rarely central to the *Letters*' conversations, thereby leaving her as a conscious presence, adjacent to the social relationships between Ignatius and the recipients. Yet details of her character are drawn from the few larger comments about her. These larger comments are integrated sporadically within the sample letters and extend beyond statements of her wellbeing or sentimental greetings. I have divided the types of references to Anne within the *Letters* into three categories. The first is recorded actions: where Ignatius comments upon something Anne has done, said or wishes to express. For example, in a letter to Mrs H--, Ignatius writes 'Mrs. Sancho is in the straw' or 'Mrs. Sancho re-joices to hear you are well – and intrusts me to send you her best wishes'.[8] There are approximately 65 instances of Anne's recorded actions.

The second type of reference to Anne are observations of Anne made by Ignatius; where Ignatius records the behaviours and sentiments of Anne without direct reference to any specific action that Anne is performing. For example, when saying to Miss Leach 'Mrs. Sancho is but indifferent – the hot weather does not befriend her ....'[9] There are approximately 47 of these observations. Finally, the third category is signatures: where Ignatius includes Anne's name in the signature of the letter. For example, where Ignatius signs letter XXXII, 'Anne and I Sancho'.[10] There are approximately five of these signatures in the published letters. Each category of reference draws Anne into the conversation/commentary as Sancho's wife and signifies how the Sanchos operated as a marital unit. Moreover, these recorded instances echo the records of Black women in Britain in this period; succinct, sporadic and selective, acknowledging moments in their lives deemed noteworthy. Nevertheless, the consequence of each reference, when collated and analysed, is a closer insight into Anne's experiences and character.

But I must first acknowledge some of the limitations of using the *Letters* as historical material. Firstly, our perception of Anne is presented by third-person commentators rather than Anne herself. All 158 letters are written by her husband, Ignatius, and are the most comprehensive materials on Anne in known records. Additionally, there are no known sources written by Anne. In this absence of voice, Anne falls into the category of dispossessed Black women, whose voices (but not necessarily agency) are left to the 'power and authority of the archive and the limits its sets on what can be known, whose perspective matters and who is endowed with the gravity and authority of historical actor'.[11] In this case, Ignatius as a man, husband and narrative lens, is this historical actor, and, predominantly, his viewpoint shapes our understanding of Anne's life, revealing but possibly concealing much about her. Also, a secondary gaze in the *Letters* is the editor, Frances Crewe-Philips, who openly expressed her desire to show that 'an untutored African may possess abilities equal to a European' alluding to her biased selection process.[12] Furthermore, despite claiming to have published only letters sent to recipients, Crewe-Philips undermines her selectivity by including unsent copies of letters to William Stevenson and Julius Soubise proving that the volumes were not merely collections of sent letters printed and bound.

Secondly, I also consider the performative tendencies of letter writing as a culture in the eighteenth century. I can only speculate on any personal alterations to Anne's character made by Ignatius and/or Crewe-Philips in the *Letters*. However, it is likely that, in the *Letters*, representations are influenced by letter writing cultures where personal identities were constructed and represented 'how writers imagine themselves, often in ideal terms and how writers think others see them'. Ignatius utilises the letter writing culture of creating identity to emphasise his 'boundaries of status, education and race' and his 'enthusiasm for, and ambition within, the cultural elite of London society'.[13] Arguably, a broad social and cultural parallel is the racially specific experience of W.E.B. Du Bois' 'double consciousness'. Ignatius would have 'this sense of always looking at oneself through the eyes of others' and be responsible for merging 'his double self into a better and truer self' as a testament to the abilities of the 'untutored African'.[14] These alterations to perceptions of Ignatius' self could equally result in Anne's representation being altered to create a conforming image of Black middling identity.

Our knowledge of Anne's actions and character are a consequence of these perspective gazes. However, these materials are still significant in conceptualising images of Anne as a historical agent. The challenge of viewing Anne, through brief, third-person sources, is the same challenge we face viewing many Black women's histories in this period. An absence of priority and focus on Black women both contemporarily and historiographically often leaves Black women's histories underrepresented in the historical conversation. Nevertheless, I draw out these histories, by recognising that each third-person source is comprised of the real actions or presence of a Black woman. Then, I isolate individual moments of Black women's agency and examine the social, political, cultural and personal circumstances that encouraged these actions and the likely results of them.[15] Using this methodological approach, I formulate a composite image of Black womanhood through a variety of themes and highlight the potential of illuminating Black women's histories in Britain.

Anne Sancho was a woman of the middling sort, a diverse social collective that, within a triadic class system, is the middle group between the aristocracy/gentry who made up 2–3 per cent of society and the working classes who made up 60 per cent. Ignatius' socio-economic position ranked within, what Davidoff and Hall distinguish as, the lower ranks of the middling sorts, because Ignatius, by 1773, operated a 'single person enterprise' (a grocer's shop), after his employment with the Duke of Montagu, 'lived in the city centre with a local social circle'. [16] As a woman of polite society, Anne would likely coordinate the household management and child rearing, while participating in social visiting cultures and in social/leisure events such as attending the Pleasure Gardens in Vauxhall.[17]

MARRIAGE

Significantly, the *Letters* provide a glimpse into the last twelve years of the Sancho marriage. Undeniably, marriage shaped the lives of Anne and Ignatius. The implication of marriage demonstrated emotional, physical and economic maturity in both Anne and Ignatius. Though the precise steps of Anne's social mobility in marrying Ignatius are unclear due to Anne's unconfirmed social standing before her marriage, for both Anne and Ignatius, 'depending upon sex', there was some discernible increase in 'wealth, status and participation in civic and social duties and rights'. For example, Anne as a wife had a 'recognised station' that we see her benefit from, receiving £500 from subscribers to Ignatius' letters. Represented often within their family home in 19 Charles Street, Westminster, Anne, as a wife, consolidated an image of an ordered middle-standing family home. Ignatius was the established domestic authority and gentleman, as a husband, father and householder. Anne, as the married housewife, was 'a pillar of wisdom and worth, with a prominent position in the hierarchical institution that society recognised as both normal and fundamental to social order, the male headed conjugal unit'.[18] As a wife, she was granted authority over the household and family and through her station, navigated and developed social relationships in society, because of and independently of Ignatius.[19] As a Black woman, her marriage exposed Anne to a level of presence uncommon for Black women within historical/literary records and provides a narrative of a Black woman's settlement and actions as a wife and mother in eighteenth-century middling society.

The language of Anne's observations and recorded actions in the *Letters* characterise elements of Anne's marital roles and the marriage's dynamics; namely, how Anne, though subject to her husband, exercised both her expected duties as a wife and independently participated in cultures of middling womanhood. Many of her recorded actions demonstrate her functionality in the household, primarily as a mother but also working within the household. Ignatius records how Anne 'read' two papers he gave her 'though it broke in upon her work' and comments on how 'the marks of the fold of Mrs Sancho's apron [were] still visible' when waiting for a guest to arrive at their home.[20] Ignatius comments on how Anne balanced household work and, on occasion, working in the shop stating, 'Mrs. Sancho has had a blessed week of it ... – it was the washing-week ... – She was forced to break sugar and attend shop.'[21] Assisting their husbands was a 'well established route' for middling wives into business enterprises.[22] Her work also likely involved household maintenance and management.

The *Letters* also offer glimpses into Anne's participation in the activities and social cultures of middling-class wives. For example, Anne coordinated and attended social visits: 'we had a good and social dinner, and Mrs. Sancho forced me to stay – for supper' and organised gifts for friends, 'Mrs Sancho would send some tamarinds 'using Ignatius as a vessel of communication.'[23] As well as visiting, Anne engaged in cultures of reading; 'Mrs. Sancho, who reads, weeps, and wonders ...' proving her literacy.[24] The letters allude to her hostess role, 'On Sunday evening we expected him – the hearth was swept – the kettle boiled – the girls were in print – and the marks of the fold of Mrs Sancho's apron still visible.'[25] Furthermore, Ignatius' observations characterise Anne as a woman of emotion, for example, Ignatius writes 'Mrs Sancho says little – but her moistened eye expresses – that she feels your friendship.'[26] These observations and actions, when gathered, humanise Anne within the image of their marital unit and frame her feminine, maternal and familial identity.

Ignatius refers to Anne as his possession when saying 'the only intrinsic nett worth, in my possession, is Mrs. Sancho – who I can compare to nothing so properly as to a diamond in the dirt –'. This statement of martial ownership demonstrates the Sancho marriage's power dynamics and how 'wives were subject to their husband's authority' but still characterising the way Anne and Ignatius were 'equal souls in the marriage … bedfellows and domestic allies'.[27] Ignatius demonstrates marital power dynamics when writing 'Nature never formed a tenderer heart … – the mother-wife-friend, she does credit to her sex.'[28] As the observer and writer, Ignatius claims authority of the text and Anne, by controlling her construction and emphasising her primary positions as a woman. However, the emphasis upon 'friendship' indicates their various forms of interaction and the complex emotions within their marital relationship. Earlier quotes from Letter LI demonstrate his dependence upon her, as his partner in both marriage and business 'She was forced to break sugar and attend shop', working in the shop when Ignatius was taken up with illness. She possesses authority in the household, 'Just upon the stroke of eleven – as I was following (like a good husband) Mrs. Sancho to bed.'[29] On many occasions, Anne inserts her sentiments into letters, extending wishes to friends: 'Mrs Sancho begs me to express her sense of your kindness ….'[30] But Anne is shown to be a woman of her own convictions, for example, disagreeing with Ignatius: 'Mrs Sancho joins me in everything but the abuse of Mr Wingrave', demonstrating that, despite their marital union, within the confines of this personal dialogue within a once private letter, she does not simply assume her husband's position/opinions.[31] The *Letters* also characterise a mutual dependence, 'Dame Sancho would be better if she cared less. – I am her barometer – if a sigh escapes me, it is answered by a tear in her eye ….'[32] Still, within the space of 'home' (theirs or another's) Anne is presented with the authority to control the actions and movements of Ignatius and the family.

By eighteenth-century social standards, Anne is presented in the *Letters* as the ideal wife, dutiful and obedient, performing the roles as mother and household manager, in conjunction with Ignatius as the patriarch. They operate happily in 'the great duty between the man and his wife … to consist in that of love … government of affection, the obedience of a complaisant, kind, obliging temper ….'[33] The effective operation of their marital unit is emphasised first by Anne being the primary object of Ignatius' affection. Ignatius, for example, describes Anne as the 'best of women', 'the chief ingredient of my felicity'.[34] Adoration and affection are the result of demarcated and apposite marital roles. Furthermore, Anne is glorified for the marital position. Ignatius asks God to 'bless and reward her! She is good – good in heart – good in principle – good by habit – good by heaven.'[35]

Still, as historians emphasise, these idealisms were not representative of how women acted in real life. Therefore, we must also consider the significance of presenting Anne as the ideal glorified wife. The Sancho household is represented idealistically in three ways: Ignatius as a man of letters and feeling, an idyllic companionate marriage between Anne and Ignatius, and a firm family hierarchy. Ignatius' house was firmly in order. It is credible that this idealistic family is the construction of Ignatius as an alteration of identity to appear more aligned with eighteenth-century middling cultures. Indeed, as both the subject, writer and observer, Ignatius could alter Anne's representation for more idealistic favourability.

Yet, it is also plausible that Anne either consciously or unconsciously tailored her actions to suit idealistic expectations of married women within her everyday life, or, for the purposes of publication, promoting or emulating actions to highlight her possession of idealistic womanly characteristics. Hill writes that 'it would have been difficult if not impossible for a woman of the middle class who could read to remain ignorant of the model to which she was expected to aspire'.[36] As a middling literate woman, raised in eighteenth-century London, Anne would not be ignorant of the feminine ideals. We can further assume that from this awareness, she may have also adopted characteristics for the sake of maintaining the position of herself and family. Either way, Anne not only physically undertook many of the actions described in the *Letters*, particularly pregnancy, childbirth and social interaction but also could have contributed to her representation within the *Letters*.

MOTHERHOOD

Extending her martial role, the *Letters* speak to Anne's experiences of pregnancy, childbirth, motherhood and child loss. Firstly, Ignatius situates Anne's position as a mother by, in some cases, addressing her welfare together with the children's welfare. For example, in 1769 stating that 'Dame Sancho will be much obliged to you for your kind mention – she and the brats are very well thank you' and then later in 1779 'The best of women – the girls – the boy – all well.'[37] These references relay the intimacy of the Sanchos as a nuclear family exclusively of his wife and children rather than the broader definitions of family which applied to seventeenth- and eighteenth-century households, including 'everyone who lived under the same household' including servants, apprentices etc.[38] This behaviour and focus aligns with the 'facet amongst the educated middling-class of increasing separation of domestic intimacy from the worlds outside of the home'.[39]

References to Anne and the children over time demonstrate her role in the creation of family and the family identity, exhibiting moments of pregnancy, birth, development and death. During the writing of the *Letters*, Anne and Ignatius had their last four children: Johnathan, Lydia, Kitty (Catherine) and Billy (William). Yet the most significant observation of Anne's experience of pregnancy is with her last child William, where she was said to have been unwell throughout the pregnancy. In a 1775 letter, Ignatius wrote that 'Mrs Sancho smiles in the pains which it has pleased providence to try her with', illuminating the abnormal pain of pregnancy. Rather than a direct reference to pregnancy, Ignatius observes discomfort and possible symptoms of pregnancy in Anne's emotional state. For example, in a letter before William's birth, Ignatius writes 'Mrs Sancho is so so – not so alert as I have known her', perhaps alluding to memory impairment as a symptom of pregnancy. Anne personifies the biological experience of pregnancy, through Ignatius' pen. The absence of Anne's other pregnancies could be linked with Anne's seasoned experiences of pregnancy and childbirth, having had seven children before William's birth. It was common for married women to be pregnant at least six times in their lifetime, but for Anne and many women, 'the experience of pregnancy differed from woman-to-woman and … from pregnancy to pregnancy'.[40]

Across the *Letters*, there are two references to childbirth. First, in a 1773 letter, Ignatius refers to the birth of Kitty; 'Mrs Sancho is in the straw – she has given me a fifth wench.' Then in 1775, Ignatius details William's birth; 'ever dear Dame Sancho was exactly at half past one, this afternoon, delivered of a – child'. The language highlights the emphasis placed on the gender of the babies with the son referred to as 'child' and the daughter, 'wench'. Ignatius further hints to the dangers of childbirth for Anne, when saying 'God grant safety and health to the mother.' Many women died during childbirth in this period. Anne, as the carrier of the child, was likely aware of this danger and confronted it emotionally and psychologically.[41]

Ignatius describes Anne's many transitions into motherhood. But the intersection of race, class and gender impose a unique challenge of identity upon the experience of childbearing. It is the conventional belief in eighteenth-century Britain that a child born within the confines of a marital unit assumes their father's name and social standing. By this standard, Ignatius would transfer upon each child his lower middling status as Black 'man of feeling'. Yet, threaded within colonial beliefs of Black mothers was the idea that with each birth, it was Black women who 'reproduce[d] the boundaries of the symbolic identity of their group'; they would pass on their own social identity/status onto their child.[42] As Ignatius' wife, Anne would pass on a middling status to each child. However, the automatic transposition of middling status from married middling parents to children should not be taken for granted. Within eighteenth-century society, Black people, particularly Black women, had many social identities; several were of a lower status.[43] Moreover, Jerry White argues that 'almost all black Londoners of African origin had, like Sancho, been captured or born as slaves'.[44] This enslaved status was not the case for most in the Sancho family, but, as stated earlier, enslaved/low status could and likely was assumed as part of a Black person's identity. These assumptions were contended with during the eighteenth century and in the present-day commentary of the eighteenth century. I even address earlier the assumed migrant status of Anne herself.

It could, therefore, be assumed that, by others, each or all the children were not of middling class but instead were one of the various other identities Black people possessed. Thus, it became important to distinguish each child both as a native Briton and as a child of middling standing and this was achieved through the *Letters'* commentary of each child's development and education.

Published references to the children's activities testify to their nurturing and education which Anne likely played a role within. Ignatius suggests Anne's nurturing parental presence after mentioning Billy's painful teething process, 'I have just wished him joy by his mother's desire, who says he took resolution at last, and walked to her some few steps quite alone.'[45] Ignatius also provides updates on his children's development to different friends; 'Billy loves flesh – Kitty is a termagant – Betsy talks as usual – The Fanny's work pretty hard' and later that year 'The children are all well. William grows … and Fanny goes on well in her tambour work.'[46] Each comment on his children's development, when collated and examined over time, track and publicise the growth of the Sancho children, in health and education, learning new skills such as playing the tambour or undertaking 'work'. Their represented skills, particularly Anne's daughters who were the oldest during the time of writing, met the educational standards of a middling woman. Indeed, 'French, dancing, music, drawing … were the ornamental accomplishment which provided the core of the education of most girls in the middle classes … along with reading, writing and elementary arithmetic'.[47] Elizabeth, Fanny and Mary all account for the learning of, at least, music and literacy. Moreover, little reference is made to tutors, nurses or assistance in the children's development, therefore, I argue that within her household/childbearing responsibilities, Anne would have likely contributed to the education of the children to a middling-class standard, with possible supplementary education given to the children with parish, charity or boarding schools, as these were common spaces of young female education during this period.[48]

Finally, the common but tragic end to this cultural and biological journey of Anne's childbearing experience is child loss. The eighteenth century saw a high infant mortality rate.[49] Paralleling this, Anne outlived all her children except one, Elizabeth, who died in

1837. Between 1768 and 1780, Johnathan, Lydia and Kitty died. Upon the death of a child, there is a small gap or mourning within the *Letters*. However, Letter XXI highlights a moment of shared grief at Kitty's death in 1779. Ignatius wrote, 'I give you due credit for your sympathising feelings on our recent very distressful situation – for thirty nights (save two) Mrs Sancho had no cloaths off.'[50] In one observation, Anne evokes an 'acute mental or physical pain' within a mourning period.[51] This rare commentary can be reiterated seven times for the deaths of her seven children, with such observations of Anne illustrating the prolonged torment of child loss and the visible emotional toil, while testifying to her maternal nature and personifying her emotional experience of motherhood.

Between the authority of her husband and the dominion over her children, Anne completes the household hierarchy and presents a rare image of the Black family (father, mother and children together) in eighteenth-century London. Characteristically, Black people appeared in contemporary materials as individuals without family or network. Historians argue that Black women often appear as wives and mothers torn from their family or as the mistress/concubine/servant adjacent to a white man or white family.[52] But Anne's actions and Ignatius' observations illustrate a Black family unit that parallels the idealistic middling family. They were a nuclear family, built within a marriage union, contrasting to the various Black family structures across the Atlantic world.[53] The *Letters* offer portraits of the Sancho family 'with common resources, problems, and dreams' as is often seen in letter writing, attending social events as a family, suffering through bouts of illness and parents demonstrating desires and aspirations for children, for example, Fanny and Betsy's education or idealising William as an heir.[54] These images of the family unit validate perceptions of the Sanchos as 'a family of cultivated Africans, marked by elevated and refined feelings.'[55] Yet, a visit to the Pleasure Gardens where the family was 'looked upon – but not much abused' illuminates more cultural realities. Despite the Sanchos appearing as a conventional middling family, their racial identities would diversify their experiences. For example, attitudes to the family at the Pleasure Gardens highlight how 'black children cannot help but learn that black people and white people occupy different structural positions' and that the Sancho family would be viewed differently, though it is difficult to discern responses of racial prejudice from fascination at the rarity of seeing a Black family of middling rank.[56]

In conclusion, after examining Anne Sancho's recorded actions and observations in the *Letters*, superficially, Ann is presented as the ideal eighteenth-century middling-class wife and mother, sentimental, dutiful and proficient. However, representations of identity and family with the *Letters* capitalise upon the writer's ability to 'imagine themselves, often in ideal terms' within contemporary letter writing cultures. Eighteenth-century ideals of womanhood were not representative of reality. But behind the idealism, the *Letters*, as a historical publication, illustrate Anne's actions and emotional integrity. Anne, as a wife and mother, was a central figure of the household, an authority over home and children, whose presence galvanised a rare image of the eighteenth-century Black family. Anne worked within the household and shop, was a marital partner and domestic ally for Ignatius, an educator for her children, and developed social relationships. Moreover, the *Letters* illustrate Anne's emotional character, taking us through her physical and emotional journey of motherhood.

Significantly, this chapter does not speak to Anne's full life, for example, examining her as a woman of society, her work as a publisher after Ignatius' death or her life before marrying Ignatius. But, instead, it characterises the already public awareness of Anne that have been in the peripheral consciousness of eighteenth-century Black British history. Here we see Anne's life and character as a social parallel to other women of a middling standing and allow us to speculate on the likely processes of integration and assimilation Anne incurred as a Black woman in this social realm. Such examination of underrepresented women like Anne presents the diverse experiences of Black womanhood in eighteenth-century London society, forcing us to question assumptive histories and explore the spectrum of Black women's histories.

NOTES

1. This chapter stemmed from my PhD research at the University of Birmingham, looking at Black women's lives in eighteenth-century London.

My thesis is titled *Mapping the Dark and Feminine: The Population of Black Women in Eighteenth-Century London*. This research is funded by the Wolfson Foundation.

2. There has been a slight confusion about the number of Anne and Ignatius' children and the dates/names/timings of their births and deaths. The Sanchos have often been recorded as having seven children. They had eight children. Mary Ann was their first child and has often been confused with Ann Alice given the similarity of their names. Mary Ann Sancho was born on 17 September 1759 and baptised in St Margaret, Westminster, on 7 October 1759, recorded 'D[aughter] of Ignatius by Ann'. She died and was buried on 22 September 1805 in the same parish. Ann Alice was born on 21 August 1763 and baptised on 18 September 1763 with her parents listed as Char Ignatius and Ann. She died and was buried in St Margaret's parish on 27July 1766; St Mary Whitechapel baptism records Year 1733–1741; Year 1739–1756 London Metropolitan Archives; London, England; Reference Number: P93/MRY1/008; P93/MRY1/009; St Margaret Westminster, Baptisms Year 1750–769; Year 1769–1786 City of Westminster Library and Archives; London, England; Reference Number: SMW/PR/1/11-VOL 11; SMW/PR/1/12-VOL.12.
3. Kate Moffatt 'A Search for Firm Evidence: Ann Sancho, Bookseller', *The Women's Printing History Project*, 25 June 2020, https://womensprinthistoryproject.com/blog/post/20 (accessed 17 September 2021).
4. Notable works include William Armistead, *A Tribute to a Negro: Being a Vindication of the Moral, Intellectual, and Religious Capabilities of the Coloured Portion of Mankind; with Particular Reference to the African Race* (New York: W. Harned, 1848); Paul Edwards and Polly Newt, *Letters of the Late Ignatius Sancho* (Edinburgh: Edinburgh University Press, 1994); Vincent Carretta, *Letters of the Late Ignatius Sancho, an African* (Ontario: Broadview Editions, 2015); Reyahn King, *Ignatius Sancho; an African Man of Letters* (London: National Portrait Gallery Publications, 1997).
5. Heidi Safia Mirza, *Black British Feminism: A Reader* (London: Routledge,1997), p. 3.
6. Moffatt, 'A Search for Firm Evidence'; Jekyll quoted in Edwards and Newt, *Letters*, p. 3.
7. Quoted from Gretchen H. Grezina, 'The Georgian Life and Modern Afterlife of Dido Elizabeth Belle', in Gretchen H. Grezina (ed.), *Britain's Black Past* (Liverpool: Liverpool University Press, 2020), p. 164.
8. Carretta, *Letters*, Letter XV, p. 51 and Letter XIX, p. 154.
9. Ibid., Letter XX, p. 56.
10. Ibid., Letter XXXII, p. 70.
11. Saidiya Hartman, *Wayward Lives, Beautiful Experiments* (London and New York: The Serpent's Tail, 2019), p. xxiii.
12. Carretta, *Letters*, p. 4.

13. Markman Ellis 'Ignatius Sancho's Letters: Sentimental Libertinism and the Politics of Form', in Philip Gould and Vincent Carretta (eds), *Genius in Bondage: Literature of Early Black Atlantic* (Kentucky: University of Kentucky Press), 2001, p. 199.
14. Susan Whyman, *The People and the Pen: English Letter Writers 1660–1800* (Oxford: Oxford University Press, 2009), p. 114; W.E.B. Du Bois quoted in Felicity A Nussbaum, 'Being a Man: Olaudah Equiano and Ignatius Sancho', in Gould and Carretta, *Genius in Bondage*, p. 56.
15. Walter Johnson, 'On Agency', *Journal of Social History*, 37/1, Special Issue (Autumn, 2003), pp. 113–24.
16. Catherine Hall and Leonore Davidoff, *Family Fortunes: Men and Women of the English Middle Class 1780–1850* (3rd edn) (London and New York: Routledge, 2019), p. 24.
17. Carretta, *Letters*, Letter XLVIII, p. 95.
18. Amanda Vickery, *Behind Closed Doors: At Home in Georgian England* (New Haven and London: Yale University Press, 2019), p. 9.
19. Amanda Vickery, *The Gentleman's Daughter: Women's Lives in Georgian England* (London: Yale University Press, 1999), p. 8.
20. Carretta, *Letters*, Letter L, p. 98; Letter XXIV, p. 159.
21. Ibid., Letter LI, p. 99.
22. Margaret R. Hunt, *The Middling Sort: Commerce, Gender, and the Family in England 1680–1780* (London: University of California Press, 1996), p. 129.
23. Carretta, *Letters*, Letter III, p. 35; Letter XLVII, p. 91.
24. Ibid., Letter XC, p. 244.
25. Ibid., Letter XXIV, p. 159.
26. Ibid., Letter XXVI, p. 64.
27. Vickery, *Behind Closed Doors*, p. 8.
28. Carretta, *Letters*, Letter XXI, p. 155.
29. Ibid., Letter XXVI, p. 64; Letter XXIV, p. 60.
30. Ibid., Letter XX, p. 155.
31. Ibid., Letter XXXVII, p. 176.
32. Ibid., Letter LII, p. 103.
33. Daniel Defoe, *Conjugal Lewdness or Matrimonial Whoredom* (1727) (Florida: Scholars Facsimiles & Reprints, 1967), p. 26.
34. Carretta, *Letters*, Letter XLII, p. 183; Letter XXX, p. 68.
35. Ibid., Letter XXVI, p. 64.
36. Bridget Hill, *Eighteenth Century Women: An Anthology* (London: Routledge, 2012), p. 16.
37. Carretta, *Letters*, Letter V, p. 34.
38. Samuel Johnson quoted in Naomi Tadmore, *Family and Friends in Eighteenth-Century England Household, Kinship and Patronage* (Cambridge: Cambridge University Press, 2001), p. 19.

39. Ruth P. Dawson, 'The Search for Women's Experiences of Childbirth and Pregnancy', in *The Bucknell Review*, 38/2 (Lewisburg, PA: Bucknell University Press, 1995), p. 105.
40. Vickery, *The Gentlemen's Daughter*, p. 100.
41. Carretta, *Letters*, Letter XXVIII, p. 77; Tyralynn Frazier in Karen T. Craddocks (ed.), *Black Motherhood(s) Contours, Contexts and Considerations* (Bradford: Demeter Press, 2015), p. 147.
42. Roxann Wheeler, 'The Complexion of Desire: Racial Ideology and Mid Eighteenth-Century British Novels', *Eighteen Century Studies* 32/3 (1999); see also Barbara Bush, *Slave Women in Caribbean Society 1650–1838* (Bloomington, IN: Indiana University Press, 1990); Jennifer Morgan, *Labouring Women: Reproduction and Gender in New World Slavery* (Philadelphia, PA: University of Pennsylvania Press, 2008).
43. Gretchen Grezina, *Black London: Life before Emancipation* (Hanover: Dartmouth College Press, 1995); Peter Fryer, *Staying Power: The History of Black People in Britain* (London: Pluto Press, 2010); J. Jean Hecht, *Continental, and Colonial Servants in Eighteen Century England* (Cambridge, MA: Department of History of Smith College, 1954).
44. Jerry White, *London in the Eighteenth Century: A Great and Monstrous Thing* (London: Bodley Head, 2012), p. 128.
45. Letter XLV, p. 90.
46. Ibid., Letter LVIII, p. 202; Letter XXXVII, p. 131.
47. Hill, *Eighteenth Century Women*, p. 45.
48. See ibid., pp. 44–68.
49. See Leonard Schwarz, 'London 1700–1840', in Peter Clark (ed.), *The Cambridge Urban History of Britain (Vol II) 1540–1840* (Cambridge: Cambridge University Press, 2000), pp. 652–3. Also see R.J. Davenport, J.P. Boulton and J. Black, *Infant Mortality by Social Status in Georgian London: A Test of the 'Epidemiological Integration' Model* (Working Paper) (London: UCL, 2013), https://research.ncl.ac.uk/pauperlives/documents/Davenportinfantmortalitybysocialstatusdraft4.pdf (accessed 10 October 2021).
50. Carretta, *Letters*, Letter XXI, p. 57.
51. Hannah Newton, *The Sick Child in Early Modern Europe* (Oxford: Oxford University Press, 2012), p. 124.
52. Gretchen Gerzina, *Black England: A Forgotten Georgian History* (London: John Murray, 2022), pp. 79–83.
53. B.W. Higman, 'The Slave Family and Household in the British West Indies, 1800–1834', *The Journal of Interdisciplinary History*, 6/2 (1975), p. 266.
54. Whyman, *The People and the Pen*, p. 117; Carretta, *Letters*, Letter XXXII, p. 69.
55. Quoted in Carretta, *Letters*, p. 349.
56. Anne Phoenix, 'Theories of Gender and Black Families', in Mirza, *Black British Feminism*, pp. 62–3.

2

Out in the English Countryside: Black People in Eighteenth-Century Warwickshire

Annabelle Gilmore

Black British history has been studied in earnest since the late twentieth century. The seminal work by Peter Fryer, *Staying Power*, explores Black history from the Roman era to the twentieth century.[1] It has continued as historians such as Hakim Adi, David Olusoga and Gretchen H. Gerzina have explored multiple aspects of the history of Black people in Britain.[2] These works have often been focused on urban environments while Black history in rural spaces has been less explored. The National Trust has also committed to researching the less explored histories of their properties, in regards to stories of slavery and empire, shown in their 2020 interim report.[3] This follows on from the research undertaken by English Heritage who explored slavery in country houses in 2013.[4] This chapter on the history of Black people in Warwickshire in the eighteenth century builds on the progress already made.

Britain's Black presence, here, refers to the pre-twentieth-century population of individuals who today would be identified as having African ancestry or heritage. There has been limited work undertaken into the history of the Black presence in Warwickshire in the early modern era. The most recent major piece of work was carried out by the Sparkbrook Caribbean and African Women's Development Initiative (SCAWDI), which undertook a significant research project aided by volunteers between 2010 and 2011, examining the Black presence in the West Midlands before 1918. The book which resulted from their work, *History Detectives: Black People in the*

West Midlands 1650–1918, is now out of print, although David Callaghan did produce a survey of the research in 2011.[5] The book is a slim volume on the region with detailed biographies of a few of the Black people discovered, making use of the limited material available. It serves as a pivotal resource for anyone wanting to discover more about the topic, spanning the entirety of the West Midlands region; including the county of the West Midlands, as well as Warwickshire, Worcestershire, Shropshire and Staffordshire with their current geographical borders. This chapter only covers the Black individuals found within the present boundaries of Warwickshire. The six individuals identified by SCAWDI in Birmingham, and one in Coventry are not discussed here.

The historic county of Warwickshire, which included Coventry and Birmingham until 1974, is in the centre of the country. The two major industrial centres were Coventry with the manufacture of cloth and Birmingham with ironworks, while the rest of the county remained predominantly agricultural. There was no real navigable water system until the developments of the canals in the mid-eighteenth century. However, due to its central location, it received a lot of road traffic from London to the north and west of the country, though the roads were often not well maintained.[6]

It is in this predominantly agricultural environment that we find hints of Warwickshire's Black presence. The earliest record currently known is Margaret Lucy. She was baptised on 1 January 1690 at Idlicote, in the south of Warwickshire.[7] The note on the records states that she was 'a Black belonging to the Lady Underhill'. It is significant that the Lucy family and Underhill family were related through a marriage in the mid-1600s between Alice, the daughter of the third Sir Thomas Lucy, and William Underhill.[8] This may provide a reason why Margaret has the surname Lucy as a reference to Alice's family.

The next mention is of Will Archus, an adult baptised in 1700 in Oxhill, also in the south of Warwickshire, and Myrtilla, who was buried at Oxhill in 1706 (or 1705 according to the Old Style calendar). Myrtilla has a little more of a description, she was a girl 'belonging' to Mrs Beauchamp.[9] Her gravestone gives a further identifier of being enslaved to Thomas Beauchamp of Nevis and baptised on 20 October the previous year. There is no evidence that connects Will Archus to Myrtilla, other than that they were both in the same parish church within five years of each other. In pure speculation, perhaps they did have the opportunity to interact, as we do not know when the two arrived at Oxhill or where Will Archus lived.

There is another passing mention in the records of Frances Warrington, baptised aged 26 in 1712 at Ilmington after escaping slavery in Constantinople. The full passage reads: 'Frances Warrington Aged 26 years a [traveller?] who three years ago made her escape from Constantinople where she had been a slave five years & an half was baptised here the 5th day of May.'[10] In this instance, it cannot be confirmed that Frances Warrington was Black as this is not specified in the record. It has been assumed simply by the description of 'slave'. However, it is possible that Frances had been the victim of Middle Eastern slavery and not racialised as Black in the modern sense of the word. It could also be possible that she was a European woman enslaved through Barbary pirates, which occurred in the early modern era in North Africa.[11] Like all the individuals here, her story is an important one to uncover as part of a history of enslavement outside the usual Atlantic system. The histories of the named women here would be particularly interesting as part of the wider Black British history because of the disparity in populations between Black men and women in the eighteenth century.[12] Understanding their experiences in the early half of the century would help in giving a voice to Black women in the period.

In 1735, a six-year-old Black boy, named Philip Lucy is baptised in the church at Charlecote Park.[13] This is a good 40 years after Margaret Lucy is baptised but with no idea of her age, it is impossible to consider a family connection. Significantly, the family at Charlecote Park are the Lucy family, who have lived there since the end of the fifteenth century and St Leonard's Church where Philip was baptised is within the boundaries of the Charlecote estate. This Lucy surname given to Philip may simply have been used to denote ownership of the boy. The name Philip is likely to also have been given to the boy once he was in Warwickshire, as part of his baptism. This was often done to Black people who were enslaved. Notably, this can be seen with Olaudah Equiano, who had a number of different names foisted on him in succession, including Jacob and Michael. The final name forced upon him was Gustavus Vassa, which he would use for the rest of his life, including on his marriage record.[14] Vincent Caretta remarks that this name was likely in reference to a Swedish king, Gustavus I, who successfully liberated Sweden from Danish rule in 1521–23. This name would have been given due to the irony of an enslaved person being named after a liberator. Caretta also notes that often enslaved people were given 'ironically inappropriate names of powerful historical figures like Caesar and Pompey to emphasise their subjugation'.[15] The name Philip does not have the same implication as Caesar or Pompey and there is no significant Philip in the Lucy family. It may be in reference to a Bible story in Acts of the Apostles, chapter 8 verses 26–39. In this story, St Philip the Evangelist baptises a eunuch from Ethiopia and traditionally, this Ethiopian was depicted as Black. This baptism of Philip Lucy may be an example of enforced Eurocentric imperialist ideas through Christianising enslaved people.

At Charlecote Park, there is also a portrait of Captain Thomas Lucy (c.1655–1688), painted by Sir Godfrey Kneller and dated to 1680.[16] Kneller was the leading British portrait painter of the day, the choice of artist was perhaps intended to emphasise Thomas Lucy's claim to status. A young Black groom is featured at the very edge of the portrait, so much so that he is not entirely fitted into the frame. He is not the focus of the painting but instead placed to portray Captain Lucy as a commanding figure for the viewer. As David Dabydeen has emphasised, Black people feature in hundreds of paintings and prints in the seventeenth and eighteenth centuries.[17] Furthermore, it was common for Black servants to be painted alongside ladies and gentlemen in English portraiture during this period and into the eighteenth century as a means of establishing a social hierarchy.[18] The Black groom in the portrait with Captain Lucy is wearing a blue coat, with what appears to be gold trim, and red stockings. These colours suggest the use of expensive materials, another sign of the Captain's wealth. Interestingly, the groom's coat does not seem to be able to button up. This gives one possible interpretation, serving again as a visual aid for the viewer, that the groom is well cared for by insinuating that he is well fed, and thus also emphasising the wealth of the Captain. On the other hand, this may just be the style of the groom's livery, as he is wearing a waistcoat that is buttoned up. However, most important is the metal collar that is clearly visible in the portrait, even if not all of the groom is. This collar is an immediate indicator of bondage. It shows that the boy is enslaved to Captain Thomas and goes beyond being a marker of wealth to show off his status. A metal collar is used in numerous portraits to indicate enslavement throughout the seventeenth and eighteenth centuries. Examples include Bartholomew Dandridge's portrait *A Young Girl with an Enslaved Servant and a Dog*, painted in 1725.[19] The boy and the dog are painted to have similar expressions of adoration towards the girl. The boy's metal collar is also decorated with a pearl. In William Hogarth's print, *A Taste in High Life* made in 1746, a young Black boy is sat on a stool in exoticised dress.[20] His collar is visible, his chin is lifted by a white woman so he is looking directly at her while smiling. Not all portraits featuring enslaved people have them looking towards the main sitter.

Often, they are placed as incidental figures, objectified to accentuate the qualities of the scene or main sitter's status. While Captain Lucy has agency in the portrait, looking out at the viewer, the groom's gaze is focused on the horse: this separates him from Captain Lucy and makes him an accessory, like the horse. Furthermore, what is not known is whether this boy was a real person or painted in as a symbol of wealth and position as was common during the era, as there are currently no known records of a Black groom at Charlecote or in association with the Captain. However, it is also worth noting that Alice Fairfax-Lucy, the wife of Brian Fairfax-Lucy, a descendant of the Captain, wrote in her collective biography of the Lucy family, first published in 1958, that Katherine, the wife of Captain Lucy, 'had her own waiting women and footmen and a black page to hand her morning chocolate'.[21] Unfortunately, the source for this offhanded statement has not yet been identified but it does give some credence to the idea that perhaps the boy in the portrait may have lived at Charlecote.

In 1756, Pulford Power, aged 14, was baptised in Alcester.[22] This is the only information available. Furthermore, SCAWDI identified John Sutcliffe Fletcher from Antigua as an enslaved person to

Vice Admiral Lord Hugh Seymour also in Alcester in 1799.[23] Yet again, this needs investigating as it may also suggest some kind of connection between Pulford Power and the Seymour family because of the proximity of his baptism location to the Seymour estate of Ragley Hall. Notably, these individuals are mostly found in the early half of the century, apart from John Sutcliffe Fletcher. This may serve as more evidence that by the latter half of the eighteenth century, Black people in the period were not staying in the countryside as they were not held in any form of service or enslavement to the country gentry. David Callaghan points out in the survey article of SCAWDI's work that in the region of the West Midlands, white sponsors of baptism become increasingly rare after the 1760s. He states that the 'evidence suggests that despite it still being a legal practice, the existence of slavery in the West Midlands was all but diminished in reality before abolition had even been suggested in parliament by William Wilberforce in 1789'.[24] Callaghan suggests that social and political changes were driving trends towards self-emancipation. John Sutcliffe Fletcher can be seen as the exception because of Lord Hugh Seymour's naval career in the Caribbean, where ideas around enslavement differed from those in Britain. In the Caribbean, chattel slavery was the norm, as enslaved people predominantly worked in plantation fields. In Britain, on the other hand, it was more likely that an enslaved person would be working in a domestic environment as a household servant alongside white English servants. Douglas Lorimer described this as a 'half-way' stage between liberty and the enslavement in the Caribbean and was cause for Black people considering themselves as liberated.[25]

The baptisms of these Black people in Warwickshire are part of the wider narrative of Black people in Britain. It was during the first half of the eighteenth century that British merchants commanded the transatlantic slave trade and it was during this period where the law surrounding conditions of enslavement were being defined. In 1677, the *Butts* v. *Penny* lawsuit took place to recover the value of goods wrongfully detained. These 'goods' being ten Africans. The ruling followed that the Africans were infidels and that as it was usual for enslaved Africans to be bought and sold by merchants, they should be considered merchandise, 'and also being

Infidels, there might be property in them to maintain Trover'.[26] This judgment, thanks to its reference to infidels, led to the widespread belief that baptism would confer free status. This led to efforts amongst white enslavers to prevent baptisms, as viewing Black people as heathens would justify enslavement.[27] From as early as the 1690s there were writers stating that once an enslaved person set foot on English soil, they could no longer be considered enslaved.[28] This was reinforced in 1706 by the Lord Chief Justice Holt, who is reported to have said, '[t]hat as soon as a Negro comes into England, he becomes free'.[29] Enslaved people continued to be brought to England by their enslavers but by 1729 there were heightened concerns over the ambiguity of their legal status. This led people with West Indian interests to petition the attorney-general, Sir Philip Yorke, and the solicitor-general, Charles Talbot, who shared their opinion that an enslaved person arriving in England, with or without their enslaver, did not have their enslaved status changed and that they could still be compelled to leave the country. The opinion also stated that baptisms of enslaved people did not confer freed status.[30] Although this opinion was only an *obiter dictum*, and thus not legally binding, it was viewed favourably by enslavers thanks to the reputation of Yorke and Talbot.

These decisions affecting the status of enslaved people in England provide some context for these baptisms of the Black individuals in Warwickshire. Margaret Lucy, Will Archus and Myrtilla were all baptised between the Holt and Yorke-Talbot statements. Without further evidence it is difficult to say with any certainty if these individuals were considered to have free status once they were baptised, or, especially in the case of Will Archus, whether they were deemed to have been enslaved upon their arrival to Warwickshire. Perhaps Will Archus chose for himself to be baptised to ensure he could not be removed from the country by anyone who may have thought he was enslaved. It may also be that in Warwickshire, away from the epicentre of decisions and opinions in London, baptism was mainly considered for its religious purposes.

Although Philip Lucy and Pulford Power were baptised after the Yorke-Talbot opinion, it was still considered by many enslaved that baptism conferred free status. This is seen in the example of Jonathan Strong. In 1767, two years after he had been in the care of Granville Sharp and his brother, William Sharp, and nursed back to health from a beating, he was kidnapped by his former enslaver, David Lisle, and sold to James Kerr on the condition that payment would be made after Jonathan was on a ship to Jamaica. Jonathan believed that this could not be possible as he had been baptised since then and implored Granville Sharp to help him.[31] Jonathan was freed and did not have to go to Jamaica but it was not exclusively because he was baptised. The Lord Mayor discharged him as he had not stolen anything and was guilty of no offence.[32] Baptisms, therefore, were of great importance to Black people in the long eighteenth century. The records in Warwickshire of these Black people show that they may have considered themselves to have had free status even if they were officially still in service. However, in contrast to this, the perceived enslavers like Mrs Beauchamp and Lady Underhill still may have not considered baptism as a precedent for freedom. Baptism records alone are not enough to develop a nuanced understanding of these Black people's status in Warwickshire.

It is unfortunate that these scant parish records are the only details to date that we have of these Black individuals in Warwickshire. What their lives were like is left to speculation based on the surrounding evidence. As these individuals are nearly all associated with country houses, or in proximity to country houses, it is not unreasonable then to imagine them as household servants. Perhaps the most famous of household servants is Francis Barber, servant to Samuel Johnson who is most well known for his contribution in developing an authoritative English dictionary. Barber was born enslaved in Jamaica in the late 1740s, he was baptised by his enslaver Colonel Bathurst and entered Samuel Johnson's household in 1752.[33] However, Barber's duties as a servant were not typical of the era, as Samuel Johnson was known for having few wants or needs.[34] Sometime after Johnson's death, Francis Barber moved, with his wife and children, to Lichfield in Staffordshire which bordered Warwickshire. He had inherited money from Johnson but struggled financially during his time in Lichfield until his death in 1801.

Francis Barber is perhaps an anomalous exception when discussing the daily routines of household servants. It was popular in the eighteenth century to have a Black servant as it was indicative of wealth and high social status, similar to their depictions in portraits, especially if they were in positions where they could be seen. The wealth of a country estate could be seen through the architecture, the objects displayed, and the number of male servants who could attend visitors. Female servants were usually not in a visible role but performed their duties in the private quarters.[35] The wording in Margaret Lucy's baptism record suggests she may have been Lady Underhill's maid. As a maid, she would have been involved in Lady Underhill's daily life, dressing her, combing her hair and tending to her personal needs. However, there has not yet been a connection found between the Underhills and the Caribbean, leaving how Margaret arrived in Idlicote a mystery. Similarly, Myrtilla may have arrived from Nevis for the same purpose, though the details are vague. It is uncertain as to how old she was when she died and the only account on her grave is that she was from Nevis and enslaved to Thomas Beauchamp. There are records of a Thomas Beauchamp in Nevis, though not within a timeline that fits with the dates for Myrtilla. In Vere Langford Oliver's *Caribbeana*, a Thomas Beauchamp is listed in the inhabitants of Nevis from 1707 to 1708. This Beauchamp is noted as having a total of 30 Black people enslaved on his property.[36] Again, a Thomas Beauchamp is mentioned in the will of James Bevon. The will is dated 18 November 1720, 15 years after Myrtilla is buried in Oxhill. James Bevon leaves his portion of the land at Saddle Hill he shared with Thomas Beauchamp. Bevon also leaves in his will money to a Black woman named Dido and her three children, one named Myrtilla. Presumably this is not the same Myrtilla who was in Warwickshire as the dates do not align. However, this does give some impression that the Myrtilla in Oxhill is perhaps connected to the Saddle Hill estate and James Bevon.[37]

Due to the proximity within Charlecote Park, Philip Lucy's age, and given surname, he may have been a page boy at Charlecote. This would have fit with the fashion for having a visible Black page and would reflect well upon the household when hosting visitors. However, this can only be speculative, since the archive makes no mention of a Black page during the eighteenth century at Charlecote. If Philip Lucy, Will Archus and Pulford Power were not in the employ of a country estate, perhaps they were employed by merchants, which may also be the reason for how they arrived in Warwickshire, or even farm labourers, but this is the least likely option. If any of these Black people were in service to gentry at the country houses, it is uncertain whether they would have earned a wage. It is only Margaret Lucy and Myrtilla whose records give any indication of enslavement. This may have affected whether they earned money from their duties or whether they were merely considered property by their enslavers. It was not impossible for enslaved servants to earn a wage, if this were the case, it may explain how, and if, these Black individuals left Warwickshire. While some Black servants earned wages, others could make money through different means, similar to how white servants could increase their income. This could have been in tips, or selling second-hand clothes given to them by their employer, or other items like wax candles.[38] With some money saved, it could have been possible to leave the Warwickshire countryside for the towns or to different counties.

The circumstances of these Black individuals are uncertain. The dates from when we know they were in Warwickshire suggest a possibility of some overlap and potential for interaction when considering the tendency for country gentry to visit each other's houses. However, in places like London or Liverpool, there were many opportunities for Black people to meet and interact with each other. This is seen in London where gatherings exclusively for Black people were held. For example, in 1764, *The London Chronicle* detailed an event in which 57 Black men and women attended a public house where they drank, ate and danced to music.[39] Or, in the case of Frances Barber, other Black servants visited him at the home of Samuel Johnson while he was in service.[40] In the countryside of Warwickshire this does not seem to be the case. Kathleen Chater remarks that there has been a stereotypical viewpoint established by earlier historians, based upon the great number of portraits similar to that of Captain Lucy and the Groom; a lone Black figure in the background of a white person or group of white people. She notes that it has led to ideas that Black people were limited to roles 'of a servant in the shadows of an aristocratic family'.[41] Instead, particularly for Black male servants, they were often employed in more visible roles. Ignatius Sancho was a butler and a valet in the Duke of Montague's household, both were servant roles where Sancho would have been seen by any guests visiting the house or outside travelling with the Duke.[42] However, Chater continues by highlighting that white servants would have been considered too ordinary and would not reflect the wealth of the sitter to be depicted in a portrait. As such, the Black servant was isolated in this instance but was otherwise in the company of other servants. However, in view of the circumstances for how these individuals may have singularly arrived in Warwickshire, their experiences may still have been quite isolating as they could not form the same connections found in London with fellow Black servants. Events in public houses or the opportunity to gather in small groups may not appear to be significant but their very existence in London highlights that they were important to Black people at the time. This may explain why all traces of these individuals disappear after their baptisms in the county, since there was no community in which they felt they belonged. As there are no records of their marriages or deaths under these names, it suggests perhaps that they left Warwickshire for different opportunities.

It is disappointing that there are no traces of these Black individuals other than what is found in the parish records. The tangible evidence of their existence raises more questions than providing a satisfactory understanding for where they fit in everyday Warwickshire. In some way, this could be looked at positively. They were simply ordinary people who lived part of their lives in Warwickshire, like any other person in the county of whom we only know their names. Yet, we know that at least Myrtilla and Margaret Lucy did live their lives in bondage. Did Myrtilla have a choice in leaving Nevis? How did Margaret Lucy arrive at the Underhill house? Did either of them have any family that they left behind? Some records have been lost or destroyed. For example, at Charlecote Park, Christina Campbell, the wife of Spencer Lucy, upon the death of her husband in 1889 set about burning inventories, letters, charters and title deeds related to Charlecote Park.[43] It may still be possible to find more information in servants' records associated with country houses. These would list the provisions for each servant, such as livery, food and wages and would work to build a bigger picture around how Black people in Warwickshire lived. Their presence is an important part of Warwickshire's history. It highlights that the county was not isolated and that it was the home for some early Black British settlement. The stories of these people are complex and do go beyond their names.

The research on Warwickshire's Black presence in the early modern era can be expanded beyond the parish records in the county. This includes scouring through the local newspapers for any references to these individuals or for any other Black people. This may be in the form of advertisements from people looking for new jobs. If the individuals already known are named in the papers but with no indications that they are Black, it may explain why a connection has not yet been made. Hue and cry advertisements for enslaved runaways have been a source of valuable information in documenting the London Black population and could potentially serve a similar purpose for Warwickshire. These hue and cry notices often give descriptions of the runaway's appearance, including what they were wearing, their last known address and where they may have ties to. This would be helpful in documenting movement patterns as well as enriching the current knowledge of livelihoods of Black people in Warwickshire.

Other potential sources are the records of law courts, perhaps in a similar frame to what is available of the digitised records of the Old Bailey proceedings.[44] These proceedings list centuries worth of court records that are focused on the non-elite of London, they provide a glimpse into these more ordinary lives through criminal trials. The records available at the Warwickshire Record Office are neither as extensive nor as accessible as the Old Bailey proceedings but may still serve a similar purpose of understanding the Warwickshire environment from a perspective outside the country house. The Old Bailey records themselves may hold some information that may aid in further research, such as whether a person on trial, or a victim, was from the Warwickshire area.

Furthermore, there may be traces in records of poor relief in the county. Poor relief was for those in need who could not work and people who could not find enough work to support themselves or their families.[45] As poor relief was provided by individual parishes after the Elizabethan Poor Law of 1601, each parish will need to be investigated individually for any traces of Black individuals. Poor relief records have been another method that has investigated history from below. Looking through these records may reveal key location information. These efforts can be extended towards investigating the Black people found by SCAWDI in Coventry and Birmingham. This may lead to further discoveries and more information while building a more detailed understanding of the Black presence in historic Warwickshire, such as what was different between life in the countryside and for those in the city.

Finally, but not exhaustively, the wills and inventories of country estates constitute an important potential source. Some of these records may never be accessible but it will be worthwhile to investigate all the remaining records of these country estates, including wills and diaries for any passing mentions. The country estate serves in some way as a depository of histories going back centuries but as with the majority of histories in Britain, these are likely to be through a white lens. If there are any leads to the named individuals here, or other Black people, in the records of these estates, such material will have to be handled with the knowledge that these are not the direct accounts of the individuals. The content from country houses may also lead to expanding what is meant by a Black presence in Warwickshire. For example, in looking into the life of John Sutcliffe Fletcher, perhaps through the records of Vice Admiral Lord Hugh Seymour, and the family seat of Ragley Hall, the expansive connections between Warwickshire and the Caribbean can be investigated through Black history. Furthermore, like Thomas Beauchamp, there were other absentee planters who lived in Warwickshire, such as the Greatheed family, who held plantations in St Kitts, and, using the proceeds of enslaved labour, purchased the estate of Guy's Cliffe in the mid-eighteenth century.[46]

It is clear that the Black presence in Warwickshire is not as numerically significant as that in London or other port cities but the effects of enslaved labour on Caribbean plantations still reverberate back into the Warwickshire county. It may also be necessary to expand the research into neighbouring counties for any evidence of the named Black people, as exploring the neighbouring counties for the names may reveal more information about these individuals. In investigating all these potential avenues, an enriched narrative of the Black presence in Warwickshire could be found.

This work would be a large undertaking but fits within the much wider framework of historical research that deepens the current understanding of Black people outside of London and the home counties. Saidiya Hartman discusses the scarcity of narratives about enslaved Africans and particularly enslaved women from their own point of view. She remarks that any details found in the archive about enslaved women in the Caribbean are shrouded in violence. The silences in the archive are deafening, leading many to rely on quantitative discussions of enslavement.[47] While Hartman is specifically discussing her experiences in writing about enslaved women in the Caribbean and the violence in the archive that she as a writer encounters, her work on a silent archive resonates here. The only records of the presence of Black people in Warwickshire in the eighteenth century are not passed down by their own hands. Instead, they have been quantified in the parish records and they are only known because the recorder thought it interesting to note their skin colour as it was deemed unusual that they were there.

This creates some dissonance when viewing this history as it is clear that Margaret Lucy, Will Archus, Myrtilla, Frances Warrington, Phillip Lucy, Pulford Power and John Sutcliffe Fletcher were all in some way othered by the community in Warwickshire but without such othering, their existence in the county might never have been known. The gaps in the archive, particularly when searching for histories of Black people, can be infuriating and tantalising in the hopes that they can be filled. Filling the gaps with assumptions, as has been done here, is not an ideal solution but it does bring some life to the people who have been named and makes tangible their histories. This work in part contributes to what Gretchen Gerzina, amongst other historians have said, that Britain's Black past is all part of British history and 'that knowing the past is one important way of shaping the future'.[48] In building upon the fragments left behind of Warwickshire's Black past, Warwickshire's history and future can be further enriched.

NOTES

1. Peter Fryer, *Staying Power: The History of Black People in Britain* (London: Pluto Press, 1984).
2. Hakim Adi, *West Africans in Britain 1900–1960: Nationalism, Pan-Africanism and Communism* (London: Lawrence and Wishart, 1998). David Olusoga, *Black and British: A Forgotten History* (London: Pan Books, 2017). Gretchen H. Gerzina (ed.), *Black Victorians/Black Victoriana* (New Brunswick, NJ and London: Rutgers University Press, 2003).
3. Sally-Anne Huxtable et al., *Interim Report on the Connections between Colonialism and Properties Now in the Care of the National Trust, Including Links with Historic Slavery* (Swindon: National Trust, 2020).
4. Madge Dresser and Andrew Hann (eds), *Slavery and the British Country House* (Swindon: English Heritage, 2013).
5. Barbara Willis-Brown and David Callaghan (eds), *History Detectives: Black People in the West Midlands 1650–1918* (Birmingham: SCAWDI, 2010). D.I. Callaghan, 'The Black Presence in the West Midlands, 1650–1918', *Midland History*, 36/2 (2011), pp. 180–94.
6. William Page (ed.), *The Victoria History of the Counties of England: A History of Warwickshire (Volume 2)* (London: Dawsons, 1965), pp. 138, 148, 172.
7. Warwickshire County Record Office (WCRO) DR0209, Parish Records of St James the Great, Idlicote.
8. Alice Fairfax-Lucy, *Charlecote and the Lucys* (London: Victor Gollancz, 1990), p. 14.
9. WCRO DR0024, Parish Records of St Lawrence, Oxhill.
10. WCRO DR0020, Parish Church of St Mary, Ilmington.
11. Miranda Kaufmann, *Black Tudors: The Untold Story* (London: Oneworld, 2017), p. 3. See also Giles Milton, *White Gold* (London: Hodder and Stoughton, 2004).
12. Kathleen Chater, *Untold Histories: Black People in England and Wales during the Period of the British Slave Trade, c. 1660–1807* (Manchester: Manchester University Press, 2009), p. 30.
13. WCRO DR0148, Parish Records of St Leonard, Charlecote.
14. Olaudah Equiano and Vincent Caretta, *The Interesting Narrative and Other Writings* (New York: Penguin Books, 2003), pp. 63–4.
15. Ibid., *The Interesting Narrative and Other Writings*, pp. 252–3.
16. National Trust, *Captain Thomas Lucy (c.1655–1684) and an Unidentified Groom*, Sir Godfrey Kneller, 1680.
17. David Dabydeen, *Hogarth's Blacks: Images of Blacks in Eighteenth Century Art* (Athens, GA: University of Georgia Press, 1987), p. 18.
18. Ibid., p. 26.
19. Yale Centre for British Art, *A Young Girl with an Enslaved Servant and Dog*, Bartholomew Dandridge c. 1725.

20. V&A Museums, *A Taste in High Life*, William Hogarth 1746.
21. Fairfax-Lucy, *Charlecote and the Lucys*, p. 159.
22. WCRO DR0360, Parish Records of St Nicholas, Alcester.
23. Willis-Brown and Callaghan, *History Detectives*, p. 4.
24. Callaghan, 'The Black Presence in the West Midlands, 1650–1918', p. 185.
25. Douglas A. Lorimer, 'Black Slaves and English Liberty: A Re-examination of Racial Slavery in England', *Immigrants and Minorities*, 3/2 (1984), p. 122.
26. Helen Tunnicliff Catterall, David Maydole Matteson and James J Hayden, *Judicial Cases Concerning American Slavery, and the Negro* (Washington, DC: Carnegie Institution of Washington, 1926), p. 9.
27. Fryer, *Staying Power*, p. 113.
28. Travis Glasson, '"Baptism doth not bestow Freedom": Missionary Anglicanism, Slavery, and the York-Talbot Opinion, 1701–30', *The William and Mary Quarterly*, 67/2 (April 2010), p. 282.
29. Fryer, *Staying Power*, p. 114.
30. Ibid.
31. Folarin Shyllon, *Black Slaves in Britain* (Oxford: Oxford University Press, 1974), p. 20.
32. Ibid., p.21.
33. Michael Bundock, *The Fortunes of Frances Barber* (New Haven, CT and London: Yale University Press, 2015), pp. 1, 28.
34. Bundock, *Fortunes of Francis Barber*, p. 55.
35. Joanna Martin, *Wives and Daughters: Women and Children in the Georgian Country House* (London: Hambledon and London, 2004), p. 121.
36. Vere Langford Oliver, *Caribbeana* (Volume III) (London: Mitchell, Hughes and Clarke 1914), p. 176.
37. Vere Langford Oliver, *Caribbeana* (Volume VI) (London: Mitchell, Hughes and Clarke 1919), p. 14.
38. Chater, *Untold Histories*, pp. 224–5.
39. Folarin Shyllon, *Black People in Britain 1555–1833* (London: Oxford University Press, 1977), p. 80.
40. Bundock, *Fortunes of Frances Barber*, p. 99.
41. Chater, *Untold Histories*, p. 222.
42. Vincent Caretta (ed.), *Letters of the Late Great Ignatius Sancho, an African* (Toronto: Broadview Editions, 2015), pp. 14–15.
43. Mary Elizabeth Lucy, *Mistress of Charlecote: The Memoirs of Mary Elizabeth Lucy* (London: Orion, 2002), p. 175.
44. Tim Hitchcock, Robert Shoemaker, Clive Emsley et al., *The Old Bailey Proceedings Online, 1674–1913*, 24 March 2012, www.oldbaileyonline.org, version 7.0 (accessed 19 January 2023).

45. Steve Hindle, *On the Parish?: The Micro-Politics of Poor Relief in Rural England c.1550–1750* (Oxford: Oxford University Press), p. 2.
46. National Archives, will of Samuel Greatheed, 1766 PROB 11/917/15. W.B. Stephens (ed.), 'The Borough of Warwick: Churches', in *A History of the County of Warwick: Volume 8, the City of Coventry and Borough of Warwick* (London: Victoria County History, 1969), pp. 522–35. *British History Online*, www.british-history.ac.uk/vch/warks/vol8/pp522-535 (accessed 26 February 2022).
47. Saidiya Hartman, 'Venus in Two Acts', *Small Axe*, 26 (June 2008), pp. 1–4.
48. Gretchen H. Gerzina (ed.), *Britain's Black Past* (Liverpool: Liverpool University Press, 2020), p. 5.

3

Chasing Shadows: Conducting a Regional Black History of Falmouth and Penryn during the Packet Boat Years of 1688 to 1850

Kate Bernstock

The Packet Boat Years mark the period in which Falmouth became home to the Lisbon and 'West Indies' packet services, carrying passengers and mail to and from those locations. The presence of these packet services sparked an economic boom in the area, which created approximately 1,000 jobs in Falmouth by the early 1800s, providing work for around one-quarter of its overall population.[1] At the same time, they inserted Falmouth and Penryn into a national discourse of information and power, with publications from *The Times* to local newspapers like the *Derby Mercury* littered with references to news from abroad brought by the Falmouth packet.[2]

Indeed, a regional history of this period debunks narratives of Cornwall as impoverished periphery and of the Black Presence in peripheral Britain as a rarity. Although the 'West Indies' packet services were only active in Falmouth between 1702 and 1705, the Empire's parasitic spread, which demanded the presence of the packets, also contributed to the area's changing identity as an international, imperial hub. For example, by 1814, rum and sugar from the Caribbean constituted two of Falmouth's principal imports.[3] Matching the import of colonial 'goods', parish and census records and other contemporary sources have revealed a growing number of enslaved, freed and free people of African descent contributing to Falmouth and Penryn's evolving identities; from Olaudah

Equiano who first set eyes on England, and indeed, on snow, when he passed through Falmouth as an enslaved child in 1755, to Maria née Edwards, a 'blackwoman' who was recorded in the 1851 census as a 'born Africa British subject' and resident of Penryn.[4]

As William Beckford, a man who derived wealth from Caribbean plantations noted dismissively, by 1787 Falmouth had become a 'society of Barbadoes Creoles and packet-boat captains'. Although those 'Barbadoes Creoles' likely refer to everyone born in Barbados and not necessarily people of African descent, this quote introduces us to the idea that Falmouth and Penryn were more ethnically diverse than we might initially expect. It also serves as evidence of the racist Archive that historians must use to spot this.[5]

Hartman explains in 'Venus in Two Acts' that it is the historian's duty to challenge the 'death sentence' of the slavery Archive, which reduces enslaved women's 'violated' bodies to an 'asterisk'.[6] In the same vein, historians of Falmouth and Penryn must be wary of the racialisation of the African descended subjects we encounter through an Archive curated by literate and influential people like Beckford, enslavers and their allies who defined Blackness as abject, as opposite to the humanity of whiteness, to defend the racial capitalism that upheld the trade in enslaved Africans. We encounter subjects who have been 'Black(ened)' by the consciously constructed prejudices of the Archive's gatekeepers.[7] It serves as a dirty window, Black(ening) the faces, hearts and minds of our subjects while also blurring their outlines, their place in society. The adjective Black(ened) is used here to emphasise that our subjects continue to be racialised through a process which Trouillot described as the power in the production of history. Writing in relation to accepted and inaccurate historical narratives produced about the Haitian Revolution (1791–1804), Trouillot's work illuminates the uneven power dynamics at play in history, where 'facts are not created equal' and the 'production of traces' is met with 'the creation of silences'.[8] Historians have a hand in defining how we see the past, and this is especially pertinent when studying a period so entwined with the British Empire, a period (and its inhabitants) made 'hostage to myth' by modern-day politicians and historians who continue to weaponise national pride of former glories at the expense of the enslaved people exploited to sustain it.[9]

In this way, historians imitate the Archive by writing about our subjects not as they were, but as imperialist, prejudiced systems of thought expect them to be; implicitly figured as the *Other.* In the context of Falmouth and Penryn, for example, the historian might limit analysis of the 'absented' and possibly enslaved 'NEGRO' Punch, who was pursued after his escape from the *Betsy* in Falmouth in March 1760, to his experience of Black Trauma. Little is known about Punch, described in an advert in the *Whitehall Evening Post* as 'a shortish well-set Fellow' who had escaped the *Betsy* dressed as a sailor before heading to London.[10] With a lens informed only by limited evidence and an assumption of trauma, the historian risks viewing him only as a victim by virtue of his rejection by colonial society, not as a multifaceted human being with an infinite number of stories to tell. Much more is known about Joseph Emidy born in West Africa between 1770 and 1775. A talented violinist, Emidy was enslaved in Guinea and taken to Portugal where he played in the Lisbon Opera before being press-ganged into the English navy in 1795. In 1799, we find him in Truro and Falmouth, playing in the Truro Philharmonic Orchestra, teaching a range of instruments including the flute to Sheffield's reformist MP James Silk Buckingham, and practising his violin in the Old Town Hall in Falmouth.[11] Unlike Punch, Emidy's narrative could be reduced to one of uplifting, Black Excellence; a two-dimensional version of his life and his person viewed through Western value systems of success, forgoing an exploration of the enslavement that led to him learning the violin in the first place.

Regional history, a study defined by nuance, provides historians with a pathway to reject such reductivity. Drawing on the work of Fuentes, who produced a subject-perspective tour of eighteenth-century Bridgetown in Barbados, this chapter will situate the African descended subjects present in Falmouth and Penryn within their geographical context, both physical and emotional.[12] Analysis will extend from the central point of community at this time, the Church, to the respective dominance of the transatlantic slave trade and the abolition movement formed in response. This regional exploration cannot summon a spot-on likeness of our subjects, but it does shine a light on their surroundings, making visible their silhouettes and, in turn, the shadows they cast on the world around them. It enables us as historians to ask questions, to chase the shadows of our subjects, while allowing them the 'complex personhood' that exists outside the boundaries of imperial fact.[13]

I also reject the Academy's (and popular media's) conceptualisation of Black British history as a neat addition to existing, grander British narratives, failing to acknowledge that when writing the history of Black Britain we must come face-to-face with the unpalatable, dark side of many moments in British history and begin to rewrite them. Cornwall, a Celtic nation forced into the geographic definition of Britishness, often against its will, was intentionally chosen as the site of exploration for this. Historic and current discourse produced in the region are preoccupied with what it means to be Cornish; rejecting the pursuit of belonging to Britain and its grander nationalist narratives. In 2011, 73,220 Cornish residents recorded either their nationality or ethnicity as Cornish not English or British. By 2014, the Cornish were recognised as a protected identity. Certainly, there is space in history to consider the place of Black subjects in hegemonic narratives of Britishness and also of Cornishness, but it is important not to let that macrocosmic approach obfuscate our understanding of them as people existing within their own microcosmic contexts too.

It is significant that the nature of the violent Archive means that most of the Black(ened) subjects discussed in this chapter are free and baptised folks, inhabiting a proximity to whiteness that meant they were deemed valuable enough to be included in the official record. For those living on the margins of society, whether hiding from the law or hidden from view by their enslavers, there will be some discussion where evidence is available. More must always be done to bring the many and complex realities of Blackness to life and it is necessary to bear in mind those who have been obscured from view by demanding answers not from them, but from the conditions that caused their obfuscation.

With 93.6 per cent of English and Welsh subjects identifying as Nominal Anglicans in 1760, it was within the space of the Church that communities were made and maintained.[14] Interestingly, the Church also became an arena for conditional assimilation within the British Empire for Black(ened) people who used Christianity to distance themselves from the perceived 'savagery' of non-Christians, despite the fact that the 1729 Yorke-Talbot opinion had stated that baptism did not translate to freedom for enslaved people. Yet this pursuit of conditional belonging would be better described as the pursuit of an impossible belonging. Indeed, the fact that William Quarme, a local rector in Falmouth from 1679 to 1728, was involved in the trafficking of enslaved Africans is indicative that religious spaces would not have been free of the violence of racialisation. It is interesting to note that the church of King Charles the Martyr, where Quarme was rector, was the same church in which Joseph Emidy married Jenefer Hutchins in 1802. Was the previously enslaved Emidy, or his future wife, the presumed white daughter of a local tradesman in a town abuzz with debate around the slave trade, aware of the church's history on their wedding day? Did they mind that a rector not one hundred years before had been invested in the trade that displaced Emidy from his birthplace?

It is through the institution of St Gluvias Church in Penryn that we learn of a number of African descended people living in the region. Samuel Steward, a 'Negro' mariner, married Ann Yendall 'of this parish, a spinster' on 22 March 1806 in the same period that Maria née Edwards was a member of the congregation.[15] Maria was, according to the 1851 census, born in Africa and baptised at St Gluvias at nine years old on 10 July 1769, likely brought to the region by way of the transatlantic slave trade.[16] Maria married three times, first to a Black mariner called John Hooper on 24 November 1778, then to John Joseph Blackall on 4 September 1787 and finally to 'William Weymouth of this parish Bachelor a Negro' on 28 June 1802. She gave birth to eight children.[17] Evidence of both families situated together at the same church may indicate that a Black Community existed in the region; yet to leave this assumption unchecked would be to fall foul of reproducing the reductivity of the Archive that makes our subjects knowable only in a state of racialisation.

It is very possible that Maria and her family were close with the Stewards, they may have shared stories about the rumour of a smuggler's tunnel, which ran from the coast to the basement of the church. Smuggling was big business in Falmouth and Penryn, evidenced by the overt presence of the King's Pipe attached to the back of Falmouth's Customs House with a plaque that states its former use 'for the destruction of contraband tobacco'.[18] Intriguingly, an issue of *The Times* published on 9 May 1786 reported that a group of men had escaped Pendennis Castle in Falmouth after attempting to smuggle goods from a ship in Falmouth's port. One of those smugglers was described as an Irishman with a 'black complexion' and a 'large flat nose like a mulatto'.[19] Was William Stone of African descent? Did the image of him create a shared intrigue amongst the Black(ened) folks of the church that allowed them to conjure themselves into its history and therefore into the history of Penryn itself?

It is of course possible that the two families stood side by side in church with nothing in common but their Blackness and positionality as mariners in a busy trading port. Indeed, standing alongside Black and white parishioners alike, would they have been more moved by the collective memory of a shipwreck on 14 January 1814? Just over a week after many households would have celebrated the Twelfth Night, 195 people were lost on board the *Queen* in a snowstorm. Struck by the loss, St Gluvias organised a collection for a memorial stone for the people lost at sea, some of whom may have been Black based on the racially mixed demographic of mariners discussed in this chapter alone. Did Maria or Samuel, moved by the loss and recognising their own connection with the port (Maria's husbands were all mariners alongside Samuel), donate to the collection? The memorial at St Gluvias is a physical reminder of the emotional collective memory, which would both have influenced and been influenced by Maria and Samuel. Indeed, by lighting a candle in honour of the complex reality that existed within the walls of St Gluvias, the fluid and contrasting shadows of our Black(ened) subjects become visible and remain just out of reach.

Falmouth and Penryn's maritime activity flourished during the eighteenth century thanks to their South Westerly position on the way to the New World, and Falmouth's ability to accommodate around 200 sailing vessels. This meant that proximity to the transatlantic slave trade was inevitable for the Black(ened) folks of Falmouth and Penryn.[20] From the transitory visit of Olaudah Equiano, who befriended the young daughter of an enslaver living in Falmouth in 1755, to the residence of Elizabeth Chegoe, Martin 'a negro' and Jacob 'a negro boy' who were all enslaved by the Corker family in Falmouth (evidence of whom can be found objectified next to sums of money in the probate inventory of the Falmouth merchant, Thomas Corker, after his death in 1703).[21] For the free and freed people of African descent, engagement with the trade in enslaved Africans might have been a daily occurrence in other ways. The maritime industry funded a range of work including chandlery, victualling and ship repair. Alongside Samuel Steward and John Hooper, another mariner of African descent, John Rodney, is referenced in the records of Budock Parish Church in Falmouth where he married Elizabeth Stotten in 1804.[22] Any or all of these mariners may have been employed by enslavers or those with a financial interest in the trade.

Indeed, enslavers and those profiting from racial capitalism held significant power in both Falmouth and Penryn. How would our Black(ened) subjects have felt walking past the 'formal garden and mulberry orchard', which belonged to the large waterfront house of Bryan Rogers, who traded in the Caribbean and colonial America, as well as acting as an agent for overseas colonial merchants?[23] Did they ever visit the Falmouth Arms, built by Edward Pearce in the 1680s, a man who was involved in two trading expeditions from Falmouth to Africa?[24] The impact of being in a region where the trade and financial profit of many of its inhabitants and politicians relied on the racialisation of African descended people as having a 'physical or mental likeness to nonhuman animals' would have been stark.[25] For smuggler William Stone and the runaway Punch, who lived on the margins of society and were pursued by the authorities, occupying a space where they were figured as commodities would have presented an immediate threat to their freedom at a time when Black(ened) people were illegally seized by greedy enslavers with little recourse to justice. One wonders whether any of our subjects were made aware of the capture and advertisement of a 'Negroe Man ... taken at Penzance ... wandering, and begging, and frightning (sic) Country People'. Listed in a notice taken from the *St. James Evening Post* in 1733, this unnamed man was taken in as a 'Ward' alongside three other 'Comrades,

Mulattoes' and his fate sheds light on the constant precarity faced by the Black(ened) people of Falmouth and Penryn, towns not far from Penzance.[26] This incident is pertinent when one bears in mind the political influence of those in whose interest it would have been to insist on the figuration of Blackness as property; from four times mayor of Falmouth Bryan Rogers to Joseph Banfield, a merchant and shipping agent in Falmouth who was a member of the Falmouth Corporation and served as mayor in 1788. With this in mind, it is important to consider whether Black(ened) folks like Emidy, operating as a tutor and performer in elite circles, internalised top-down racist messaging to define himelf as separate from outsiders like William Stone and Punch, reproducing anti-Blackness as a form of survival.

There are many unknowns about our Black subjects, enslaved and free; their emotional response to living in a town dominated by the transatlantic slave trade and even their own opinions of the trade. It is by accepting that we may not have answers directly from the mouths of our subjects, and instead establishing as nuanced a picture of their world as possible, that their many possible realities begin to take shape.

Balancing out the nefarious presence of enslavers and their allies in this period were a growing number of Quaker abolitionists. Following the passage of the Toleration Act of 1689, a Quaker House was established in Falmouth, providing a space for those who adhered to the ethical standard that had spearheaded the abolitionist movement by way of the Society for the Abolition of the Slave Trade formed on 22 May 1787. In Falmouth, ten members of the Quakers, the Fox family joined the Society in the same year (half of whom were women).[27] The family were influential in the area and in 1788 the second George Crocker Fox canvassed support for abolition, returning a number of abolitionist petitions to Parliament from Falmouth and Penryn. To get a sense of the scale of the abolition movement in the region, Fox stated that he requested signatures from 'creditable townsmen and inhabitants'. These may have included three members of the Quaker merchant Tregelles family in Falmouth and Peter Price, a corn and flour merchant living in Penryn in 1791.[28] It is possible that Maria née Edwards would have purchased flour from Price and, at a time when the transatlantic slave trade was hotly debated in Cornwall, with *The Royal Cornwall Gazette* printing a number of articles on topics from emancipation to the consequences of granting freedom, she may have discussed abolition with him.[29] It is also possible that Price and even Maria and her husband, John Joseph Blackall, joined the consumer boycott of Caribbean sugar led by abolitionists the following year.

Even if the Black(ened) folks living in Falmouth and Penryn were not politically engaged with abolition, or were indeed opposed to it, the presence of abolitionists in town may have offered some respite. Elizabeth Elliot was a bookseller in the late eighteenth century, she sold foreign language books, sheet music and musical instruments, wares that MacKenzie argues may have brought Joseph Emidy to her shop.[30] Elliot was an abolitionist who in 1791 published *A Satirical Poem on Slavery*, which featured an introductory letter addressed to leading abolitionist William Wilberforce. Did her sympathies inform a dynamic of equality between herself and Emidy, which may not have existed in many of the colonial spaces of Falmouth and Penryn?[31] It is important not just to consider the possible friendship between Emidy and Elliot, but also the evidence of a number of interracial marriages between Emidy and Jenefer Hutchins, Maria and her second husband, and the mariners John Rodney and Samuel Steward and their locally born wives. Interracial marriage, particularly between the working classes, was so popular in fact that in 1769 the abolitionist lawyer Granville Sharp commented on what was, in his opinion, the unfortunate presence of 'mixed people or Mulattoes, produced by the unavoidable intercourse with their white neighbours' in England.[32] As much as this is further proof of the racialisation of our subjects, it is also evidence of another story, one of resistance to top-down racial separatism and an acceptance of the *Other* by those whose opinions, worth less than the educated elite, are no longer extant.

Yet the fact that the famed abolitionist Granville Sharp held such prejudiced opinions, and indeed described the presence of Black servants in Britain as 'a national inconvenience' in the same piece of writing, is evidence that the presence of abolitionists in Falmouth and Penryn did not translate directly to straightforward acceptance for our subjects.[33]Although abolitionists were anti-slavery they were not necessarily anti-racist; the Fox family were known to be close friends with Henry de la Beche, a man who enslaved 207 people on a Jamaican plantation.[34] The fact that the Fox family's ethics did not prevent them from sharing a mutual respect with a man known for being 'no friend to slavery' yet who opposed its abolition for financial reasons is a clear indicator of the paternalistic value that they placed on Black(ened) people. It is no surprise that William Quantamissa and John Ansah, the two Princes of Ashantee given as a peace gesture to British forces by the King of Ashantee, laughed 'in a knowing manner' whenever slavery was alluded to during their visit to Falmouth in 1840 where they were accompanied by the abolitionist Caroline Fox.[35] Is it possible that, being forced to convert to Christianity and adopt the manner of British gentlemen, the Princes were aware that they were being used as part of Britain's wider civilising mission, seen as a benevolent alternative to slavery yet which continued to value Black folks only in so far as they could prove their distance from 'savagery'. This was a more subtle but no less destructive racism.

Conducting a regional history of Falmouth and Pernyn during the Packet Boat Years empowers the historian to reject the reductive polarities and continued racialisation that Black(ened) historical subjects faced on their journey through the Archive into the history of Britain, an Imperial state. By enabling a nuanced, subject-perspective study of the period and its people, regional history allows the complexity of our subjects' context to shine, casting their shadows, formed of endlessly possible shapes, onto the pages of a new kind of British history as a result. Reflecting on Bhabha's theory of mimicry (the 'ironic compromise' in which the coloniser requires assimilation from the colonised while still branding them as an 'outsider'), the historian might ask how much of our Black(ened) subjects was lost to mimicry in Falmouth and Penryn.[36] We might also ask how much more could be lost by squeezing our subjects' personhood's to fit within the confines of an academic project that exists in a Britain operating in the shadow of its colonial past.

NOTES

1. Megan Lowena Oldcorn, *Falmouth and the British Maritime Empire* (PhD dissertation, University of the Arts London and Falmouth University, 2014), p. 9.
2. 'Express from Falmouth', *The Times*, 29 September 1834, p. 4; 'Extract of a Letter from Falmouth, Nov 23', *Derby Mercury*, 27 November 1778, p. 3.
3. Charlotte MacKenzie, 'Cornwall's Untold Histories – the African Diaspora and Black Identities', Institute of Cornish Studies (2020), www.youtube.com/watch?v=QYVBLUqeuAg (accessed 3 May 2022).
4. Olaudah Equiano, *The Interesting Narrative of the Life of Olaudah Equiano, or Gustavus Vassa, the African. Written by Himself. Vol. I* (Chapel Hill, NC: University of North Carolina Academic Affairs Library, 2001), p. 104; 'Marriage of William Weymouth and Maria Blackall', 28 June 1802, *Register of marriages and banns of marriage, St Gluvias Parish Church 1789–1812* (2021), https://kresenkernow.org/SOAP/detail/34c2094d-98c6-4f4b-b2c4-826290d00275/?tH=%5B%22blackall%22%5D (accessed 10 May 2022).
5. William Beckford, *Italy, Spain, and Portugal, with an Excursion to the Monasteries of Alcobaça and Batalha* (London: Richard Bentley, 1840), p. 183.
6. Saidiya Hartman, 'Venus in Two Acts', *Small Axe*, 26 (2008), p. 2.
7. Zakiyyah I. Jackson, *Becoming Human: Matter and Meaning in an Antiblack World* (New York: New York University Press, 2020), pp. 10–11.
8. Michel-Rolph Trouillot, *Silencing the Past: Power and the Production of History* (Boston, MA: Beacon Press, 1997), pp. 29 and xxiii.
9. Priya Satia, *Time's Monster: How History Makes History* (Cambridge, MA: Belknap Press, 2020), p. 5.
10. *Whitehall Evening Post*, 'ABSENTED from on Board the Betsy', 18 March 1760, Runaway Slaves in Britain: Bondage, Freedom and Race in the Eighteenth Century, www.runaways.gla.ac.uk/database/display/?rid=297 (accessed 10 May 2022).
11. Richard McGrady, 'Joseph Emidy: An African in Cornwall', *The Musical Times*, 127 (1986) p. 619; Richard McGrady, *Music and Musicians in Early Nineteenth-Century Cornwall: The World of Joseph Emidy – Slave, Violinist and Composer* (Exeter: University of Exeter Press, 1991), p. 41.
12. Marisa J. Fuentes, *Dispossessed Lives: Enslaved Women, Violence, and the Archive* (Philadelphia, PA: University of Pennsylvania Press, 2016).
13. Avery F. Gordon, *Ghostly Matters: Haunting and the Sociological Imagination* (Minneapolis, MN: University of Minnesota Press, 2008), pp. 4–5.
14. Clive D. Field, 'Counting Religion in England and Wales: The Long Eighteenth Century, c. 1680–c. 1840', *The Journal of Ecclesiastical History*, 63 (2012), p. 711.

15. 'Marriage of Samuel Steward and Ann Yendall', 22 March 1806, *Register of marriages and banns of marriage, St Gluvias Parish Church 1789–1812*, https://kresenkernow.org/SOAP/detail/34c2094d-98c6-4f4b-b2c4-826290d00275/?tH=%5B%22blackall%22%5D (accessed 10 May 2022).
16. 'Baptism of Maria Edwards', 10 July 1769, *Register of baptisms, marriages and burials, St Gluvias Parish Church 1747–1809*, https://kresenkernow.org/SOAP/detail/d2f49a09-e8ef-44a8-9c0e-631251a0ed86/?tH=%5B%22Black%22%2C%22history%22%5D (accessed 10 May 2022).
17. 'Marriage of William Weymouth and Maria Blackall'; Kresen Kernow, email to author, 11 May 2021.
18. Sam Willis, 'The Archaeology of Smuggling and Falmouth's King Pipe'. *Journal of Maritime Archaeology*, 4/1 (2009) p. 53.
19. 'The Happy-Go-Lucky Affair,' Cornwall Smugglers, http://cornwallsmugglers.com/happy%20go%20lucky.htm (accessed 10 May 2022).
20. Alex M. Jacob, 'The Jews of Falmouth – 1740–1860'. *Transactions (Jewish Historical Society of England)*, 17 (1951–52), p. 63.
21. MacKenzie, *Merchants and Smugglers in Eighteenth Century Cornwall*, p. 29; Equiano, *The Interesting Narrative of the Life of Olaudah Equiano, Vol. I*, p. 107.
22. 'Marriage of John Rodney and Elizabeth Stotten', 10 March 1804, *Register of marriages and banns of marriage, Budock Parish Church*, https://kresenkernow.org/SOAP/detail/a7f38831-169d-489b-8b3d-717b3826dc0d/ (accessed 10 May 2022).
23. MacKenzie, *Merchants and Smugglers in Eighteenth Century Cornwall*, p. 19.
24. Ibid., p. 45.
25. Jackson, *Becoming Human*, p. 22.
26. 'This Is to Give Notice', 14 June 1733, Runaway Slaves in Britain, www.runaways.gla.ac.uk/database/display/?rid=417 (accessed 26 May 2022).
27. MacKenzie, *Merchants and Smugglers in Eighteenth Century Cornwall*, pp. 194–5.
28. Ibid., p. 195; 'Universal Business Directory of 1791: Penryn', Penryn Cornwall: History and Genealogy, www.penryncornwall.com/universal-1791.htm (accessed 10 May 2022).
29. Oldcorn cites a number of *Royal Cornwall Gazette* articles discussing these topics in Oldcorn, *Falmouth and the British Maritime Empire*, p. 174.
30. MacKenzie, *Merchants and Smugglers in Eighteenth Century Cornwall*, pp. 192–3.
31. Elizabeth Elliot, *A Satirical Poem on Slavery* (Falmouth: E. Elliot, 1791).
32. Daniel Livesay, *Children of Uncertain Fortune: Mixed-Race Jamaicans in Britain and the Atlantic Family, 1733–1833* (Chapel Hill, NC: University of North Carolina Press, 2018), p. 120.
33. Ibid., p. 120.

34. Ibid., p. 177.
35. Oldcorn, *Falmouth and the British Maritime Empire*, pp. 181–3.
36. Homi K. Bhabha, *The Location of Culture* (Abingdon: Routledge, 1994), p. 122.

4

'Comrade Algerine Sankoh of West Africa': Pan-Africanist and Britain's First Black Revolutionary Socialist?

Christian Høgsbjerg

On 19 March 1908, one 'Comrade Algerine Sankoh of West Africa' addressed a public meeting of Kirkdale branch of the Social Democratic Federation (SDF), which met at 132 Kirkdale Road in Liverpool, on 'Socialism and the Negro Race'. The SDF was Britain's first ever Marxist organisation founded in 1881; it existed until it was renamed the British Socialist Party in 1911.[1] Though few, it seems, realised its historic significance at the time, this was possibly the first time an African addressed a public meeting of a revolutionary socialist organisation in Britain. The claim that Sankoh was 'Britain's first Black revolutionary socialist' needs to acknowledge the presence in Britain for periods from the 1860s to the 1880s of the Cuban-born Paul Lafargue (1842–1911), son-in-law of Karl Marx and the grandson of a mixed heritage refugee from Haiti, who always took pride in his African heritage and who could be said to be 'politically Black'.

Algerine Kelfallah Sankoh has been a long neglected figure in both Black British history and the wider history of Pan-Africanism, remembered if at all for his later life as a leading member of the Sierra Leone 'Saro' community in Port Harcourt in the Niger Delta. As Mac Dixon-Fyle's work on the Potts-Johnsons family shows, from 1932 Sankoh was a respected columnist and editor of the recently launched *Nigerian Observer*, and from 1938, Vice-Principal at Enitonna High School. After his death on 14 November 1940, the *Nigerian Observer* reported 'Professor' Sankoh, the

'Schoolmaster and Journalist' and 'editor of the *Nigerian Observer*, 1932–37' had died, 'about 63 years of age'.[2] As Dixon-Fyle noted in 1999, 'Sankoh's life deserves review in a biographical study'.[3] It is sadly impossible to give that full biographical portrait here. Rather, our aims are more modest, to outline Sankoh's early life and Pan-Africanist activism, and his shift towards ideas of revolution and socialism while in Britain during the 1900s.

EARLY LIFE IN SIERRA LEONE

Algerine Kelfallah Sankoh was the adopted name of Isaac Augustus Johnson, born in Sierra Leone around 1882.[4] He attended what became Methodist Boys High School, Freetown, which had been established by missionaries as Wesleyan Methodist Boys High School in 1874 to inculcate a pride in God, country and race, later recalling his religious upbringing, with regular Bible readings.[5] Freetown had been established in the eighteenth century by British humanitarians as refuge for former slaves, maroons etc. – and those from Nova Scotia who fought for Britain during the American War of Independence. A colonial literary elite emerged here, shaped by British colonialism and missionary activity, and with a strong identity with Christianity, European dress and the English language.[6]

Yet Sankoh was also shaped by more radical, early Pan-Africanist ideas, and recalled having 'a master' who he cooked for and heard talking about 'Yoruba diplomacy'.[7] One of his parents was friends with the pioneering Caribbean-born Pan-Africanist Edward Wilmot Blyden (1832–1912), an important intellectual influence in Sierra Leone in the late nineteenth and early twentieth centuries until his death in Freetown in 1912. As he later recalled of Blyden, 'there is much I could say from personal knowledge of the doctor, whose company I was privileged to enjoy very frequently through his friendship with one of my parents … In Free-Town, Sierra Leone there is a drinking Fount erected to his memory.' He recalled Blyden had conceived of a West African university, so indirectly may be credited for Kings College, Lagos. 'I should like our young men to know that Edward Blyden was black, as black as the blackest of us.'[8] Sankoh's early life then saw him inculcated into a rich intellectual counter-culture, one that challenged any idea of racial inferiority with respect to Africans, and so in implicit and sometimes explicit opposition to the prevailing ideas of British colonialism.

> When I was a boy I used to be all glee at hearing the stump speeches delivered by some of my country's leaders. These ancient orators of ours and they were not a few (perhaps some of them are alive today) used to talk of 'Africa the grey-haired mother of civilisation'. They talked of how she has had her day and will have her day again. In other words she has had her innings, has been bowled out and will at the second innings do wonders. New Africa is preaching it today and Old Africa is saying 'Amen' to it, but with tons of reservations.[9]

White European settlers and colonialists, who often died of various tropical diseases, called Sierra Leone a 'beautiful charnel house', but by the late nineteenth century it had been established as a British crown colony, one that celebrated Christmas, Easter, New Year and Empire Day (the birthday of Queen Victoria). It also marked Pope Henessey Day every year on 22 August, which Sankoh recalled as 'the people's day in the beautiful charnel house'.[10] As Odile Goerg has noted, this festival 'started as a tribute to Governor Pope Hennessy at the time of the abolition of unpopular taxes, it continued to be celebrated as both a commemoration and a way of affirming some kind of autonomy vis-à-vis the colonial power'.[11]

STUDYING AT WILBERFORCE UNIVERSITY IN OHIO

In 1899, aged about 18, Sankoh seems to have won a scholarship to study in the US, at Wilberforce University, Ohio. Named after the famous British abolitionist and religious thinker, Wilberforce was the first college to be owned and operated by Black Americans, having been founded in 1856 by a unique collaboration between the Cincinnati Conference of the Methodist Episcopal Church and the African Methodist Episcopal Church (AME) to provide classical education and teacher training for young Blacks. As W.E.B. Du Bois, who taught at Wilberforce from 1894 to 1896, later noted, it had an 'extraordinary geographical situation ... practically in the longitudinal center of the Negro population of the United States, and yet in latitude North of Mason and Dixon's line'. Du Bois was 'thrilled by the natural beauty of this place and uplifted by the romantic history of its founding'.[12] In 1898, Wilberforce had about 20 faculty, 334 students and 246 graduates, and had a programme of scholarships for African students in place, organised by the AME Church's Mission to Africa.[13]

Accordingly, Sankoh recalled how he crossed the Atlantic en route to Wilberforce, meeting the African American boxer Frank Craig (1868–1943), 'The Harlem Coffee Cooler', who had been based in London for several years and where he had in 1898 won the English middleweight championship, after already winning the title of world middleweight champion back in 1894 on the way. 'I once met Frank Craig, the world's light weight champion boxer, I think it was in 1899 on board the SS *City of Rome*, on a journey from Greenock [Scotland] to New York USA. He first loaned me a copy of Dante's *Inferno*. I was interested in it.'[14] In 1934, Sankoh recalled

> I was a stripling of a lad when along with two other friends and one of 1500 passengers I sailed from Greenock in Scotland on the SS *City of Rome* bound for New York via Newfoundland. We had a thrilling experience off the banks of Newfoundland, where we encountered some Icebergs which nearly sent us to old *Davy Jones locker* (the bottom of the sea). About 4 days afterwards we came in sight of the historic *Statue of Liberty*. We were in Hudson Bay. It was really a thrilling sight. Quite enthralling! I asked whether the Statue was the mother of Uncle Sam. I was a rather precocious youth then![15]

We know little of Sankoh's time at Wilberforce University, though he later recalled a time 'when I was studying, or pretending to study, Logic'.[16] In the US, he clearly developed his knowledge about African American history, learning about figures such as Phyllis Wheatley, reading Beecher Stowe's *Uncle's Tom's Cabin* and seeing a dramatisation of it as a 'young chap' when 'in exile in one of the American colleges'.[17] He was also impressed by Oliver

William Holmes, whose *The Autocrat of the Breakfast-Table* he read in 1900.[18] While in America he met Paul Lawrence Dunbar (1872–1906), 'the Poet-Laureate of the Negro Race in America', and who he heard tell the story of how he became noticed while working as an elevator boy in city business just scribbling a poem.[19] Other African American intellectuals he met in this period who made an impact on him included Kelly Miller (1863–1939), Professor of Sociology at Howard University and known as 'the Bard of the Potomac', and William Sanders Scarborough (1852–1926), an African American Professor of Classics at Wilberforce University.[20]

Sankoh also decided to travel close to, and then over and beyond the Mason and Dixon line, visiting first Kentucky, and then Atlanta in Georgia, possibly to visit the AME Church there. He later recalled meeting Henry McNeal Turner (1834–1915), an important African American bishop who had established and developed the AME Church across Georgia as well as encouraging links with West and South Africa, and thought him inspiring, 'brimful with hopes for the future of Africa' and a 'silver tongued orator'.[21] 'He used to say that every Negro Christian should sing "Wash me and I shall be blacker than a crow" instead of singing "Wash me and I shall be whiter than snow"'.[22] Turner had notably preached that God was Black, scandalising some but appealing to others at the first Black Baptist Convention in 1895. As he put it, 'we have *as much right* biblically and otherwise to believe that God is a Negroe, as you buckra or white people have to believe that God is a fine looking, symmetrical and ornamented white man'.[23] Yet Sankoh's trip to Georgia was memorable for other reasons, for, as he recalled, while riding 'the Jim Crow car' he was nearly lynched. As he wrote in April 1934, 'Lynching is illegally hanging and burning a man by irresponsible parties without due trial by the courts of the land. This is the American style.' Indeed, when the topic of lynching arises, 'my memory goes back to 34 years ago' to 'a subject I never like to think of. It always makes me get *the blues* somehow.' He remained haunted by his experience of seeing murderous American racism up close in Kentucky. 'There I would either have been lynched or I would have lynched and saved the Devil the trouble of claiming as his a few grizzle faced, tobacco-chewing Yankees', 'those horrible fellows'.

> Alexandre Dumas in his book *The Three Musketeers* has an interesting character D'Artagnan whose father charged him on leaving his village home for Paris to endure nothing from any man save the Cardinal and the King. D'Artagnan took every gaze for a challenge and every smile for an insult. I took less than these for more than these. He swore once by God's blood! I did not swear but I thought hell fire to be a fit place for any and every American bearded or beardless who dare ask me exchange my coach for the Jim Crow Car. I was up against it and right in the Dixon and Mason's line. I had either to defy Uncle Sam and wear his beard or get into the Jim Crow Car. Discretion in more ways than one and on many occasions is the better part of valour. I was hundreds of miles from New York city where I boarded the coach I was asked to vacate. I would not and will not walk back to New York nor would a question of refund of fare be considered if it even arose.[24]

In the American South and still in what he called the 'Jim Crow car', Johnson (Sankoh) 'travelled to Atlanta, Georgia, a luke-warm bed of lynching'.

> There I almost had the pleasure of being lynched for daring to come to the assistance of a care free and veritable careless American who along one of the *dug outs* I would call the negro houses and homes along Decatur Avenue, was being beaten beyond pleasure point by a gang of irresponsible white ruffians. There is such a thing as bed fellows in degradation and misery; strange bedfellows they may be, but they are nevertheless real comrades.[25]

'DRIFTING' TOWARDS POLITICS IN LIVERPOOL

After studying at Wilberforce University, Sankoh returned to Britain, and in the summer of 1902 was resident in Liverpool, an important port for trade with colonial Sierra Leone.[26] He soon met an 'older Parisian man' in an old second-hand bookshop along Pembroke Place, Liverpool. 'Our acquaintance developed into friendship – a true, real one', while 'the owner of the bookshop was a man I had learnt to admire, if not to respect. I admired him for his profound knowledge of books.'[27] The owner suggested he buy John William Draper's *A History of the Intellectual Development of Europe* (1863), though Sankoh recalled: 'I would have none of that stuff. I had already decided on Europe's intellectual and other developments since I landed in Liverpool.' Instead, he felt 'I and my people I decided needed to know our psychology and that of other races etc, before developing my intellect to the degree I had been impressed [by] England's.' His French friend recommended instead *The Psychology of Peoples: Its Influence on Their Evolution* (1898) by the French polymath Gustav Le Bon, author of the best-seller *The Crowd: A Study of the Popular Mind* (1895), which clearly made an impression.[28] Sankoh also visited France as a tourist with his French friend in July 1902.[29] In Liverpool, then Sankoh took the opportunity to continue reading widely, remembering Picton Reading Room and Hornby Library as a model of what a public library could be like.[30]

Sankoh's reading habits started to challenge his religious beliefs, and shaped his growing interest in political ideas. As well as some classic works of scholarship and literature Sankoh later recalled also reading 'a disreputable few, exceptionally bad authors' who 'I should never have read'.

> I recall writers of this class as Tom Paine, Robert Ingersoll, and many others. The result of my reading those books was not the best. I was really drifting; at least my religious ambition was. I was getting to lose hold of myself and the religious foundation that had been laid in me.[31]

Sankoh read Sir Thomas More's *Utopia* in 1904, which 'fascinated me as did Oscar Wilde's *De Profundis* for which I entertained and hold great prejudice'. *Utopia* 'took me some time however to digest … I at first swallowed it with the proverbial "grain of salt" because the ideal city and state of man Sir Thomas More depicted I considered was gross impossibility. But time brings about changes …'[32] He recalled being particularly impressed by the anarchist Prince Peter Kropotkin's collection of anthropological essays *Mutual Aid: A Factor of Evolution* (1902).

> Some years ago I read Kropotkin's book *Mutual Aid*. I considered it a wonderful book, and others, especially Press Reviewers of books, considered it so too. He dealt with man, beginning with savages, and he marshals a mass of striking and suggestive evidence to show that mutual aid is found among cannibals and the lowest races of mankind.[33]

Sankoh also visited London, stopping at *Madame Tussaud's* wax house, and looking at himself in a distorting mirror.[34] Though he does not dwell on it at length, he clearly also experienced racism in Britain, as he movingly reminisced about when contrasting the open racism of the US with the more subtle variety in Britain.

> Lynching law is not an American law although in many states in the American Union it is practiced and silently approved by those who ought to have known better, just as there is no English law that enacts that an African or any negro should be judged and treated a social leper in London the world's metropolis.[35]

THE ETHIOPIAN PROGRESSIVE ASSOCIATION

It was perhaps partly in response to such racism in the early twentieth century that 'Ethiopianism', a form of early Pan-Africanism, became popular in Britain, especially among African and Caribbean students.[36] In 1904, Johnson (Sankoh) helped found the Ethiopian Progressive Association (EPA) in Liverpool with other West Africans and West Indians, mainly as Hakim Adi notes, 'students at the various colleges', and eventually published a quarterly, *The Ethiopian Review*.[37] This is not the place to detail the EPA's activism, which aimed according to its initial constitution in November 1904 'to create friendly feeling and intercourse among all its members residing in Liverpool'; 'To create a bond of union between (a) all other members of the Ethiopian race at home and abroad; (b) to further the interest and raise the social status of the Ethiopian race at home and abroad; and to strengthen the friendly relationship of the said race and other races of mankind'; and 'To discuss at each meeting matters of vital importance concerning Africa in particular, and the Negro race in general'. Other early

EPA activists and supporters included Africans like J.M. Whitfield, Rev. E.D.L. Thompson and Rev. J.P. Richards from Sierra Leone; Kwesi Ewusu, J.A. Abraham, C. Bartels-Kodwo, A.W. Neizer, James Hutton Mills, I. Minnow, Rev. T.E. Ward and K.S.E. Insaidoo from the Gold Coast, S.N. Kitson from Fernando Po (Bioko), J.A. Caulcrick from Lagos and Dr H.B. Gabashane from South Africa. West Indians such as Jonathan Knight from Barbados, Dr G.D. Hamilton and F. Bailey from Jamaica and R.R. Mirranda from Cuba also played an important role. The EPA aimed to 'instill into all its members the necessity for cultivating manly principles, thereby impressing in the hearts of all those with whom it is their opportunity to associate the true efficiency and worth of their misunderstood race', and membership was open to 'all men of true moral worth and character, irrespective of position or circumstance'.

They took as their slogan, 'Non sibi sed patriae et humanitati', 'Not for ourselves, but for our country and humanity'. After elections, Sankoh – or as he was still known, Isaac Augustus Johnson, was elected President, testament to his dynamism and intellectual capacities.[38] As Danell Jones notes, on one level the EPA approach was not particularly radical, and they felt 'assured of the good will of the educated class of the British nation' and believed they would win respect regardless 'of colour or nationality' by possessing exemplary 'character, intelligence, and efficiency'. They were committed to teaching people 'how to get recognition constitutionally' and actively working 'to prepare the minds of the African students in England to receive the gospel of united effort on which the salvation of the African race depends'.[39]

In July 1905, the *Sierra Leone Weekly News*, a major paper on the West Coast of Africa having been established in 1884 with the help of Blyden, carried a 'Presidents' message to the members of the Ethiopian Progressive Association'. After speaking of the honour of his election as EPA President, Sankoh noted: 'The twentieth century dawns on us as a free race and people, for "children of freedom", as a race cognizant of the … changes of the past, of the wonders … of the present, and grand promises of the future.' He praised the courage of Black Americans, noting: 'No race of cowards ever succeed, or bring any project to a successful end.' 'Our race is one of which we should be justly proud of. We should have more race pride: have more self-reliance.' He stressed that 'our duty is to God, ourselves and our country'. He devoted attention to outlining the horrific reality of Belgian colonialism in the Congo, praising the work raising awareness by 'our much esteemed friend and sympathiser, E.D. Morel editor of the *West African Mail*'. It is perhaps worth quoting the close of the address to get a sense of Sankoh's developing political consciousness:

> Like Spartan youths let us devote our lives to our country's good, and the world's advancement. We are claiming, and should claim, recognition as men and honourable men. This is an inalienable right. In demanding recognition we must do so on grounds of merit and efficiency. We should be unwilling to be recognised by any man on grounds of favour and sympathy. Those days of racial life are passed. These questions confront us – 1) What will we do for ourselves? 2) Will we sit and allow ourselves to be dragged once more into disguised slavery? 3) Will we sit and allow other nations to deprive us of our country? These are questions that we must of necessity answer, or our doom is inevitable ...
>
> Yours for the future of the Negro race,
>
> I.A. Johnson.[40]

This piece drew a response on 7 October 1905 from one Rev. Charles W. Farquhar, a Barbadian who after a period as a priest in Conakry, French Guinea, in 1890 as part of the Society for the Propagation of the Gospel had become a teacher in Sierra Leone. Farquhar discussed his experiences in the African Association in London which had been founded in 1897 by the Black Trinidadian Pan-Africanist Henry Sylvester Williams and which Farquhar had visited to give talks and sermons in 1898 and 1899 as one of its 'leading men'.[41] Farquhar somewhat patronisingly suggested the students should instead form a social club rather than one with any political agenda, which was to reflect on things above their concerns. Sankoh, writing from the EPA's base at Association Room, Daulby Hall, Daulby Street, Liverpool, fired off a letter in response to Farquhar to defend the EPA which was published in the *Sierra Leone Weekly News* in late November 1905:

> We as African students will, in our feeble way, as we are doing, try to show to the traducers of the African race that the Negro and the African of the twentieth century mean to demand their God-given rights. We are here as students and not as social club promoters and merry-makers. Are we young men representatives of a race and one worth working for and fighting for – to spend our spare moments around the billiard table or in dancing halls? Our racial life and career demand more from us.
>
> The members of the Ethiopian Progressive Association do not claim competency in discussing Negro affairs. We do not deny and we will never deny that there are latent talents in the Negro race. We do not expect to create material fetters with which to bind the African in his action but we are trying to prepare the minds of the African students in England to receive the gospel of united effort on which the salvation of the African race depends.
>
> Does he [Farquhar] know that Negroes were refused admission to a 'Workhouse' in Liverpool on account of their colour? Does he know that men of his own colour were denied a night's lodging for the same reason?
>
> Does our critic know that we have in our roll residents of Liverpool? Does he know that our Vice-President, Dr G D Hamilton, MA, MD, MRCS, LRCP, etc, has a home in Liverpool, having an extensive practice in the city, as well as our Assistant Secretary, Treasurer, Editor of the *Ethiopian Review* and two thirds of our members who are residents in Liverpool?[42]

Sankoh continued, noting that the EPA founders were 'patriotic sons of Africa' who founded the EPA 'not because we have no social pleasures from White homes, for we seek no such transitory pleasures, but we founded the Ethiopian Progressive Association on broader principles than epicurean and bacchanalian pleasures'.

> The Ethiopian Progressive Association through the columns of the *Ethiopian Review* means to try to teach the Ethiopian how to gain recognition constitutionally … If he must fight at all, he must first be taught the lesson of united effort which the Ethiopian Progressive Association means to try to teach the African. The Ethiopian Progressive Association has been meeting with

> encouragement throughout the Coast in England and America (North and South).[43]

Once again the contradictions of the EPA come through, on the one hand, wanting to take the non-violent moral high road as honourable Christian men, but also angry about the institutional racist colour bar in Britain and imperial domination in Africa. As Adi notes, the EPA supported the 1906 Zulu or Bambatha Rebellion in Natal, challenged discrimination in the West African medical service, and opposed the 'pacification' campaigns in Nigeria. They admired the achievements of Africanus Horton and Edward Blyden and celebrated a glorious African past before colonialism.[44] On 14 February 1906, Johnson and Ewusi wrote to Du Bois about the EPA, sending a copy of their constitution.[45]

Such anti-imperialist ideas were also to take a growing anti-capitalist direction. Black activists in Britain were beginning to establish connections and links with the modern socialist movement during the first decade of the twentieth century, when the British Empire was growing to the very height of its power and when European socialists were beginning to develop a theory of 'imperialism'. On 3 August 1906, the Nigerian nationalist Prince Bandele Omoniyi (1884–1913), while studying at the University of Edinburgh, had written an article in *The African Mail* which had linked socialism with 'the equality of freedom and opportunity to all coloured races'. A year later, on 16 August 1907, Omoniyi published another article, 'The Regeneration of Africa' in the Independent Labour Party's paper, the *Labour Leader*, which Hakim Adi notes

> was probably the first ever written by an African to appear in an openly socialist journal ... evidently Socialism and the Labour Movement interested Omoniyi sufficiently for him to write a book on the subject, *Socialism Examined*, which unfortunately has not yet come to light. Even these tenuous links do show something of a new departure for West Africans ...[46]

Bandele Omoniyi would soon join the EPA around Sankoh in Liverpool and publish *A Defence of the Ethiopian Movement* (1908).[47]

It is then as one of the leading Pan-Africanist activists in Britain that we find the notice for one 'Comrade Algerine Sankoh of West Africa' speaking to Kirkdale SDF on 'Socialism and the Negro Race' in March 1908.[48] Over a year later, in June 1909, Sankoh went public about his change of name, with a notice in the *Sierra Leone Weekly News* running over several issues from 19 June 1909 onwards noticing that Isaac Augustus Johnson of Freetown, Sierra Leone, 'now resident of Liverpool, in the county of Lancashire, England do from the subscribed date, relinquish and renounce the above name for Algerine Kelfallah Sankoh by which name I desire to be addressed and known'.[49] The decision to adopt a more African name like Sankoh was a trend among some of his contemporaries, particularly those connected to the Dress Reform Society of Freetown, which had been founded in 1887. For example, A.E. Metzger became A.E. Tuboku-Metzger, while later, in the 1920s, Etheldred Nathaniel Jones became Lamina Sankoh.[50] Tellingly Sankoh gave his address for correspondence as 'Clarion Club, Liverpool', probably Liverpool Clarion Club House, Halewood, revealing of his continuing connection with socialists in Liverpool organised around the popular *Clarion* newspaper established in 1891 and edited by Robert Blatchford.[51] On 30 June 1909, Sankoh also joined the freemasons, one of the few organisations in Britain at that time outside of the socialist movement that didn't operate a 'colour bar'.[52]

While back briefly in Sierra Leone during 1909, *Britons through Negro Spectacles*, a book by a compatriot and friend of Sankoh's, A.B.C. Merriman-Labor, was published.[53] On 18 September 1909, Sankoh reviewed his friend's pioneering take on Britain from an African perspective in the *Sierra Leone Weekly News*.[54]

> Beneath the roof-tree of European Empires we may all meet, but in the heart of every member of the wide dominion lies an affection for his own race, his own country, his own people and ineradicable belief in its particular destiny. Intelligent Colonials, especially in Western Africa are no longer content to be sleeping partners in the problems of their respective Colonies. We congratulate Mr Merriman-Labor on his laudable efforts and shake hands with him across the sea for the masterly and

> statesman-like manner in which he has handled the vital questions of the race. We recommend the book as an introduction to his future works on African sociology, a concise and well written guide to London, in story-form, a work of exceptional merit, a much needed addition to African and general literature.[55]

In October 1909, Sankoh followed this up with a longer three-part piece for the *Sierra Leone Weekly News*, 'The Old and the New'. This once again highlighted the appalling human rights abuses in the Congo Free State under King Leopold's despotism, praised Morel's work and railed against the social Darwinist theory of 'the survival of the fittest', declaring there was a need for 'a new hope' for Africans.[56] Though writing in a publication that would be subject to British colonial state censorship, the final part – with which it seems fitting to conclude – gives us perhaps the clearest sense of what would now become more or less his mature political and intellectual outlook. Fittingly, given Sankoh's recent SDF connection, he made a call for 'revolution':

> Africa needs revolution before evolution in matters political, social and ecclesiastical. As Robert Blatchford in Britain timely and wisely tells his people, revolution by force of arms is not desirable nor feasible; but there is another kind of revolution from which we hope great things. This is the revolution of thought. Let us once get the people, or a big majority of the people to understand themselves, to believe in themselves and to work for themselves, and the real revolution is accomplished. In free countries, as our British West African colonies pose and profess to be, the Almighty voice should be the voice of public opinion. What the public believe in and demand, if conscientiously born, and constitutionally sought for, has got to be given. And who is to refuse? Neither King nor Parliament can stand against a united and resolute community of British subjects. And do not suppose that brute force, which is powerless to get good or to keep it, has power to resist it or destroy it. Neither truncheons nor bayonets can kill a truth. Believe me, we can overcome the constable, the soldier, without shedding one drop of blood or breaking one pane of glass or losing one day's work.

> Our real task is to win the trust and help of the people – I do not mean the Colonists black and white only, but also the aborigines – and the first thing to be done is to educate them; to teach them, and to educate them what we mean. To make it quite clear to them what we are, and what we are not. Our method must be persuasive; our cause must be justice; our weapons must be the tongue and the pen: our final or New Hope must be good will to all, and ill will for none. Believe me, as soon as we can command capital; as soon as we are able to obtain a release from the prison of our egregious poverty, the colour-question will hear its death-knell and the corpse of race prejudice will be borne with funeral steps to the grave of oblivion and forgetfulness.[57]

NOTES

1. *Justice*, 14 March 1908, p. 12. I am grateful for correspondence with Mac Dixon-Fyle, and am indebted to Shina Alimi, and the Centre for Memory, Narrative and Histories' Research Support Fund at the University for Brighton, without whom the necessary research for this chapter at the National Archives, Ibadan, would have been impossible.
2. *Nigerian Observer*, 16 November 1940, p. 1.
3. Mac Dixon-Fyle, *A Saro Community in the Niger Delta, 1912–1984: The Potts-Johnsons of Port Harcourt and Their Heirs* (Rochester, NY: University of Rochester Press, 1999), p. 242.
4. United Grand Lodge of England Freemason Membership Registers, 1751–1921.
5. 'Judas and Co', *Nigerian Observer*, 15 April 1933, p. 5.
6. Dixon-Fyle, *A Saro Community in the Niger Delta*, pp. 8–9. See also Christopher Fyfe, *A History of Sierra Leone* (London: Oxford University Press, 1962).
7. *Nigerian Observer*, 21 March 1936, p. 5.
8. *Nigerian Observer*, 26 September 1936, p. 5. On Blyden, see Gilbert M. Khadiagala, 'Edward Wilmot Blyden: Pan-African Pioneer', in Adekeye Adebajo (ed.), *The Pan-African Pantheon* (Manchester: Manchester University Press, 2021), pp. 73–87.
9. *Nigerian Observer*, 29 February 1936, p. 5.
10. 'Children's Day', *Nigerian Observer*, 20 May 1933, p. 5.
11. Odile Goerg, 'Between Everyday Life and Exception: Celebrating Pope Hennessy Day in Freetown, 1872–c. 1905', *Journal of African Cultural Studies*, 15/1 (2002).
12. W.E.B. Du Bois, 'The Future of Wilberforce University', *The Journal of Negro Education*, 9/4 (October 1940), pp. 553–4.

13. James T. Campbell, *Songs of Zion: The African Methodist Episcopal Church in the United States and South Africa* (New York: Oxford University Press, 1995), pp. 259–60; John R. Hawkins (ed.), 'Our Schools from Latest Reports', *The Educator*, 1/1 (1898), p. 47.
14. *Nigerian Observer*, 30 May 1936. See also 'Ring Legends: Frank Craig', *Black Then*, 21 August 2019, https://blackthen.com/ring-legends-frank-craig/ (accessed 8 December 2021).
15. 'Lynching and Lynch Law', *Nigerian Observer*, 28 April 1934, p. 5.
16. *Nigerian Observer*, 29 February 1936, p. 5.
17. *Nigerian Observer*, 15 August 1936, p. 21. For his reference to Wheatley, see *Nigerian Observer*, 19 September 1936, p. 11.
18. *Nigerian Observer*, 21 August 1937, p. 11.
19. *Nigerian Observer*, 19 September 1936, p. 11.
20. Ibid., p. 11.
21. 'The Cry of Youth', *Nigerian Observer*, 10 April 1937, p. 11.
22. 'A New Idea', *Nigerian Observer*, 1 April 1933, p. 5.
23. Stephen Ward Angell, *Bishop Henry McNeal Turner and African-American Religion in the South* (Knoxville, TN: University of Tennessee Press, 1992), p. 261.
24. Lynching and Lynch Law', *Nigerian Observer*, p. 5.
25. 'Lynching', *Nigerian Observer*, 5 May 1934, p. 5.
26. For advertisements relating to Liverpool companies, see *Sierra Leone Weekly News*, 9 October 1909, p. 2.
27. *Nigerian Observer*, 14 March 1936, p. 5.
28. Ibid., p. 5.
29. *Nigerian Observer*, 28 March 1936, p. 5.
30. *Nigerian Observer*, 8 February 1936, p. 12.
31. 'Authors I Admire', *Nigerian Observer*, 14 August 1937, p. 11.
32. 'Sir Thomas More's *Utopia*', *Nigerian Observer*, 17 July 1937, p. 11.
33. 'Spending', *Nigerian Observer*, 14 July 1934, p. 5.
34. *Nigerian Observer*, 27 January 1934, p. 5.
35. 'Lynching', *Nigerian Observer*, p. 5.
36. On 'Ethiopianism', see Hakim Adi, *Pan-Africanism: A History* (London: Bloomsbury Academic: 2018), pp. 16–18.
37. Hakim Adi, *West Africans in Britain, 1900–1960: Nationalism, Pan-Africanism and Communism* (London: Lawrence & Wishart, 1998), p. 11.
38. *The Constitution of the Ethiopian Progressive Association* (Liverpool: D. Marples and Co, 1905), https://credo.library.umass.edu/view/pageturn/mums312-b002-i204/#page/7/mode/1up (accessed 8 December 2021).
39. Danell Jones, *An African in Imperial London: The Indomitable Life of A.B.C. Merriman-Labor* (Oxford: Oxford University Press, 2018), p. 82.
40. *Sierra Leone Weekly News*, 22 July 1905, p. 4. On the Congo, see Adam Hochschild, *King Leopold's Ghost: A Story of Greed, Terror, and Heroism in Colonial Africa* (London: Pan, 2006).

41. 'The Ethiopian Progressive Association', *Sierra Leone Weekly News*, 7 October 1905, p. 3. On Farquhar and the African Association, see Marika Sherwood, *Origins of Pan-Africanism: Henry Sylvester Williams, Africa and the African Diaspora* (New York: Routledge, 2011), pp. 42–3, 241–2.
42. *Sierra Leone Weekly News*, 25 November 1905, p. 5.
43. Ibid., p. 5.
44. Adi, *West Africans in Britain*, p. 12.
45. Jeffrey Green, *Black Edwardians: Black People in Britain 1901–1914* (Abingdon: Routledge, 2012). The EPA also approached Booker T. Washington. Ibid., p. 11; Herbert Aptheker, 'W. E. B. Du Bois and Africa', in Robert A. Hill (ed.), *Pan-African Biography* (Los Angeles: Crossroads Press, 1987), p. 101.
46. Hakim Adi, 'Bandele Omoniyi – a Neglected Nigerian Nationalist', *African Affairs*, 90 (1991), pp. 591–2.
47. Ibid.
48. *Justice*, 14 March 1908, p. 12.
49. *Sierra Leone Weekly News*, 19 June 1909, p. 8. See also similar notices on 26 June and 8 July 1909, p. 12.
50. Dixon-Fyle, *A Saro Community in the Niger Delta*, pp. 34, 93.
51. 'Liverpool Clarion', *Country Standard*, 31 May 2010, http://country-standard.blogspot.com/2010/05/liverpool-clarion.html (accessed 8 December 2021).
52. United Grand Lodge of England Freemason Membership Registers, 1751–1921.
53. Jones, *An African in Imperial London*, p. 82. The work has recently been republished with a new introduction by Bernadine Evaristo. See A.B.C. Merriman-Labor, *Britons through Negro Spectacles* (London: Penguin, 2022).
54. Jones, *An African in Imperial London*, p. 140.
55. *Sierra Leone Weekly News*, 18 September 1909, p. 4.
56. Kelfallah Sankoh, 'The Old and the New', *Sierra Leone Weekly News*, 9 October 1909, p. 5; 23 October 1909, p. 5; and 30 October 1909, p. 5.
57. Sankoh, 'The Old and the New', *Sierra Leone Weekly News*, 30 October 1909, p. 5.

5

Dusé Mohamed Ali, the *African Times and Orient Review* and the British Government

Rey Bowen

Dusé Mohamed Ali (1866–1945) was a Sudanese-Egyptian, who was raised and lived in the UK between 1876 and 1921. He was the co-founder and editor of the journal *African Times and Orient Review (ATOR)*,[1] one of Britain's earliest periodicals owned by Africans and published in London between 1912 and 1920. As a supporter of Egyptian nationalism, he is unheard of, or not mentioned, in contemporary Egyptian politics of his day; and his significance is in Britain, the English-speaking African diaspora and Pan-Islamic world. Between 1882 and 1909, Ali spent much of his time as an actor, playwright, journalist and traveller.[2] As an actor, he invariably played 'dark parts' and had roles in several plays as a Black slave and as Othello. On his first visit to the US, between 1886 and 1898, he won success as 'The Young Egyptian Wonder Reciter of Shakespeare'. During this period, Dusé travelled throughout the country and to various countries in the Caribbean, as well as South and Central America, before returning to Europe. This contact made him consciously aware of the precarious circumstances of Africans in the diaspora. His writing career began by penning letters to the British Press. From 1909 until 1911, he became a writer for a famous British journal, *The New Age*. By his mid-40s, with a wealth of experience, Ali emerged onto the 'world scene as an avid Pan-Africanist. Pan-Africanism is a movement that took on many forms to unite people of African descent, whether in the diaspora or on the continent. Such unity would enable the various peoples of African descent to combine their efforts to build social, economic, cultural and political liberation to fight European imperialism, discrimination and colonialism and provide economic self-sufficiency through business practices among all Africans.[3] Ali was also an ardent Pan-Orientalist, a supporter of people living in the East or Orient. He championed the unity of the group of countries, peoples and cultures located in the regions referred to as the Near East (now the Middle East) and the Far East. In the early twentieth century, such countries included those in the Ottoman and Persian Empires, South and South East Asia, China and Japan. In Ali's estimation, the East needed a unified effort to counter this imperialist onslaught, particularly against the hegemony of the British Empire.

Shortly before attending the Universal Races Congress (URC) in 1911, Ali contacted John Eldred Taylor. The URC was the idea of Felix Adler and Gustave Spiller and took place at the University of London between 26 and 29 July 1911.[4] The international conference convened as many ethnic groups and nations that existed at the time

> to discuss, in the light of science and modern conscience, the general relations subsisting between the peoples of the West and those of the East, between the so-called white and the so-called coloured peoples, with a view to encouraging between them a fuller understanding, the most friendly feelings, and the heartier co-operation.[5]

There were over two thousand delegates in attendance from all over the globe. Taylor, a Sierra Leonean businessman and colleague, knew Ali as they were both members of the Imperial African Club. The club was a fraternity of European and African intellectuals working together for the advancement of British West Africans.[6] Ali and Taylor co-founded the *ATOR* a year later in July 1912.

Ali became a known agitator, and he used the *ATOR* to fight anti-racist, anti-imperialist and anti-colonialist campaigns that attempted to thwart the advance of political, social and cultural injustices throughout the world for people of colour. For example, in the first issue of the *ATOR*, Ali reported the public floggings of two African railway employees at Zaria in Nigeria for not bowing before a British administrator. The Colonial Office was not impressed, nor was Ali taken lightly by the War Office's MI5 or Scotland Yard's Special Branch. The British intelligence agencies investigated Ali to establish his nationality, concerned about his public support of Pan-Islamism, a modern ideology that called for the socio-political solidarity among Muslims across the world. The philosophy was state policy during the declining years of the Ottoman Empire, especially at the beginning of the twentieth century.[7]

Moreover, his endorsement of Pan-Ethiopianism, an early form of Pan-Africanism with its most recent origins in the establishment of African-run Christian churches, influenced by African American and African Caribbean missionaries, illustrated his commitment to African solidarity.[8] The authorities took note of the *ATOR*'s anti-British sentiments, Turcophilia, pro-Egyptian and pro-Indian nationalism, and continual support of Africa for the Africans.

ALI'S NATIONALITY

Dusé Mohamed Ali was not a British subject, and he did not have proof of his Egyptian origins. The British government had their doubts, especially during World War I, while the Foreign and Colonial Offices had difficulty accepting his nationality. This impediment would delay Ali from receiving a passport to travel to West Africa. However, it is worth looking into Ali's origins because, when the UK entered World War I on 4 August 1914, all foreign nationals were considered suspicious. The consensus is that Ali was born on the 21 November 1866 in Alexandria, Egypt. Scotland Yard surveillance records also agree to Ali's birth year of 1866.[9] The Special Branch section of New Scotland Yard reported that he arrived in 1876 at the age of ten and then in 1886 travelled to the US before returning to England in 1898.[10] According to Ali, he was sent to live and study in England by his father in the care of Captain Dusé, a French army officer.[11]

Moreover, at the time of his request for a passport on 22 September 1914 when attempting to make his first trip to West Africa, he had no birth certificate to prove he was an Egyptian national. For example, in a letter dated 22 September of that year, Ali wrote to The Secretary of State for the Colonies, Lewis Vernon Harcourt, for 'safe conduct from Gambia to Calabar'. He intended to travel the following November to survey the local conditions and to solicit funds for his journal.[12] Assessing his suitability to travel, Sir George Fiddes, the Under-secretary of State, regarded Ali as an agitator:

> His paper is a notorious disseminator of sedition & lies, mainly circulated among Mohammedans. A good deal of space is devoted to Indian & Egyptian grievances and there are a number of paragraphs in Arabic. It is a strong supporter of the 'Pan-Ethiopianism' or Africa for the Africans.[13]

On 26 September, the Colonial Office drafted a response to inform Ali that his request to obtain safe conduct through British West Africa during the war was not possible and that the Under-secretary of State 'can take no action in this matter'. As far as Harcourt was concerned, Ali was an undesirable and the real reason he was travelling to British West Africa was to stir up unrest. To that end, Harcourt sent an internal memo suggesting that it would be in the interest of the colonial authorities:

> to keep watch on his movements & conduct if he arrives. If he arrives but does not land in a colony, or if having landed he leaves for another colony, the Governor of the first colony should inform the Governor of the second of his departure and destination.[14]

Copies of the memo marked 'confidential' were sent to the governors of the Gambia, Sierra Leone, the Gold Coast and Nigeria. Such a predicament made it difficult for Ali to obtain travel documents. In effect, it was to be another five years before he would have documentation to prove he was Egyptian by birth, attained by Ahmed Zaki Abushady (Abushady Bey).

In 1917, Ali applied again for a passport to travel in West Africa but he was unsuccessful. He made another attempt to gain travel documents in August 1919. He wrote to the then Foreign Secretary, A.J. Balfour, explaining his current predicament. Again, he was required to prove his Egyptian nationality. Because he had no birth certificate, Ali was registered as Turkish. It is clear from his letter to the Foreign Secretary that he was becoming frustrated at being unable to apply for a passport because of what amounted to being classed as an alien subject, even though he had registered with Brixton police station as an Egyptian national. Ali turned to his old ally, Colonel Aubrey Herbert, a diplomat and ex-president of the Albanian Committee with family connections to the Prime Minister Herbert Asquith. Herbert called on his contact in the Foreign Office in support of Ali's passport application. His recorded testimonial states that:

> Dusé Mohamed Ali
> Lt Col Aubrey Herbert called to-day to speak about the case of this man. He said that he believed he was of negro descent, via America, but he was born in Egypt & he claimed to be an Egyptian subject. He had been informed by the Foreign Office that, in view of his long absence from Egypt, he was not regarded by the Egyptian Govt as an Egyptian subject & would appear to be of Ottoman nationality. Col Herbert seemed puzzled to know why Ottoman any more than some agreeable nationality had been selected for the man if he could not be recognised as an Egyptian.[15]

Ali wrote that the police told him 'they had instructions from the Home Office to demand that I should re-register as a Turkish subject. Inasmuch as the Egyptian Government know nothing about me.'[16] Although Ali was not given an adequate explanation for being designated Turkish by the British government, Herbert received a written reply to his enquiry. W. Stewart of the Foreign Office mentioned Ali's previous unsuccessful application for a passport in 1917. He continued by stating that if Ali 'asks us to assist him with some form of emergency passport for the purpose of a particular journey he has in contemplation I dare say we might be able to help him, but we can do nothing at present'. Stewart was adamant that

> the Egyptian Govt ... are disinclined, in the absence of an Egyptian law of nationality, to recognise as Egyptian subjects persons claiming that nationality who have been long absent from Egypt & maintain no close connexion with the country. It is assumed that all persons who claim Egyptian nationality were Ottoman subjects prior to the declaration of the Protectorate, &, if they are not now recognised by the Egyptian Govt, they remain Ottoman subjects. This is the reason Dusé Mohamed is regarded as such.[17]

According to Ali in a letter sent to the Foreign Office in August 1919 in support of his passport application, he had proof he was Egyptian. He had obtained a duplicate birth certificate from the city of his birth in Alexandria and had left a copy at the British police headquarters at New Scotland Yard. Ali wrote:

> This certificate was obtained for me from Alexandria, my birthplace, by Abushady Bey, Advocate of Cairo ... It should be known to you that to procure an Egyptian birth certificate one must not only know the full name of one's father, but one must also know the name of the midwife by whom one was delivered, and who is responsible for the registration of all births with which one is directly concerned.[18]

What is more, between the years 1914 and 1919 Ali would be refused travel documents no matter who endorsed his application. It was to take another year before Ali's birth certificate was acknowledged and during the summer of 1920, he successfully applied and received his passport and made his first trip to West Africa.[19] Ali found difficulty acquiring a British passport because of the introduction of the British Nationality and Status of Aliens Act 1914, which came into force on 1 January 1915. The Act made it more difficult for non-British subjects to apply for a British passport, especially if they were not born within the British colonies, a status Ali did not meet.[20]

PAN-ISLAMISM AND TURCOPHILE

Other causes that Ali supported, under the broader umbrella of Pan-Asian solidarity, included that of fellow Muslims who were either Indian or Egyptian nationalists. Ali's additional involvements included helping to organise the London branch of the All-India Muslim League and the newly arrived Ahmadiyya Movement, a messianic Muslim movement. Thus, to strengthen his commitment to Islam Ali became a Turcophile, supporting the largest Islamic state of the period. His early commitment to Turkey became a serious issue once war was declared, at which point he became involved with the politics of the Ottoman Empire. For example, he became a founding member of an international organisation, the Anglo-Ottoman Society, an outgrowth of its earlier incarnation, the Ottoman Committee and the Ottoman Association.[21] The society's aim was 'defending the interests of the Ottoman Empire and the Caliphate'.[22] The objectives of the society were stipulated in a circular that was received at the Foreign Office in late January 1915:

> (1) To advocate a speedy restoration of peace with Turkey on terms which shall assure the independence and development of the Ottoman nation.
> (2) To promote the establishment of a more sympathetic understanding between the two nations.
> (3) Or, for brevity, the establishment of pacific relations and a sympathetic understanding between Turkey and Great Britain.[23]

Another example of a Pan-Islamist and Turcophile organisation Ali belonged to and co-founded was the Albania Committee, a pro-Turkish organisation. The group's membership included African, Indian, Albanian Muslims and British sympathisers. This commitment to the political affairs of Muslims in Albania came as a result of the Balkan Wars (1912–13). Initially, the first conflict was an effort to dissolve the power of the Ottoman Empire led by the Balkan League (Greece, Bulgaria, Serbia and Montenegro) to establish individual nationalism of those states belonging to the League.[24] Albania, the state in the area with the most significant majority of Muslims, was a threat. Consequently, the Albanian Committee's aims and objectives were the independence of Albania and to protect the rights of the Muslims and Jews against the aggression of the Balkan Christians.[25] Ali announced his commitment to the group in the December 1912 to January 1913 edition of the *ATOR*; he claimed there was a conspiracy of silence when it came to discussing the politics of Albania.[26] Nevertheless, the Foreign Office found Ali to be a valuable tool in tempering the behaviour of at least two members of the Albania Committee. For example, they had become aware of two Indian seditionists within the group who were originally members of the British branch of the Muslim League. The charge of sedition amounted to treason against the British government. The traitorous couple were the brothers Shaukat Ali and Muhammad Ali,[27] who had spoken publicly in favour of the Turks.

Six years later, in a conversation between Colonel Aubrey Herbert, Albanian Committee member (and friend of Ali), and Mr W. Stewart of the Foreign Office, the latter notes:

> Col Herbert said that when some years ago he was President of a society, he had had certain dealings with Dusé Mohamed, & he had found him useful for speaking with Indian seditionists who were frequent callers upon him (Col H). Therefore, without knowing very much of the man he could say that what he did know of him was in his favour.[28]

One might conjecture that Herbert, collaborating with the British intelligence services, may have considered Ali, out of the many Muslims under surveillance, malleable. By maintaining Ali's trust and acting as a go-between, Herbert may have found Ali suggestable to mitigating the behaviour of extremist sections of the Albanian Committee. For example, to keep the Ali brothers in check during those turbulent times of the Balkan War. Still, during this period at the onset and throughout the war, Ali immediately became a suspicious target of the British government. Consequently, the British authorities intensified its surveillance and harassment of him. In his biography, Ali discussed how the police would visit his office at all hours of the day upon some flimsy excuse until I requested

Scotland Yard to leave a plain clothes officer permanently stationed at my office to closely scrutinise all visitors. The annoyance ceased, but a detective was always stationed across Fleet Street who carefully scrutinised all visitors to 158 Fleet Street.[29]

A report by the Department of Intelligence at New Scotland Yard reveals that Ali had been under surveillance since 1914:

> On the 22nd December 1914 in consequence of information received from M.I.5. (g) War Office, that Dusé Mohamed was in communication with the young Turks and the National Societies of Egypt, aided by one Prince Omar Toussoum, President of the 'Egyptian Society' his premises at 158 Fleet Street, were visited by the City Police, but on search being made, nothing incriminating was found.[30]

Ali was under surveillance: interviewed by the police, the *ATOR* office searched, and his mail opened. In a later MI5 report lodged at their office on 7 February 1915, the agent explains that:

> The office of the *African Times and Orient Review* was searched by the Police, nothing incriminating was found. It is said that inflammatory literature and some incriminating papers were removed secretly to Liverpool by an Egyptian named Degouski Effendi and an Indian named Zaffer Ali Kahn, the Editor of the Lahore paper 'Zemindar'. This statement does not appear to have been confirmed.[31]

The Egyptian went unnoticed, but the poet and journalist, Zafar Ali Khan was an anti-imperialist and a campaigner for the Pakistan Movement, an organisation opposed to the British Raj.[32] In any event, the report had more detail of the connection between Ali and Prince Omar Toussoun. The prince was the grandson of an ex-ruler of Egypt, Said Pasha (1854–1863). He was a multi-linguist speaking Arabic, Turkish, French and English. He was an active supporter of Turkey during the Italo-Turkish War of 1911–12.[33] It seems that in the aftermath of the 1911 Italo-Turkish War, where Italy invaded Ottoman-ruled Libya, Ali had been implicated in collecting money for the procurement of arms for the rebel forces against the Italians. The MI5 missive declared:

> Information has reached us that Dusé Mohamed assisted the Turkish officers with the Senussi Arabs against the Italians, probably through a Prince Omar Tousson who … has been detained in France. He is believed to have collected money in England, which was sent out via Egypt to Tripoli, and have been active in 1913 in providing Arabs in Tripoli with arms.[34]

Moreover, the government intercepted letters between Ali's wife, Beatrice, and his close friend Ahmed Zaki Abushady (Abushady Bey). He was the Abushady Bey who was able to obtain a duplicate birth certificate from Alexandria.[35] The authorities knew that Abushady had sent 'her an English translation of verses from the Arabic of "Shawky Bey"'. Shawky Bey or Ahmed Shawqi (1866–1945) was an Egyptian poet laureate known as 'The Prince of Poets'. He is reputed to be the most prominent of all modern poets and dramatists in the Arab literary world. An anti-colonialist, Ahmed Shawqi was exiled by the British to Andalusia in southern Spain.[36] Ali's wife, Beatrice, regularly published poetry and features in the *ATOR* and was eager to read the verse of Shawqi. The Foreign Office reported that:

> The verses were composed for school students and urged the young generation of Egyptians to cease to be slaves and by sacrificing themselves for the Motherland to restore the ancient glories of Egypt.[37]

Ali even had the ire of the India Office because of a publication issued from his Fleet Street address. The item was a translation of Pierre Loti's *Turquie Agonisante* (*Turkey in Agony*),[38] a critique of Western European's general acceptance of Italian rule in Ottoman Libya and the Balkans War. Loti, who was Louis Marie-Julien Viaud, became a French naval officer and a novelist. His was sympathetic to the Ottoman cause. A dispatch, dated 28 May 1914, from the Government of India expressed that:

> The Bombay Government have recently brought to notice the importation of a book entitled 'Turkey in Agony' being a translation of a work by Pierre Loti (Turquie Agonisante) and published for the Ottoman Committee by the African Times & Orient Review Ltd ... The local Government desired action to be taken under the Sea Customs Act against the work, but the Government of India have decided to refrain from doing so, looking to the eminence of the author, the auspices under which the translation was produced, and the fact that it seems inexpedient to revive the bitter memories of the Balkan War, which have to some extent subsided, by bringing again into prominence stories of atrocities and the like.[39]

The dispatch acknowledged that the book would 'do a certain amount of harm and it is likely that it will be quoted from in the Muhammedan Press'. The hesitancy over banning the importation of the book was because those involved in its translation and production included Charles Stourton (1867–1936), whose peerages included Lords Mowbray and Stourton and Charles Cochrane-Baillie, Lord Lamington (1860–1940), the first two members of the Ottoman Association and the latter a member of the Ottoman Committee. Lord Mowbray and Stourton was the President of the Anglo-Ottoman Association. While Lord Lamington was an ex-Governor of Bombay, he was a President of the Anglo-Ottoman Society, an incarnation of the Anglo-Ottoman Association/Committee.[40] However, the Government of India were unhappy about the book because it also contained 'various attacks on H.M.G (e.g. at pages 175 & 179) and the whole trend of its criticisms is against Europe and Christianity'.[41]

Ali was becoming increasingly cautious over his successful campaigning journalism. Aside from inaugurating the formation of the Anglo-Ottoman Society, the renamed Ottoman Committee,[42] and attracting distinguished British membership, there were other successes. For example, he was responsible for exposing the Zaria (Northern Nigeria) case, in which native African clerks were mistreated by white colonial administrators. The colonial machinations of the case were uncovered in the House of Commons, and to the readers of the *ATOR* throughout the British Empire.[43]

Another campaigning first was the reporting of the case of African Jamaican, Leila James, who was dismissed by the Jamaican Education Department in 1920. In 1912, James was the first African Jamaican to win a scholarship for girls to study abroad at a university.[44] Then, there was the example of Indian suffragette and writer Mrinalini Sen (1879–1972). Sen, a leading advocate for the Bangiya Nari Samaj women's group in Bengal, argued about the unfairness of not allowing Indian women to vote, when they own property and still had to pay taxes – two prerequisites for suffrage.[45]

In the *ATOR*, Ali warned that 'we learn from authentic sources that we are "black listed", both at the British Foreign and the Colonial Office. To be "black listed" means that we shall be watched.'[46] He may have learned about his journal's blacklisting through his connection with MPs such as Josiah Wedgewood, Joseph King, Aubrey Herbert, or the politician Lord Lamington (Charles Cochrane-Baillie), the latter two were members of the Anglo-Ottoman Society. Ali suspected that the *ATOR* was being 'black listed' and it was banned throughout the British Empire shortly after the August 1914 edition, only to be permitted to return in January 1917. According to Superintendent Quinn of the Special Branch of New Scotland Yard, the

> 'African Times and Orient Review' appeared to have a fairly good circulation in Africa and among the Orientals abroad until the outbreak of the War, when owing to its circulation being prohibited, in Africa and India, its last publication appeared on the 18th August 1914 and Dusé Mohamed, who had invested his money in the concern, seems to have lost his entire fortune in the venture.[47]

It may seem that eventually, the government's recourse to Ali's continual criticism of British colonial rule in Africa and India was to remove his public voice and also his livelihood.

PAN-AFRICANISM CONNECTIONS TO THE UNIVERSAL NEGRO IMPROVEMENT ASSOCIATION

MI5 also monitored Ali's connections in the US, especially with John Bruce and Marcus Garvey. John Edward Bruce (1856–1924) was an African American journalist, historian, civil rights activist and Pan-Africanist. Since the 1870s, he had founded several newspapers and contributed to more than one hundred periodicals. Bruce was a regular contributor and served as the American agent for the *ATOR*. Under the auspices of Bruce, Ali was to make connections to Arthur A. Schomburg, the researcher and bibliophile, through the Negro Society for the Historical Research, founded in 1911.[48] Marcus Garvey (1887–1940) was an African Jamaican political leader of the Universal Negro Improvement Association (UNIA), a Black nationalist and Pan-Africanist organisation based in New York. Garvey's efforts produced a transnational, anti-imperialist and self-help movement for the salvation of Africans in Africa and the diaspora.[49] Bruce introduced Garvey to prominent people in New York and wrote for the UNIA's newspaper the *Negro World*.

When Ali arrived in New York in July 1921, he would first contact John Edward Bruce before eventually reuniting with Garvey who was the leader of the UNIA. During his involvement with Garvey, Ali became the editor of the *Negro World*. Under Ali's editorship, the newspaper 'gained distinction'.[50] He would rise in the movement and become head of its African Affairs unit before he parted company with the UNIA and moved onto another phase of his life. Before arriving in New York, he had been approached by Garvey in a letter dated 18 July 1919.[51] In the correspondence Garvey asked Ali to book the Royal Albert Hall and Caxton Hall for meetings he would hold of the UNIA and African Communities League.[52] Ali did not reply because he was under interrogation by MI5 about his connection with Garvey and Bruce.

Unknown to Garvey at the time, all three men were under surveillance. For example, on 5 November 1918, S. Newly, under the auspices of the director of the Special Intelligence Bureau (MI5), Colonel Sir Vernon George Waldegrave, had written to the American Military Intelligence inquiring about the relationship of the three men. After requesting information from his counterpart in the War Department in Washington, DC, Newly describes the founder of the UNIA and then explained that:

> Marcus Garvey … is also believed to run a newspaper called 'The Negro World'. Another person possibly connected with this Society is John Edward Bruce … This man is in regular correspondence with a mongrel Soudanese-Egyptian named DUSÉ MOHAMED [Ali], who has been living in England for many years. This man dabbles in any sort of mischievous agitation which comes to hand and out of which a little money is to be made.[53]

MI5 continued their surveillance of Ali and his connection with Garvey. According to the MI5 file, Ali was interrogated and explained that he knew little about Garvey except that he worked at the *ATOR* for about three months before losing his job due to unsatisfactory conduct. In 1913, during his first visit to London, Garvey worked as a messenger boy for Ali at the Fleet Street Office of the *ATOR*.[54] Ali was known to help out Africans and others of colour living, working and studying in London. Aside from providing Garvey with a written reference to use the Reading Room at the British Museum, Ali published an early article by Garvey in the October 1913 edition of the *ATOR*.[55] In any case, the American Military Intelligence were now carefully monitoring Garvey and Bruce. In an internal memo in response to MI5's request for information on the duo, the Americans acknowledged that they contacted Garvey and knew of Bruce.[56]

Consequently, Ali's role as an agitator is confirmed by British government sources, including the Colonial Office and Foreign Office, New Scotland Yard's Special Branch Division and MI5. He made enemies within the British Raj, and even the American Military Intelligence service kept a watchful eye on his movements. He was aware that he was under surveillance and by late spring 1921 would leave the UK to seek a future initially in the US but becoming a permanent resident in West Africa.

British intelligence surveillance records of Ali start at the beginning of his career as the editor of the *ATOR* in 1912. Once his anti-imperialism campaigns in his journal became widely circulated, especially in British West Africa (Sierra Leone, Gold Coast (Ghana) and Nigeria), South Africa and India, he was viewed as an agitator. At the onset of World War I, the tone of *ATOR* continued to provoke the indignation of the British government. Ali's support of Pan-Islamism and the Ottoman Empire was problematic, but by 28 October 1914, when the Ottoman Empire entered the war on Germany's side, Ali's stance became untenable. To make matters worse, only a few weeks previously, on 22 September, Ali had applied for a passport to travel to British West Africa to promote the *ATOR* and its business.

In British law, Ali was Turkish and, therefore, a member of the Ottoman Empire, which severely restricted his movements. If the Foreign Office allowed Ali to land in British West Africa, the relevant governors of each colony would be made aware of the potential he has to cause mischievous activities. As the war continued, so the harassment of Ali and many of his co-workers increased. British law enforcement agencies' surveillance of Ali's business activities continued to such an extent they would regularly raid the *ATOR* offices at Fleet Street to search for discriminating evidence. Eventually, the British government banned Ali's paper during the war, which wreaked havoc on the *ATOR*'s circulation and his livelihood. Consequently, as an African living in Britain during the Edwardian period, Dusé Mohamed Ali's significance lay in his pioneering investigative journalism and Pan-Africanism. He was an anti-imperialist and anti-colonialist, providing an uncompromising alternative viewpoint to the prevailing attitude of his day that was disrespectful to people of colour.

NOTES

1. In 1920 the *ATOR* was rebranded the *Africa and Orient Review (AOR)*.
2. I. Duffield, *Dusé Mohamed Ali and the Development of Pan-Africanism 1866–1945*, PhD thesis (University of Edinburgh 1971), pp. 24–36.
3. H. Adi, *Pan-Africanism: A History* (London: Bloomsbury Academic, 2018), pp.16–18.
4. G. Spiller (ed.), *Papers on Inter-Racial Problems, Communicated to the First Universal Races Congress, Held at the University of London, July 26–29, 1911* (London: P.S. King & Son, 1911). Universal Races Congress, *First Universal Races Congress pamphlet*, 1911. W. E. B. Du Bois Papers (MS 312). Special Collections and University Archives, University of Massachusetts Amherst Libraries.
5. Spiller, *Papers on Inter-Racial Problems*, p. xiii.
6. *The Sierra Leone Weekly News*, 22 April 1911, p. 5.

7. J. Hirano, 'Historical Formation of Pan-Islamism: Modern Islamic Reformists Project for Intra-Umma Alliance and Intra-Madhāhib Rapprochement', December 2008, https://repository.kulib.kyotou.ac.jp/dspace/bitstream/2433/155788/1/ssh_010.pdf (accessed 19 January 2023).
8. Adi, *Pan-Africanism: A History*, p. 16.
9. A confidential report of Dusé Mohamed, by Mr Nathan, War Office, to Mr G Clarke, Foreign Office, 7 February 1914, TNA, FO 371/2355/15047.
10. Supt. P. Quinn, Special Branch, New Scotland Yard, Dusé Mohamed, 27 March 1916, TNA, FO 371/3728/114805/19.
11. M. Abdelwahid, *Dusé Mohamed Ali 1866–1945: The Autobiography of a Pioneer Pan African and Afro-Asian Activist* (Trento, NJ: Red Sea Press, 2011), p. 32.
12. Letter, Dusé Mohamed to Harcourt, 22 September 1914, TNA, CO 554/23/36403.
13. Sir George Fiddes, minute 1, 25 September 1914, TNA, CO 554/23/36403.
14. Memo from L. Harcourt to the Governors of the Gambia, Sierra Leone, Gold Coast and Nigeria, 2 October 1914, TNA, CO 554/23/36403.
15. Conversation with Lt Colonel Aubrey Herbert and W. Stewart, 27 September 1919, TNA, FO 372/1274/135061.
16. Letter, Dusé Mohamed Ali to Rt. Hon. A.J. Balfour, the Secretary of State for Foreign Affairs, 9 August 1919, TNA, FO 371/3728/114805.
17. Letter, W. Stewart to Lt Colonel Aubrey Herbert, 29 September 1919, TNA, FO 372/1274/135061.
18. Letter, Duse Mohamed Ali to Rt. Hon. A.J. Balfour, The Foreign Secretary. 9 August 1919, p. 3, TNA, FO 371/3728/114805
19. 'The Editor Abroad', *Africa and Orient Review*, I/12 (December 1920) pp. 53–6.
20. British Nationality and Status of Aliens Act 1914, www.legislation.gov.uk/ukpga/Geo5/4-5/17/enacted (accessed 28 January 2021).
21. Duffield, *Dusé Mohamed Ali and the Development of Pan-Africanism 1866–1945*, p. 445.
22. A. Field, 'The Ottoman Committee', *African Times and Orient Review* (November–December 1913) p. 184.
23. Anglo-Ottoman Society Circular, 158 Fleet Street, January 1915, TNA, FO 371/2482/9577.
24. R. Hall, 'Balkan Wars 1912–1913', https://encyclopedia.1914-1918-online.net/pdf/1914-1918-Online-Balkan_wars_1912-1913-2014-10-08.pdf (accessed 26 January 2021).
25. Duffield, *Dusé Mohamed Ali and the Development of Pan-Africanism 1866–1945*, pp. 431–2.
26. Ibid.
27. Ibid., p. 438.

28. Conversation with Lt Colonel Aubrey Herbert and W. Stewart, 27 September 1919, TNA, FO 372/1274/135061.
29. D.M. Ali, 'Leaves from an Active Life', in M. Abdelwahid, *Dusé Mohamed Ali: 1866–1945* (Trenton, NJ: Red Sea Press, 2011), p. 163.
30. Memo, Supt. P. Quinn, Special Branch, New Scotland Yard to Loder, The Director of Intelligence, 15 August 1919, TNA, FO 371/3728/114805/19.
31. M.I.5 (g), report on Duse Mohamed, enclosed in P. Nathan, M. I. 5 (g), War Office, to G. Clarke, Foreign Office, 9 February 1915, p. 2, FO, 371/2355/15047.
32. R. Khan, 'Maulana Zafar Ali Khan – the History Make', *The Nation*, https://nation.com.pk/27-Nov-2012/maulana-zafar-ali-khan-the-history-maker (accessed 1 February 2021).
33. S. Hamouda, *Omar Toussoun Prince of Alexandria* (Alexandria: Bibliotheca Alexandria, 2004), pp. 35, 58.
34. M. I. 5 (g), War Office, to G. Clarke, Foreign Office, 9 February 1915, p. 3, TNA, FO 371/2355/15047.
35. See E. Abdul-Latif, 'Ahmad Zaki Abu Shadi', in E.K. Akyeampong and H.L. Gates (ed.), *African Biography*. Vol 1. (Oxford: Oxford University Press, 2012), pp.130–1.
36. N.Y. Al-Rifai, 'The Influence of Greco-Roman Literature on the Poetry of Ahmad Shawqi', *Advances in Social Sciences Research Journal*, 5/6 (25 June 2018), pp. 358–78.
37. M. I. 5 (g), War Office, to G. Clarke, Foreign Office, 7 February 1915, p. 4, TNA, FO 371/2355/15047.
38. P. Loti, *Turkey in Agony* (London: African Times and Orient Review, 1913).
39. Government of India, Home Dept. Simla, 28 May 1914, to India Office, enclosed in A. Hirtzel, India Office, to G.K. Clark, Foreign Office, confidential, 17 June 1914, TNA, FO 371/2135/27468.
40. J. Heller, *British Policy towards the Ottoman Empire, 1908–1914* (Abingdon, Oxon: Routledge, 2014), p. 203. J. Schneer, *The Balfour Declaration: Origins of the Arab-Israeli Conflict* (London: Bloomsbury, 2011), p. 247.
41. Government of India, Home Dept. Simla, 28 May 1914, to India Office, enclosed in A. Hirtzel, India Office, to G.K. Clark, Foreign Office, confidential, 17 June 1914, TNA, FO 371/2135/27468.
42. *ATOR*, 2/37 (November–December 1913), p. 184; Schneer, *The Balfour Declaration: Origins of the Arab-Israeli Conflict*, p. 248.
43. *ATOR*, 1/1 (July 1912), p. 8.
44. *AOR*, 1/7 (July 1920), pp. 31–2; H Altink, '"The Case of Miss Leila James B.A.': Class, Race, Gender and National Identity in Early Twentieth-Century Jamaica', http://community-languages.org.uk/SCS-Papers/Altink07.pdf (accessed 20 February 2022).

45. M. Sen, 'The Indian Reform Bill and the Women of India', *AOR*, 1/2 (February 1920), pp. 15–16; G. Forbes, *Women in Modern India* (Cambridge: Cambridge University Press, 1996), p. 103. See also S. Mukherjee, *Indian Suffragettes: Female Identities and Transnational Networks* (New Dehli: Oxford University Press, 2018), passim; P. Ravichandran, 'The Indian Suffragists: Claiming Their Rights in Britain and India', Oxford Human Rights Hub, 5 March 2018, http://ohrh.law.ox.ac.uk/the-indian-suffragists-claiming-their-rights-in-britain-and-india/ (accessed 20 February 2022).
46. 'The Editor', *ATOR* (5 May 1914), p. 147.
47. Supt. P. Quinn, Special Branch, New Scotland Yard, Duse Mohamed, 27 March 1916, p. 2, FO, 371/3728/114805.
48. R.L. Crowder, *John Edward Bruce: Politician, Journalist, and Self-Trained Historian of the African Diaspora* (New York: New York University Press, 2004), p. 117.
49. H. Adi and M. Sherwood, *Pan-African History: Political Figures from Africa and the Diaspora since 1787* (London: Routledge, 2003), p. 76.
50. R. Hill (ed.), *The Marcus Garvey and Universal Negro Improvement Association Papers* (Vol. I) (Berkeley, CA: University of California Press, 1983), p. 521.
51. Duffield, *Dusé Mohamed Ali and the Development of Pan-Africanism 1866–1945*, p. 551.
52. R. Hill, *The Marcus Garvey and Universal Negro Improvement Association Papers* (Vol. I), p. 465.
53. DNA, The National Archive, Washington, DC, RG 165, File 10218-261/9, 5/11/1918, cited in Hill, *The Marcus Garvey and Universal Negro Improvement Association Papers*, p. 314.
54. C. Grant, *Negro with a Hat: The Rise and Fall of Marcus Garvey* (London: Vintage, 2009), pp. 38–40.
55. M. Garvey, 'The British West Indies in the Mirror of Civilization', *ATOR*, II/16 (Mid-October 1913), pp. 158–60. Hill, *The Marcus Garvey and Universal Negro Improvement Association Papers*, p. 26.
56. DNA, The National Archive, Washington, DC, RG 165, File 10218-261/27, 11/12/1918, cited in Hill, *The Marcus Garvey and Universal Negro Improvement Association Papers*, p. 322.

6

Dark Lovers and Desdemonas: Gender, Race and Pan-Africanism in Britain, 1935–45

Theo Williams

In October 1959, the British Jewish activist Dorothy Pizer wrote to the African American author Richard Wright. Pizer was the widow of George Padmore, the Trinidadian socialist and Pan-Africanist who had died the previous month. She had played a crucial role in producing Padmore's influential writings, often collecting material, typing his manuscripts and editing his work. She wanted to publish a new edition of Padmore's 1956 book, *Pan-Africanism or Communism?* and asked if Wright, a friend of the couple and a famous writer, would be able to write the foreword to the new edition. Pizer already had in mind what Padmore would have liked the foreword to say. However, as articulately as Pizer was able to express these ideas herself, she still believed Wright was the best person to write the foreword. As she explained to him: 'Your name would lend it prestige. My own has no selling value.'[1]

Pizer was one of a number of British women who were deeply involved in Pan-Africanist activism between 1935 and 1945. This period, bookended by the Italian invasion of Ethiopia and the Fifth Pan-African Congress, was one of the most productive phases of the movement's history. In Britain, it was spearheaded by a group of activists that formed a series of organisations named the International African Friends of Ethiopia (IAFE, formed in 1935), the International African Service Bureau (IASB, formed in 1937) and the Pan-African Federation (formed in 1944). The central figure in this activist circle was George Padmore, and his comrades included Peter Abrahams (from South Africa), Amy Ashwood Garvey (from Jamaica), C.L.R. James (from Trinidad), Chris Jones (from Barbados), Jomo Kenyatta (from Kenya), Ras Makonnen (from British Guiana), Kwame Nkrumah (from the Gold Coast) and I.T.A. Wallace-Johnson (from Sierra Leone). These organisations joined a rich mix of Black political activism in Britain, which included slightly older organisations such as the League of Coloured Peoples (LCP) and the West African Students' Union (WASU).[2] Britain was home to several Black female activists and intellectuals during the 1930s and 1940s, including not only Ashwood Garvey, but also Constance Horton and Una Marson, among others. Nevertheless, the vast majority of Britain's Black population in this period was male. Even in 1951, after female migration to the metropole began to increase, the government census found that 63 per cent of those from the Caribbean and 81 per cent of West Africans in Britain were men.[3]

Underpinning this chapter is a plea for historians of ideas to work at the field's intersections with social history. Michael Goebel, in his study of anticolonialism in interwar Paris, has convincingly argued that historians 'need to attend to the social bedrock of ideas'. He insists that the 'intellectual history of anti-imperialism' is rooted in the 'social history of migration'.[4] I contend that Goebel's approach becomes even more important when we consider the history of women's contributions to metropolitan anti-imperialist movements (or, for that matter, the history of ideas more broadly). Women – including Black women like Ashwood Garvey and Marson, as well as white women like Dorothy Pizer and Dinah Stock – played central roles in Pan-Africanist activism and organising. They acted as hosts and created activist spaces, they collected and edited material, and they were often writers and journalists in their own right. This labour has remained relatively unacknowledged, and male Pan-Africanists have been somewhat complicit in this lack of acknowledgement. Furthermore, intellectual production is also, in a broader sense, always a collective effort. It is informed by a complex tapestry of conversations, experiences and environment. The subsequent attribution of a text to a single 'author' expunges this collective production, and is particularly likely to efface women's labour. It is therefore vital that historians of ideas, as well as performing close readings of published texts, aim to reconstruct the process of intellectual production by adopting social history methods. Through using material like diaries, memoirs and private correspondence, historians can begin to see how wider networks and social contexts have produced the big texts – such as C.L.R. James' *The Black Jacobins* or Jomo Kenyatta's *Facing Mount Kenya* – that command so much of our attention. When we do so, we see the role of women's labour and gendered activist practices in producing such texts.

Ashwood Garvey was the only Black woman who was a central member of the group of radical Pan-Africanists who are the main focus of this chapter. In London, she co-founded the International African Friends of Ethiopia alongside James in 1935, and also ran the International Afro Restaurant on New Oxford Street and the Florence Mills Social Parlour on Carnaby Street.[5] As Minkah Makalani has argued, Ashwood Garvey was a 'tireless organizer' who in opening such venues created 'centers of activism' that were invaluable in producing and maintaining the dynamism of Black radical politics in London.[6] She was born in Jamaica to a middle-class family in 1897. She met Marcus Garvey in 1914, and they were married in 1919. She was a leading figure in Garvey's Universal Negro Improvement Association (which claimed a global membership in the millions) and a director of the Black Star shipping line. Her marriage was short-lived, and in 1922 she arrived in London, where she helped Ladipo Solanke to establish the Nigerian Progress Union – a forerunner of WASU – in 1924. After a decade away from Britain, she returned to London in 1934, accompanied by her partner, the Trinidadian musician and activist, Sam Manning.[7] It was in the context of the impending Italian invasion of Ethiopia that Ashwood Garvey founded the IAFE and began operating her club and restaurant. At an IAFE rally in Trafalgar Square on 25 August 1935 – attended by approximately 500 people – she shared a platform with the likes of C.L.R. James, Chris Jones, Jomo Kenyatta, George Padmore and Arnold Ward. She declared in her speech that 'No race has been so noble in forgiving, but now the hour has struck for our complete emancipation. We will not tolerate the invasion of Abyssinia.'[8]

The IAFE was headquartered at Ashwood Garvey's International Afro Restaurant, and in creating such a space, Ashwood Garvey did much to foster the organisation's development. The creation of such activist spaces is the kind of under-acknowledged labour often performed by women. Some of Ashwood Garvey's comrades wrote about her in their reminiscences. James, in his unpublished memoirs, remembered her as 'a very powerful personality' who had a wealth of political experience, while Peter Abrahams recalled her being 'a gay spirit filled with pealing laughter'.[9] However, as Marc Matera has observed, the reminiscences of Abrahams, James and Padmore make little mention of Ashwood Garvey.[10] As discussed more thoroughly below, Ashwood Garvey suffered a similar marginalisation to many white female associates of Pan-Africanists. Nevertheless, Ashwood Garvey remains a key figure in Pan-Africanist history. After spending World War II in Jamaica and the US, she returned to Britain to attend the Fifth Pan-African Congress in Manchester in October 1945. In a session about the Caribbean, she outlined a Black feminist position, stating that 'Very much has been written and spoken of the Negro, but for some reason very little has been said about the black woman.'[11]

Ashwood Garvey was not the only female Pan-Africanist in Britain during this period. Constance Horton was born in Sierra Leone in 1918 into a family of the Krio elite (descendants of previously enslaved people who settled in Freetown and its surrounding areas). Horton first came to Britain in 1935, and was recorded as attending a meeting of the League of Coloured Peoples on 25 August 1935. During 1936 she toured the US, and was radicalised by her experience of Jim Crow laws. She returned to London in the autumn of 1936, where she met her compatriot, I.T.A. Wallace-Johnson. Through Wallace-Johnson, she met Kenyatta, Padmore and the British feminist, socialist and anti-imperialist, Sylvia Pankhurst, and became more heavily involved in Pan-Africanist activism. She was only in Britain for a short time, and in October 1937, Horton (now using her married name of Cummings-John) returned to Sierra Leone, where she continued to work alongside Wallace-Johnson as a leading figure in the West African Youth League. She won a seat in the Freetown municipal council elections in 1938 and was elected as mayor of

Freetown in 1966, becoming the first Black female mayor of an African capital city.[12]

The Jamaican poet and playwright, Una Marson, was a contemporary of Ashwood Garvey and Horton. The middle-class daughter of a Baptist minister, Marson was born in 1905 in Saint Elizabeth parish, and received a colonial education at Hampton School in Malvern. In early adulthood, she published a feminist magazine, *The Cosmopolitan*. She first came to Britain in 1932, and lived for a time with Harold Moody, the Jamaican physician and founder of the LCP, at his Peckham home. She joined the LCP and became an occasional editor of its journal, *The Keys*, where she also published some of her poetry. As well as devoting herself to feminist causes, she developed Pan-Africanist and anticolonial sympathies during her time in London, especially after the invasion of Ethiopia. She was, therefore, in Imaobong Umoren's words, a 'race woman internationalist'.[13] She worked for the BBC during World War II, where she produced the landmark programme *Caribbean Voices*, which promoted the work of a number of emerging Caribbean writers.

As Matera has observed of women like Ashwood Garvey, Horton and Marson, these Black female activists were from 'relatively privileged backgrounds'. They 'applied the skills acquired in their upbringing as young women of the educated elite to expose the racist underpinnings of extant models of colonial respectability and femininity and to challenge the categorical distinctions of the racializing project of colonialism'.[14]

What role did gender play in shaping the contours of the British Pan-Africanist movement during the 1930s and 1940s? Michelle Ann Stephens has used the phrase 'revolutionary masculinity' to characterise the ideas and activism of Caribbean figures such as Marcus Garvey, C.L.R. James and Claude McKay.[15] For Stephens, there were both radical and reactionary impulses behind these men's politics. While they promoted global Black sovereignty, their vision of transnational Blackness often excluded women, or relegated them to a subordinate role. Of particular relevance to the present chapter is Stephens' analysis of James' play *Toussaint Louverture*, performed in London in 1936 and starring the African American activist and performer Paul Robeson as the eponymous Haitian revolutionary leader. Stephens argues that for James 'the figure of the black sovereign Toussaint L'Ouverture becomes in James's hands not just a figure for a revolutionary masculinity but the representative leader playing out the tensions and the possibilities inherent within the race, for leadership and self-government'.[16]

Striking a similar note, Matera argues that it was not only Black nationalist men who disparaged the role of Black women in political movements, but also that this attitude was replicated among more radical and internationalist Black male figures. He observes, for example, 'Padmore's erasure of African and Caribbean women in London', and contends that this reveals that Padmore and his comrades' 'conception of revolutionary black masculinity differed little from bourgeois nationalist masculinity'.[17] Christian Høgsbjerg, meanwhile, has countered that 'Padmore's criticism of black American upper class women' was 'clearly shaped above all by his own radical politics', and that Matera's more general argument is rendered somewhat unconvincing by 'the comparative rarity of black women in London in this period' and Peter Abrahams' references to the high regard in which Padmore held Communist women.[18] Padmore was perhaps a poor example for Matera to pick, in part for the reasons cited by Høgsbjerg. However, Matera is right to observe that the reminiscences of Padmore and his colleagues understate the contributions of women such as Ashwood Garvey to British Pan-Africanist politics. Furthermore, charges of patriarchal gender politics are more convincing when applied to some of Padmore's colleagues and to British Pan-Africanist activism institutionally.

It should be noted that radical Pan-Africanist organisations such as the International African Friends of Ethiopia and the International African Service Bureau held at least a theoretical commitment to women's equality, and had no doubt encountered Marxist arguments for women's liberation. This can be seen, for example, in the regular 'Women's Page' in the IASB's journal, the *African Sentinel*. However, it is difficult to infer much feminist influence on their writing and activism in broader terms. Intentionally or otherwise, societal gender relations were often reinforced and reproduced in these groups. For instance, Ras Makonnen remembered of Ashwood Garvey's Florence Mills Social Parlour that 'you could go there after you'd been slugging it out for two or three hours at Hyde Park or some other meeting, and get a lovely meal, dance and enjoy yourself'.[19] Ashwood Garvey was most often portrayed by her male comrades as occupying the role of the feminine nurturer and caregiver, and was likely prevented from adopting a more active leadership position in the group because of a gendered marginalisation. According to the *African Sentinel*, at an IASB meeting in September 1937 several male members gave political reports while the audience was 'refreshed by the service of tea, prepared by Mrs. Amy Ashwood Garvey', who does not seem to have given a report.[20] The *African Sentinel* either misleadingly omitted details of further work performed by Ashwood Garvey, or accurately reported her performing a markedly gendered role. A generous reading could point to Ashwood Garvey's profession as a restaurateur as justification for this division of labour, but James similarly remembered of Padmore and Pizer's household:

> The Padmore hospitality was famous. The constant stream of visitors stayed to lunch or to tea or to dinner, sometimes to all three. Dorothy, a fine cook, bore this burden (George washed up, the discussion for the time being moving into the kitchen). Dorothy was constantly on the move between the kitchen and the excitement in the living room. A woman of capacity, a Londoner of unusual sophistication, she had ambitions of her own both in literature and business. She suppressed them in the interests of African emancipation, more concretely helping George.[21]

This was a relativly familiar form of patriarchy, and such a gendered division of labour was largely unremarkable in 1930s Britain. As Ashwood Garvey created centres of activism in her club and restaurant, so too did Pizer in her flat on Cranleigh Street in Camden; this was a kind of activist labour coded as feminine. Pizer's intelligence was respected, and Padmore at least washed up, even if Pizer took responsibility for all the cooking. It is, though, especially illuminating that James linked Pizer's sacrifices for the sake of African emancipation to a personal support of Padmore; many Pan-Africanist men made personal sacrifices for their political cause, but for Pizer, as a woman, this was linked to a support of her male partner. If, as later generations of feminists would argue, the personal is political, there were some clear political failings in the private lives of Pan-Africanists. James' white lover, Louise Cripps, writing about their relationship later in life, believed that James saw her 'in the role of a faithful Krupskaya to his role of Lenin'.[22] She observed that although 'he made the correct statements of belief in the equality of the sexes on the platform, he evidently found it difficult to follow personally'. He 'felt the man needed to be the dominant partner' (although Cripps acknowledged that this extended to James' relationships with both men and women; James always 'wanted to be the leader').[23]

Relationships, both political and romantic, between Black radical men and white radical women were commonplace. Pan-Africanists often depended on white women to type their work, prepare stencils for mimeographs or fund their activism. Cripps wrote in her memoir that she helped to edit and proofread James' novel, *Minty Alley* (1936), and went to the British Museum to help with the research for *The Black Jacobins* (1938).[24] James later remembered of Pizer that she was instantly sympathetic to the IASB's politics, had a Marxist background and was well read. She helped Padmore with his books, translated them into French and German, and for years worked as a secretary 'so that the household might have a steady income'.[25] Several other white women, such as Nancy Cunard, Mary Downes, Ethel Mannin and Sylvia Pankhurst, frequently collaborated with Pan-Africanists and aided or funded their activism in various ways. Financial support was especially welcome, as many Pan-Africanist activists were consistently short of money. Reflecting on the work of the West African National Secretariat, the British-based organisation founded by Kwame Nkrumah in the aftermath of the Fifth Pan-African Congress, Nkrumah wrote in his autobiography that

> Even if we had difficulty in warming our bodies round a fire, our hearts were constantly warmed by the ever ready offer of help by several English girls. These girls – most of them of good class families – used to come and type for hours on end in the evenings and they never asked a single penny for their work. The best we could do for them was either to put them in a taxi and pay their fare, if we happened to be in funds or, which was

> more often the case, to accompany them to the tube station and wave them goodbye. I did one day go to the cinema with one of them, however, because I remember as we were about to go in an Englishman made some scathing remark about the girl being in the company of a black man (only that was not the expression he used). The next thing I knew was that the girl had given him a resounding slap on the face and told him to mind his own business and not to use such offensive language.[26]

Makonnen postulated that for white women, 'One way of rejecting the oppression of men was to associate with blacks.'[27] The reaction of Nkrumah's companion to the comment of the male English cinema-goer – a comment rooted in white supremacist patriarchy – lends credence to this interpretation. While Nkrumah commented on the relatively privileged backgrounds of many Pan-Africanist white female associates, Makonnen noted that 'Jewish girls' were particularly sympathetic to the cause.[28] Indeed, British Pan-Africanism drew support from both apostate aristocrats like Nancy Cunard and working-class Jews like Dorothy Pizer (as well as from women of more intermediate social status). While male Pan-Africanists' memoirs often provide an illuminating insight into white female support of the movement, Makonnen's description of women like Dinah Stock as 'the typical English type of devoted girl' reduces these women's political determination to a personal attachment, which is something of a trope in male Pan-Africanist reminiscences of this period.[29]

Stock played a crucial role in the publication of Kenyatta's *Facing Mount Kenya* (1938), an anthropological study of the Kikuyu (the nation to which Kenyatta belonged). She was an Oxford graduate, born of Irish parentage in England in 1902.[30] She was also a journalist and had been an anticolonial activist since the 1920s, long before she met Kenyatta and his comrades. Kenyatta and Stock's relationship is particularly interesting given that Ralph Bunche, the African American political scientist who kept a detailed diary of his 1937 stay in London, recorded that Kenyatta spoke of his distrust of almost all white men.[31] White women were deemed less invested in racism and imperialism than their male counterparts, and as such more likely to be genuine allies. Stock was introduced to Kenyatta in May 1937 at a meeting in Trafalgar Square. William McGregor Ross, a colonial reformer upon whose financial generosity Kenyatta had relied in his early years in London, had broken with Kenyatta in 1935, so the destitute Kenyatta was happy to take a room in Stock's flat in Camden, on the same street as Padmore and Pizer's.[32] Reginald Reynolds, a left-wing activist who had worked closely with Stock over the previous decade, never doubted Kenyatta's 'political convictions' but had doubts about him ('mostly petty things – conceit and snobbery, for example'). Stock, conversely, had 'a higher opinion of Jomo'.[33]

When Kenyatta met Stock, he had only a collection of anthropological essays. It was Stock who arranged the essays into publishable form, a task which, according to Makonnen, took her only 'about three weeks'.[34] Unfortunately, Makonnen's is the fullest account of Stock's involvement in the book's production, but, as it is feasible that male activists trivialised the role played by women in intellectual production, it is possible that her role was more significant. Kenyatta, however, when penning the acknowledgements for the book, neglected to thank Stock for her role. White women, while willing and committed participants in Pan-Africanist work, were often intellectually marginalised in the group. The lack of recognition of Stock's labour in the published version of *Facing Mount Kenya* is a particularly sharp reminder of the need to look beyond texts themselves in order to understand women's contributions to the development of anti-imperialist thought. Nevertheless, there were countervailing tendencies. Stock served on the editorial committee of *Pan-Africa*, the journal launched by Makonnen in January 1947. When she left for India that summer, the editorial team complimented her to the fullest: 'We think of her not as a European, but as a person with all the characteristics of true greatness.'[35] Padmore, in *Africa and World Peace* (1937), thanked Pizer for gathering material, typing the manuscript, and performing 'other thankless literary chores in connection with this work'.[36]

Several relationships between Black men and white women, including those of Padmore and Pizer, and of James and Cripps (though possibly not that of Kenyatta and Stock), were examples of a phenomenon in which the boundaries between political and romantic relationships were blurred. Bunche believed Padmore's 'choice of a woman' to be incongruous with his racial politics, mistaking Padmore's materialist analysis of racism and imperialism with a racial essentialism.[37] Furthermore, as a working-class Jew, Pizer had personal experiences of oppression and racism. In a letter to Nancy Cunard written later in her life, she recalled growing up 'in London's East End, amid poverty and sickness and racial animosities'.[38] The 'whiteness' of Jewish women who associated with Pan-Africanist men needs to be qualified in such terms.

Bunche recorded Padmore saying to him that 'Englishmen don't want Negroes to fool with their women – even the radicals.'[39] However, Makonnen noted that he and Padmore, unlike some other Black men, did not believe that it was a 'revolutionary act' to sleep with white women.[40] That Padmore had a 20-year, apparently monogamous, relationship with Pizer suggests that their relationship was not based on a fantasy of anticolonial sexual revenge. Even so, sexual encounters between Pan-Africanist men and white women could adopt a racialised character. Louise Cripps recalled in her memoir the evening that she and James went to see a production of *Othello*. After the performance, they slept together for the first time. In bed, James called her 'Desdemona'. Cripps afterwards lay awake happily thinking about the fact that she now 'had a dark lover'.[41] It should be noted here that Cripps was not alone in writing about James in such a manner, even if her words have a different register given the sexual nature of their relationship. Stephen Howe has observed how James features as 'an exotic curiosity' in the reminiscences of several left-wing British figures he met during the 1930s, such as Ethel Mannin, Reginald Reynolds and Fredric Warburg.[42]

In his novel *A Wreath for Udomo* (1956), Peter Abrahams savaged Padmore and Pizer's relationship. By the 1950s, Abrahams had become disillusioned with the direction of the Pan-African movement. His novel offered a critical history of, and gloomy forecast for, the movement. Padmore, fictionalised as Thomas Lanwood, is portrayed, in Marc Matera's words, as 'a tragic figure of impotent black masculinity' whose relationship with Pizer conceals 'a more profound attachment to Britishness'.[43] Pizer ('Mary Feld' in the novel) is depicted as a domineering woman who has no respect for Padmore/Lanwood.[44] This perhaps says as much about Abrahams' race and gender politics as it does about Padmore and Pizer's relationship. If, as discussed above, the Pan-Africanist movement was characterised by revolutionary Black masculinity, Abrahams may have seen Pizer as compromising Padmore's Pan-Africanist credentials. However, Abrahams further problematised British Pan-Africanist gender relations. A white female character in the novel, Lois Barlow, challenges Michael Udomo (who most closely resembles Kwame Nkrumah) for thinking her 'the primitive backward woman'.[45] Abrahams portrays Black men's attraction to white women as inherently racialised. Udomo enters a relationship with Barlow, but cheats on her with another white woman in the group after being excited by her 'mass of corn-coloured hair'.[46] Udomo's fetishisation of white women mirrors Cripps' fetishisation of James as her 'dark lover'. To Abrahams it seemed that various types of relationships between Black men and white women were problematic. Udomo's trysts caused an unnecessary distraction for the group and hurt innocent white women. At the same time, Padmore/Lanwood's 20-year relationship with Pizer/Feld left him resembling 'a white man with a black skin'.[47]

Abrahams' own romantic experiences in London likely informed these ideas. His landlady, Dorothy Pennington, was a Communist Party member. He drunkenly slept with her shortly after arriving in London and they married two weeks later. He remembered that Padmore 'approved of the marriage', as Pennington was 'a good comrade'. Padmore often visited the couple at their flat in Belsize Park, where 'sometimes he and Dorothy talked about me almost as though I was not there'. He believed that Padmore had wanted his marriage to Pennington to happen, seeing it as a means of 'control'.[48] The couple separated shortly after the end of World War II, and Abrahams resented what he saw as Padmore's attempts to pressure him into the sort of personal–political relationship that Padmore and Pizer had. Indeed, while Abrahams was married to Pennington, Padmore worked closely with Cunard and Pizer on *The White Man's Duty* (1943). The book took the form of a series of conversations between Cunard and Padmore, which were conducted in the spring of 1942 and typed up by Pizer. In contrast to Abrahams, Cunard wrote to Pizer in the months after Padmore's death that Padmore and Pizer were 'a superb team'.[49]

Carol Polsgrove observes that 'Viewing the Pizer-Padmore relationship from the vantage point of a later day, it would be tempting to see Padmore as exploiting Pizer's talent and interest in writing for his own purposes.' However, she argues that Padmore also 'open[ed] a door to her', giving her 'the opportunity to create books, albeit as a junior partner'.[50] Of course, these are not mutually exclusive observations, and Pizer was granted more intellectual acknowledgement than other women associated with the group. Activists like Pizer and Stock, brilliant writers in their own right, dedicated much of their political energy to aiding men, sometimes without being publicly acknowledged. This had lasting effects on literary careers, as we can see from the sketch with which I began this chapter. Pizer's plea to Richard Wright in October 1959 to contribute a foreword to the new edition of *Pan-Africanism or Communism?* was a melancholic epilogue to the story of one woman's sacrifices in the cause of African liberation.

Through using the methods adopted by this chapter, we can analyse the ways in which the intersections of race and gender shaped the Pan-Africanist movement in Britain, and begin to reconstruct the role played by women in Pan-Africanist activism. By looking beyond the big texts themselves, women's contribution to the history of ideas comes into sharper focus, as does the ways in which activist labour was often deeply gendered. For instance, a reader of Kenyatta's *Facing Mount Kenya* will come away completely ignorant of Dinah Stock's role in its production. Historians must turn instead to Makonnen's memoirs to begin to reconstruct the book's development. This approach is not a panacea. Many of the sources we are left with – the reminiscences of James, Makonnen, Nkrumah and Padmore, and the diary of Ralph Bunche – were still produced by men. Women associated with the Pan-Africanist movement have left behind fewer sources, although the memoirs of Louise Cripps and Constance Horton, and the correspondence between Nancy Cunard and Dorothy Pizer, offer notable exceptions. Even then, what do we make of the fact that Horton wrote of her association with Padmore, while she is absent from Padmore's reminiscences? What do we make of Cripps' claims to have contributed to the production of *Minty Alley* and *The Black Jacobins*, while James himself is silent on the matter? We are left to grapple with the past in a dimly-lit room, cross-referencing sources, reading against the archival grain, and occasionally even making educated guesses. The history of the Pan-Africanist movement in Britain is all the richer for us doing so.

NOTES

1. Dorothy Pizer to Richard Wright, 20 October 1959, Richard Wright papers, box 103 folder 1521, Beinecke Rare Book and Manuscript Library, New Haven, CT.
2. For more on Black politics in Britain during this period, see Hakim Adi, *West Africans in Britain, 1900–1960: Nationalism, Pan-Africanism and Communism* (London: Lawrence & Wishart, 1998); Christian Høgsbjerg, *C. L. R. James in Imperial Britain* (Durham, NC: Duke University Press, 2014); Leslie James, *George Padmore and Decolonization from below: Pan-Africanism, the Cold War, and the End of Empire* (Basingstoke: Palgrave Macmillan, 2015); David Killingray, '"To Do Something for the Race": Harold Moody and the League of Coloured Peoples', in Bill Schwarz (ed.), *West Indian Intellectuals in Britain* (Manchester: Manchester University Press, 2003); Minkah Makalani, *In the Cause of Freedom: Radical Black Internationalism from Harlem to London, 1917–1939* (Chapel Hill, NC: University of North Carolina Press, 2011), ch. 7; W.O. Maloba, *Kenyatta and Britain: An Account of Political Transformation, 1929–1963* (Cham: Palgrave Macmillan, 2018); Marc Matera, *Black London: The Imperial Metropolis and Decolonization in the Twentieth Century* (Oakland, CA: University of California Press, 2015); Carol Polsgrove, *Ending British Rule in Africa: Writers in a Common Cause* (Manchester: Manchester University Press, 2009); Anne Spry Rush, 'Imperial Identity in Colonial Minds: Harold Moody and the League of Coloured Peoples, 1931–50', *Twentieth Century British History*, 13/4 (2002), pp. 356–83; Daniel Whittall, *Creolising London: Black West Indian Activism and the Politics of Race and Empire in Britain, 1931–1948*, Doctoral thesis (Royal Holloway, University of London, 2012).
3. Matera, *Black London*, p. 100.
4. Michael Goebel, *Anti-imperial Metropolis: Interwar Paris and the Seeds of Third World Nationalism* (Cambridge: Cambridge University Press, 2015), p. 3.
5. For more on Ashwood Garvey, see Keisha N. Blain, *Set the World on Fire: Black Nationalist Women and the Global Struggle for Freedom* (Philadelphia, PA: University of Pennsylvania Press, 2018); Minkah Makalani, 'An International African Opinion: Amy Ashwood Garvey and C.L.R. James in Black Radical London', in Davarian L. Baldwin and Minkah Makalani (eds), *Escape from New York: The New Negro*

Renaissance Beyond Harlem (Minneapolis, MN: University of Minnesota Press, 2013), ch. 3; Tony Martin, *Amy Ashwood Garvey: Pan-Africanist, Feminist, and Mrs. Marcus Garvey No. 1: Or, a Tale of Two Amies* (Dover, MA: Majority Press, 2007); Matera, *Black London*, pp. 104–11.

6. Makalani, 'An International African Opinion', pp. 86–9.
7. Blain, *Set the World on Fire*, pp. 13–19.
8. Ritchie Calder, 'Trafalgar Sq. Warning against Invasion', *Daily Herald*, 26 August 1935, p. 3; 'Friends of Abyssinia', *Manchester Guardian*, 26 August 1935, p. 8.
9. C.L.R. James, 'Autobiography, 1932–38', p. 51, C.L.R. James papers, box 4 folder 7, Rare Book and Manuscript Library, Columbia University, New York; Peter Abrahams, *The Coyaba Chronicles: Reflections on the Black Experience in the Twentieth Century* (Kingston, Jamaica: Ian Randle Publishers, 2000), p. 36.
10. Matera, *Black London*, p. 107.
11. George Padmore, *Colonial and… Coloured Unity: A Programme of Action: History of the Pan-African Congress* (1947), reprinted in ed. Hakim Adi and Marika Sherwood (eds), *The 1945 Manchester Pan-African Congress Revisited* (London: New Beacon Books, 1995), p. 98.
12. For more on Constance Agatha Cummings-John, see LaRay Denzer (ed.), *Memoirs of a Krio Leader* (Ibadan: Sam Bookman for Humanities Research Centre, 1995).
13. Imaobong D. Umoren, *Race Women Internationalists: Activist-Intellectuals and Global Freedom Struggles* (Oakland, CA: University of California Press, 2018).
14. Matera, *Black London*, p. 144.
15. Michelle Ann Stephens, *Black Empire: The Masculine Global Imaginary of Caribbean Intellectuals in the United States, 1914–1962* (Durham, NC: Duke University Press, 2005). While Stephens is primarily interested in these men's time in the US, it is worth noting that all three also lived in Britain for a time.
16. Stephens, *Black Empire*, p. 206.
17. Matera, *Black London*, p. 142.
18. Christian Høgsbjerg, 'Recovering the Afro-Metropolis before Windrush', *Anthurium: A Caribbean Studies Journal*, 13/1 (2016), article 5; Abrahams, *Coyaba Chronicles*, p. 42.
19. For more on T. Ras Makonnen, see Kenneth King (ed.), *Pan-Africanism from within* (London: Oxford University Press, 1973), p. 130.
20. 'Our Activities: Stemming the Tide', *African Sentinel* (October–November 1937), p. 10.
21. C.L.R. James, 'Notes on the Life of George Padmore', pp. 54–5, C.L.R. James papers, box 5 folder 21.
22. Louise Cripps, *C. L. R. James: Memories and Commentaries* (New York: Cornwall Books, 1997), p. 19.

23. Ibid., p. 145.
24. Ibid., p. 19.
25. James, 'Notes on the Life of George Padmore', p. 54; C L.R. James, 'George Padmore: Black Marxist Revolutionary – a Memoir' (1976), in *At the Rendezvous of Victory* (London: Allison & Busby, 1984), p. 260.
26. Kwame Nkrumah, *The Autobiography of Kwame Nkrumah* (Edinburgh: Thomas Nelson and Sons, 1957), p. 56.
27. Makonnen, *Pan-Africanism from within*, p. 147.
28. Ibid., p. 71.
29. Ibid., p. 146.
30. For more on Stock's life, see Basil Clarke, *Taking What Comes: A Biography of A.G. Stock (Dinah)* (Chandigarh: Publication Bureau, Panjab University, 1999).
31. Ralph Bunche, 1937 Annual Diary, 7 April, Ralph J. Bunche papers, box 279 folder 1, Charles E. Young Research Library, University of California, Los Angeles.
32. Jeremy Murray-Brown, *Kenyatta* (London: George Allen and Unwin, 1972), p. 182; Clarke, *Taking What Comes*, p. 83.
33. Reginald Reynolds, *My Life and Crimes* (London: Jarrolds, 1956), p. 152.
34. Makonnen, *Pan-Africanism from within*, p. 162.
35. *Pan-Africa*, August 1947, p. 3.
36. George Padmore, *Africa and World Peace* (London: Martin Secker and Warburg, 1937), p. 9.
37. Bunche, 1937 Annual Diary, 18 April, Ralph J. Bunche papers, box 279 folder 1, Charles E. Young Research Library, University of California, Los Angeles.
38. Dorothy Pizer to Nancy Cunard, 28 April 1961, Nancy Cunard collection, Harry Ransom Center, The University of Texas at Austin.
39. Bunche, 1937 Annual Diary, 18 April.
40. Makonnen, *Pan-Africanism from within*, p. 147.
41. Cripps, *C. L. R. James*, p. 57.
42. Stephen Howe, 'C. L. R. James: Visions of History, Visions of Britain', in Bill Schwarz (ed.), *West Indian Intellectuals in Britain*, p. 161.
43. Matera, *Black London*, p. 233.
44. Peter Abrahams, *A Wreath for Udomo* (1956; reprinted London: Faber and Faber, 1965), pp. 44–8.
45. Ibid., p. 15.
46. Ibid., p. 20.
47. Ibid., p. 193.
48. Abrahams, *Coyaba Chronicles*, pp. 40–1.
49. Nancy Cunard to Dorothy Pizer, November 1959, Nancy Cunard collection, Harry Ransom Center, The University of Texas at Austin.
50. Polsgrove, *Ending British Rule*, p. 84.

7

A Luta Continua: The Political Journey of Manchester's Black Women Activists, 1945–80

A.S. Francis

On 30 January 2001, the late community activist Elouise Edwards delivered a speech at the dedication of the Kath Locke Centre. Based in the inner-city district of Hulme in Manchester, the Centre offers holistic health and wellbeing services to the local community. It was named in honour of Kath Locke, one of Manchester's most long-standing and fervent Black radical activists of the twentieth century. Edwards, who alongside Locke was one of the leading Black women activists in Manchester during the 1960s–1980s, was the perfect candidate for such a speech. She utilised the life's work of Locke to encourage audience members, particularly those of African descent, to take up their positions in the ongoing struggles for justice and liberation:

> I have called our journey with this icon of ours, A Luta Continua: the struggle continues, as we are still caught up in a struggle for survival. However, we need to be reflective and consider what has been achieved. Mistakes have been made, but it is only with collective responsibility that we begin to see radical change … And so again I say A Luta Continua and hope this journey today will prompt those of you who are beneficiaries of the past struggle into taking your place in the war that has been waged against us.[1]

Accompanying this call to continue the fight for reparatory justice, Edwards nostalgically recounted the various ways in which

Manchester's tight-knit group of Black women activists collaborated in a political struggle to defend the rights of Black people locally, and as part of the global Black liberation struggle. Edwards demonstrated the dynamic organising methods which her and other women undertook, as much as she emphasised the great bonds and friendships which were forged in the process. In tracing her relationship with Locke, Edwards recalled their first encounter in the late 1960s, their subsequent journey together as mothers rallying to protect their children from the racism of the British school system, as facilitators and leaders of local Black women's organisations, and the challenges these organisations faced.[2] Indeed, Edwards' speech revealed how, as working-class Black women, they supported and empowered each other in a society which endeavoured to constrain them on multiple levels. Her call to review these struggles in order to continue them was of a similar nature to that of the authors of *The Heart of the Race*, who in 1985 emphasised the need for those who were triply oppressed in Britain on the basis of race, class and gender to 'take stock of our experiences, assess our responses – and learn from them'.[3] This chapter is therefore a response to Edwards' call to consider the challenges and achievements of a ferociously committed generation of Black women activists.

FERTILE GROUND

Given Manchester's long history of radical political activity, it is perhaps unsurprising that this city was such a hotspot for women-led Black activism in the late twentieth century. Local Black women in Manchester began working together from at least the late 1960s, to develop self-help initiatives for the wider Black community, and carved greater space in the Black movement for women while doing so. It was a natural location for such political bonds between Black women to develop and flourish. These Black women activists came from a diverse scope of national backgrounds and age ranges. Women born in Britain to African or Caribbean parents, and women who migrated from either the African continent or the Caribbean during the post-war wave of migration to Britain, pooled together their experiences, mentored each other, and collectively grappled with the tumultuous political climate of the late twentieth century. Manchester, like other British port cities such as Liverpool and Cardiff, contained a notable population of Africans, including West African seamen and their families. Prior to the post-World War II influx of Caribbean migrants, many of these port cities' Black residents hailed directly from the African continent.[4]

Three sisters, Kath Locke, Coca Clarke and Ada Phillips, all participated in the Black women's organising movement in Manchester. All three sisters have since passed away, however both Locke and Clarke were interviewed on several occasions during their lives, providing us with a valuable record of their personal experiences, opinions and perspectives as British-born African-descended women, who were born and grew up in Manchester, which informed their political outlook and commitment to grassroots activism. The task of recovering the contributions and experiences of the youngest sister Ada, who passed away in the late 1970s before she could tell her story, is a greater challenge. The sisters' father Anya Azura, or Alfred Lawrence as he was known in Britain, was from Calabar, Nigeria. He worked as a seaman and occasional playwright/performer. According to Locke and Clarke, he arrived in Cardiff as a cabin boy in 1907 aged around 19, and some years later relocated to Manchester where he married Ada Bate, a local English woman.[5] From this marriage came daughters Kath (1928–1992), Coca (1933–2019) and Ada (?–1978).

Lawrence's additional work as a playwright encouraged the sisters to celebrate their African identity. He included African dances in his shows and hired Black women from areas such as Cardiff and Liverpool to perform them in his productions. As Clarke recalled, this work provided another option in their very limited employment opportunities on account of their gender, racial and class status: 'It was the only thing Black girls could do in them days really, because you could not get a job in a shop, or a decent job. It was either stuck in a factory or doing something like this' (*sic*).[6] The dances featured in these shows were not specific to Calabar or Nigeria, but were inspired more generally by the African continent.[7] One might surmise that it was Lawrence's intention to showcase an all-embracing conception of

African culture to his audiences in Britain, and to celebrate Africa in a broad sense, regardless of the audience members' familiarity with specific regional or national cultures.

Naturally, the productions had a large personal impact on the sisters, demonstrated in the detail in which they talked about their father and his work in interviews. To Clarke's knowledge, Lawrence was the first Black man to produce African shows in England, and this was only one aspect of his efforts to instil pride in his daughters and African descendants in Britain:

> we were kind of political all our lives, in the sense that we knew we were Black. A lot of Black children in those days didn't accept the colour themselves, but we were brought up to be proud that we were African. We had to walk straight ... and [he'd say] 'don't let anybody touch your hair, you're not freaks!".[8]

Given that not before the 1970s (and even then), it was extremely uncommon for Black people to feature in non-derogatory roles in much of the available entertainment of the time, the African-centric plays produced by Lawrence, alongside his insistence that his daughters refuse to allow others to dehumanise them, made a positive contribution to their sense of identity and belonging which put them in good stead as Black activists in later years.

In 1933, the family relocated to Blackpool, and it was here that Locke and Clarke recall their traumatic experiences of racial abuse from schoolteachers, neighbours and fellow children. In Manchester, according to Locke, there was at least safety in numbers, but 'in a place like Blackpool, where they'd never seen any black people before, I used to spend my evenings crying quite a lot because of the tormenting I used to get.'[9] The prejudice that the sisters experienced outside of Manchester led to a heightened sense of awareness of their racialised identities, which isolated them from the rest of the community. For Clarke, her negative experiences of school in Blackpool not only left her with bad memories, but she also left school unable to read or write and had to teach herself in later years. Whereas Locke's experiences in school led her to become politically active from as early as 16 years old:

> I did become politically aware at an early age, partly because of my experience in the schools ... particularly to do with my identity, we had African names and [the teachers] refused to call us by our African names, they said they were heathen, so we had to use Anglicised names. That was a stepping-over of my parents' authority. So, it showed me the powerful and the powerless, and it was a very simple political lesson.[10]

By 1945, at the age of 17, Locke was attracted to the ideas of Communism, and hoped to join the Communist Party of Great Britain (CPGB) once she reached the voting age of 21. However, after attending a demonstration in Manchester, attended by Africans and English Communist Party members, she was struck by a dismissive attitude towards Black peoples' desires to separate from the largely white delegation and march autonomously. Locke was initially flattered when a white demonstrator turned to her and asked what she made of the suggestion, but after telling him that she agreed with the Africans, she recalled:

> He said to me 'Come the revolution, we'll give you your freedom!' and I thought 'well, everybody's born free' and there was a contradiction there, and it was a dogmatic contradiction ... so I didn't join the Communist Party ... it was only one person but I thought, well, after asking my opinion he still went on and overlooked it.[11]

Locke's recollection of this exchange between herself and a white Communist Party member is demonstrative of a problem that African, Caribbean and Asian people often encountered in attempting to engage in struggle with some English people who held reductionist attitudes towards the role of racism in society, and disagreed with the desires that many Black people had to organise autonomously around issues which centrally affected them.[12]

The two elder sisters were also politicised by encounters with African and Caribbean political figures visiting their family home, thanks to their father's links with the Pan-African movement. Although Lawrence was illiterate, he was nonetheless viewed as a 'politician in his own right' and maintained connections with

Africans throughout England.[13] This brings us to the Fifth Pan-African Congress, held in Manchester's Chorlton Town Hall during October 1945. The proceedings included powerful demands for an end to imperialism, colonialism, racism in all its manifestations, and capitalist exploitation. Locke, as the eldest sister, remembered the impact that the Congress had on her as a teenager. She recalled that it altered how she viewed herself as an African descendant growing up in Britain, leading her to re-evaluate her understanding of Africans and African descendants not solely as a minoritised group in England, but as a global community: 'you as a child met these strong characters ... and you realised we were not a minority, we were a majority' (*sic*).[14] Indeed, the reasons for the Congress being held in Manchester had much to do with the notable presence of politically active working-class Black people, as stated by one of the Congress's main organisers, local Pan-Africanist and business man, Ras Makonnen: 'Manchester had become quite a point of contact with the coloured proletariat in Britain, and we had made a name for ourselves in fighting various areas of discrimination.'[15]

One meeting between the organisers of the Congress took place in the sisters' family home. Although, according to Clarke, the sisters' gender, likely in conjunction with their young age, prevented them from being included in the conversations taking place: 'Africans in them days, even today, don't like women in the politics. You are supposed to sit back. So, with us being girls, we were not pulled into it' (*sic*).[16] Indeed, it was during the Fifth Pan-African Congress's proceedings when Amy Ashwood Garvey, the first wife of Marcus Garvey and illuminating Pan-African activist in her own right, called attention to the fact that 'for some reason very little has been said about the black woman', who 'has been shunted into the social background to be a child bearer'.[17] Ashwood Garvey's role in the Congress loomed large on Locke. During the 50th anniversary celebrations of the Congress in 1995, she helped organise the installation of a commemorative plaque outside Chorlton Hall and ensured Ashwood Garvey's name was included on it.[18] Despite gendered exclusions from political discourse as an adolescent, Clarke was actively disrupting patriarchal notions of women as passive and peaceful: 'I have fought all my life. I'm a woman, but I've had to stand up and fight like a man, from being young … You was fighting the establishment, you was fighting your teachers, you was fighting your playmates' (*sic*).[19] For example, in 1961, Clarke was arrested for fighting a woman who racially abused her on the street.[20] Ignoring Locke's advice to pay a fine and move on, Clarke insisted on hiring a lawyer and proceeded with the trial. The proceeding judge was unsympathetic to racism, and instead of finding justice Clarke received a suspended sentence. Her persistence to defend herself both on the street and in court speaks to her commitment to stand up against racism, even if the consequences proved unfavourable.

NEW AGE OF BLACK RADICALISM AND THE UCPA

1967 is a noteworthy year not only for the history of Black radical politics in Britain generally, but that of contemporary Black activism in Manchester. It is in this year that Black Power figurehead Stokely Carmichael visited Britain and delivered a speech at the Dialectics of Liberation Conference in London. This had a large mobilising effect for Britain's Black Power movement. In this same year the United Coloured People's Association (UCPA) was founded in London and became Britain's first official Black Power group.[21] Meanwhile, the strong sense of community present in Manchester's Moss Side was under threat from the authorities. Due to the post-war influx of Caribbeans to Britain, and the established presence of Africans, many of the Victorian-era terrace houses in the area were occupied by Black families.[22] Moss Side was by this time, home to 60 per cent of Manchester's Caribbean population.[23] These terrace houses became the target of a regeneration or 'slum clearance' scheme by the city authorities. The notable number of Black owner-occupiers in Moss Side was a key impetus for the local council's decision.[24] Local residents including Clarke, Locke, Edwards and her husband, the prominent Garveyite activist Beresford Edwards, formed the Moss Side People's Association and the Moss Side Housing Action Group. Despite the group's efforts, the demolitions went ahead. Alongside peoples' homes, the established sense of community was upheaved – as Locke told a journalist at the time: 'it gets you very angry … it's not an ideal community, but it is a community where people know one another and we don't want to move out. We've got a lot of old people, we've got a lot of Black people, who feel very strongly about it.'[25] There were also economic consequences for the dispersed families, who received much less via compulsory purchases than the houses were actually worth.[26] In some cases, owner-occupiers received as little as £50 for their houses, which couldn't cover a full month's rent for a flat in the new social housing blocks the council erected as alternatives.[27] Although the Housing Action Group ultimately failed to prevent the demolitions, it demonstrated the community's capacity for organised resistance against local authorities.

Around the same time, Ron Phillips of the UCPA in London travelled to Manchester to expand the UCPA's endeavours. He soon came across Locke and Clarke. Both sisters regarded this encounter as an important moment in the trajectory of Manchester's Black radical organising network. Locke recalled 'there was an organisation that sounds very liberal now: Universal Coloured People's Association. But it was the most militant organisation of the time … We organised a branch here and a branch in Liverpool, and it took off."[28] Although Phillips' arrival to Manchester provided a catalyst for developing a Black Power outlet in Manchester, the sisters' ability to pool people together for a membership base facilitated its success, as we can surmise from Clarke's recollection: 'everywhere we went we bumped into this guy … it turned out he was political. And he wanted to know the grassroots people of Moss Side because he did not know anybody.'[29] The sisters invited him to their family house and assembled other people to form a membership. What became the Manchester branch of the UCPA offered a new basis for unity between people of different nationalities, as Clarke stated,

> it was the first time, when we did get the thing off the ground, I had ever seen Africans and all the types of West Indians – I'm talking about Trinidadian, Jamaican, St Kitts, and [those of us] that were born here, all together sitting down talking … We found that every one of us had the same thing in common. We were Black, regardless of where we were from.[30]

The UCPA's Manchester chapter was registered at 22 Monton Street, the sisters' family home. The elder sisters were central organisers of the group, and their home was a trusted space for local Black activists, as it had been during the Fifth Pan-African Congress.

The UCPA filled a void in the Black organising movement and provided a home for radical activists who saw promise in the message of Black Power. It soon attracted Elouise and Beresford Edwards. Elouise had migrated from Guyana to Manchester with her son in 1961 to join Beresford, who came to pursue a career in the printing industry.[31] They settled in Moss Side and quickly became prominent members of the Black activist community. Their house was a beacon in the North West for activists and intellectuals who were passing through during their travels, such as Bernard Coard, who visited their home around the time of his 1971 publication *How the West Indian Child Is Made Educationally Subnormal in the British School System.*[32] The first time Locke met Edwards was at a meeting of local activists at the house of 'Mama' Ruby Inniss. Born in 1912, Mama Inniss arrived in Manchester in 1959 from Aruba, and was a well-respected elder in the Black women activist network.[33] Edwards recounted this encounter with Locke in her 2001 speech:

> Funny enough, we disagreed at that meeting … Angela Davis was the topic of conversation, as well as the Soledad Brothers. The Afro hair style was the reason for our disagreement. I felt that it was fashionable at the time and that it would soon become extinct, Kath felt it was a 'statement' and would continue to live on. We argued. However, we met up again as we were part of the UCPA. Ron Phillips was the lead person in the group.[34]

As Edwards became more involved with the organisation, the two began a lifelong friendship and political partnership. Although Phillips was initially the lead organiser of the group, he was eventually expelled on 10 May 1970. In a statement released by the UCPA entitled 'The exposure and expulsion of a con (Ron Phillips) by UCPA', the grounds for his expulsion were listed under four aspects of the UCPA's work he had seemingly failed: the organisation, the people, the youth, the women. In sum, he was accused of drifting from the UCPA's aims as an organising, mobilising and safeguarding force for Black working-class people. Perhaps the most relevant of these listed factors – for our purposes – is the accusations of his mistreatment towards women:

> Ron Phillips' behaviour towards several black women, (and white women too), shows quite clearly that he believes that women are a commodity to be used as toilet paper. This hypocrite has used the 'charm' of a criminal thereby deceiving several vulnerable women. The UCPA will never condone such criminal behaviour. Black consciousness demands that black women be treated with the dignity and honour which is theirs.[35]

The statement was written by members of the Manchester branch, and again the sisters' family address was printed at the bottom. The sisters were therefore involved in organising Phillips' expulsion. Expulsions from Black radical organisations under such circumstances were not uncommon. In most organisations, men acting promiscuously or disrespectfully towards women was condemned. In the case of the Black Panther Movement (BPM) in London, there was a policy against such behaviour. Altheia Jones-LeCointe, the BPM leader, gained a reputation for her intolerance of misogyny. In the examples of the UCPA and BPM, misogynistic behaviour received harsher punishment when women were in the leadership core.

In July of 1970, the UCPA – including its Manchester chapter – transformed into the Black Unity and Freedom Party (BUFP). This was an outcome of the growing disparities in the political orientations of UCPA members and the Black Power movement generally. Such disparities led to the establishment of several splinter groups, including the BPM in 1968, and the Black Liberation Front in 1971. The BUFP was informed by Marxist-Leninism and Maoism, with a commitment to worldwide socialist revolution. Naturally, people involved in the organisation were vehemently opposed to the global capitalist, white supremacist system.[36] The London and Manchester branches of the BUFP maintained a close relationship. While Phillips might have been viewed as the central figure of the Manchester branch in its UCPA era, Locke was regarded as its leader from its rebirth as the BUFP. Harry Goulbourne, who was a BUFP member in its initial years, addressed inaccuracies in historical memory by emphasising that Phillips was not a recognised member of the BUFP, and that 'the actual leader was a woman [Kath Locke], her father was West African. She had a strong family background … A very dynamic woman.'[37] Goulbourne's recollection of Locke acknowledged her individual qualities as a vital force in the movement, in conjunction with her family's continental and Pan-African roots. Given Goulbourne's acknowledgement of Locke's heritage and her family's political background, it is probable that these details of her life provided her with currency as a leader in the movement.

Emphasising her pride in her African heritage, Locke wrote under the name 'Kanto Labinjoh' in the BUFP's *Black Voice*. In the summer of 1970, she wrote an article entitled: 'Moss Side – Deprived, Capitalist, Racist'. She described her family's experiences of racism at the hands of Moss Side's poverty-stricken white residents and argued against class-reductionist attempts to ignore the prevalence of racism among working-class communities:

> I have lived in various places in this country, and I will not argue with the fact that Moss Side is fairly tolerant and racism is not rife, on the surface. But I will argue with those people who say that racism does not exist[t] because, having to live in concentrated poverty, we are all deprived. This idea is false; for just under the surface it can be found in many subtle instances of discrimination. But we in this community like to bury our heads in the sand and refuse to face reality.[38]

In line with the BUFP's revolutionary ideology, Locke declared that 'the capitalist system must be totally destroyed. The foundations will have to be dug out and replaced by a truly humane socialist system, for only then will we be assured of our human dignity.'[39] Identifiably, in the BUFP, Locke was able to further her participation in the struggle for socialist revolution, a mission she had begun but was discouraged from as a 17-year-old prospective Communist Party member. The BUFP also provided a framework for Locke and others to explore the interconnected relationship between racism and capitalism.

AUTONOMOUS WOMEN'S ORGANISING

During his teen years, Edwards' son struggled in the school system and was labelled – as were many young Black children – 'educationally subnormal' (ESN).[40] In 1966, prior to the UCPA's existence, Edwards had begun attempts alongside another local mother, Alice Evans, to convince the headteacher of the Princess Road Primary School to hold an event to showcase Black history and culture. The school wasn't committed to the idea, and Edwards' attempts to convince a local school weren't successful until 1977, when the first Roots Festival was convened at Ducie High School.[41] However, the eleven-year delay in action by local schools didn't prevent Edwards, and other concerned parents and activists, from tackling the issue of education in the interim. Just like in many other regions in Britain, people took matters into their own hands by forming supplementary schools.[42] It is due to the direct experiences that local parents had with the school system which prompted them to organise a supplementary school in St James Church, Moss Side, in 1967, the first such school in the area.[43] The supplementary school attracted women and men to become involved, but it was run mainly by the men. It was agreed by some of the women that there was a necessity to design autonomous women's models of organising within the Supplementary School Movement. Edwards recalled: 'we recognised that the women did not play a major role because of the dominance of the men … We realised that our children were not being taught their history, their culture.'[44] As a result, a women's organisation was set up to discuss education, and create a dialogue between parents and schools: Black Women's Mutual Aid (BWMA).

The BWMA's membership included Edwards, Locke, Liverpool-born Black activist and Communist Dorothy Kuya, and former member of the Black Panther Movement and Squatters Rights activist Olive Morris. Morris was already an established community activist in Brixton, South London, and relocated to Manchester in 1975 to attend university. Not long before her untimely death at the age of 27 in 1979, she travelled to China to lead a students' tour. Morris and Locke shared a similar affinity for Marxism and Maoism, and Locke was persuaded by Morris to also travel to China and lead a workers' tour: '[Olive] was like a daughter to me … she encouraged me to go, and it was interesting … it was like a child leading a parent'.[45] This cross-generational mentorship is indicative of the environment that organisations like the BWMA provided – space for women to support each other's self-development. However, the BWMA ran into difficulties due to backlash from some men in the community. Edwards recalled that some of the men who witnessed the women of the BWMA gather saw it as a negative initiative, and there were suspicions that the organisation had an anti-male agenda. Some women's involvements in the group even provoked domestic abuse from their disapproving male partners.[46] The BWMA then became stagnant, and eventually fizzled out. This signified the women's first major hurdle in their attempts to organise autonomously.

Another important site of community organisation was the West Indian Centre on Carmoor Road. As a young person growing up in the local area, Diane Watt frequented the Centre and took part in its supplementary school, describing it as the 'hub of everything that was going on'.[47] The Centre, located close to the University of Manchester, was a site of interaction between local residents and African students, which was one of its most important aspects, according to Watt: 'it was the site for fundraising events and events to highlight liberation struggles in Africa. And so, what they succeeded [in] was to bring together the local community and the student body … that was their space for helping to raise awareness about the struggles that were taking place in their countries'.[48] In earlier years, the more radical sections of the Black activist community ran into problems with organisers of the West Indian Centre, due to political differences. For example, Clarke, alongside other mothers both white and Black, attempted to take over the premises and reinvent it as a playgroup for Black children. After members of the West Indian Centre, who Clarke referred to as 'the Elitist blacks', called the police, Clarke received a permanent injunction forbidding her to return to the site. Prior to Clarke's interventions, the Centre's main contributions were hosting dances, but from her perspective 'it wasn't constructive'.[49] As time went on, the Centre evolved into something more than just a social initiative. It provided a youth club, supplementary school, workshops and partnered with African students to publicise liberation struggles taking place on the continent.[50] It was this more political version of the Centre that Watt, as a younger member of the Black women's activist network, frequented.

REACHING A HEAD

In 1974, the Manchester Black Women's Co-operative (MBWC) held its official opening, although the actual start date for the organisation is recorded as 1975. Paying homage to women leaders in the Black movement, the event featured Altheia Jones-LeCointe as guest speaker.[51] The MBWC was the next attempt, after BWMA, at autonomous Black women's organising. As described by Watt, the Co-operative 'was established to create a self-help educational programme within the community geared especially to the needs of young mothers'. The MBWC ran an office skills training programme and provided opportunities for young people to get involved with community initiatives.[52] It was largely directed by the youngest of the three sisters, Ada Phillips, who acted as the MBWC's first chairwoman. By this time Ada had married Ron Phillips after returning to Manchester from several years of living abroad in the US – hence her lack of involvement in the UCPA and BUFP. The two were also house parents for the George Jackson House Trust (GJHT), which provided accommodation and guidance for vulnerable Black youth. The MBWC, like the BWMA, became a site where Black women from different age groups and generations came together and mentored each other. Watt became involved with the MBWC, after being encouraged to do so by Ada: 'I became more grounded when [I met Ada] and she wanted to find out what I was doing, and then she told me that they were setting up the Manchester Black Women's Co-operative.'[53] Watt was studying secretarial work, and joined the MBWC as an employee, marking her entry into Black women's-centred activism. Alongside their involvement in GJHT, and Ada's leading position in the MBWC, the Phillips were both ardent Pan-Africanists. Ron in particular, who spoke on behalf of the British delegation at the 1974 Pan-African Congress in Dar-Es Salaam, Tanzania. He was instrumental in founding the Pan-African Committee, which then became the Pan-African Congress Movement (PACM) in 1977. The Phillips' commitment to Pan-Africanism fed into both the GJHT and the MBWC.[54]

According to Watt, while Ada was the group's chairwoman, the organisation reflected the fact it was a women's-centred organisation.[55] However, contradictions were exposed after her passing in 1978. The dominance of Ron Phillips' voice became more apparent and he began attempts to bring the MBWC under the umbrella of GJHT. This threatened the autonomous nature of the MBWC, and spurred the women involved to conduct what they described as a 'period of self- criticism'.[56] They suggested that the MBWC had failed in its plan to develop into a trusted, community-facing organisation, and it needed to better reflect the views of the women already involved, as well as those it sought to attract.[57] The MBWC released a position paper, which firmly articulated the women's frustrations about the group's lack of progress:

> The white capitalist media portray black women in degrading conditions. Until black women aspire above these conditions and start to educate themselves, these oppressive conditions will continue. The Co-operative was a start in this direction. The need for a Women's Co-operative is greater now than it was five years ago because these conditions have not improved. The Black Women's Co-op is the only training scheme which is staffed and controlled by women. It was never conceived that men would be dictating the ideology and activities of a women's Co-op. Women need to achieve success in the field of education, authority without the psychological control of men. We need to be able to stand up as equals.[58]

Such self-criticism was met with heavy resistance from men of the GJHT, and it was this resistance which fuelled the women to stand their ground, as Watt recalled: 'once you enter into a struggle, and you find that there's an opposition – and the opposition is groundless – that made us even more determined to exercise our voice'.[59] Because some of the MBWC's activities and equipment had been financed by grants from the Commission for Racial Equality under the auspices of the GJHT, Phillips was able to claim that the MBWC was its subsidiary group. A meeting was planned by the MBWC, open to local women, for 26 October 1979. The meeting's aim was 'to give other women confidence in themselves to see women staffing and controlling the organisation'.[60] On the day of this meeting, all the women of the MBWC received notifications of their suspension with immediate effect and were locked out of the MBWC premises.

The women responded with a ten-day, ten-night occupation of the premises, supported by other Black women's organisations, including the Organisation of Women of African and Asian Descent (OWAAD). On 1 January 1980, MBWC was rebirthed as the Abasindi Co-operative. This signified a collective resolution to persevere with their aim of building a truly independent Black women's initiative. The women involved in its rebirth were Kath Locke, Duduzile Lethlaku, Yvonne Hypolite, Maria Noble, Popgee Manderson, Madge Gordon, Abena Braithwaite, Shirley Inniss and Diane Watt.[61] The choice of name – Abasindi – meaning 'Survivors' in Zulu – represented the group's embrace of their own struggle which brought them to that particular moment, and connected this with the struggles for liberation taking place in Southern Africa and elsewhere.[62] This rebirth meant that women could organise in line with their own needs and politics. One lesson learned from the whole debacle was the value of steering clear of state grants. Abasindi raised money to fund their activities through independent means, such as making and selling clothing, hair plaiting, and generally relying on their own skillsets.

CONCLUSION

The creation of the Abasindi Co-operative brings us to the high point in these women's struggles for liberation, at personal levels as well as community wide. The various initiatives that were driven by Kath Locke, Elouise Edwards, Coca Clarke, Diane Watt, Ada Phillips and others were important stepping stones in a shared trajectory. With each organisation founded, each obstacle confronted, and each solution sought, this network of committed Black women activists continued to push, critique and develop themselves in a profoundly holistic and collectivist arrangement. Each step of the way, the necessity to support and champion the needs of working-class Black women was regularly articulated both in the words and deeds of these women. From as early as 1945, Clarke was aware of the exclusion of women and girls within Pan-African discourse. During the Black Power era, Locke, Clarke and other members of the Manchester UCPA branch fought to safeguard the position of women in the movement. As in the case of the BWMA, the need for women's autonomous organising was not always respected by the wider community. In 1979, these contentions eventually erupted, and provided a clean break in the form of Abasindi. But the struggles waged by these women were about more than solely Black women's empowerment: they were about justice, liberation for all, and challenging the white supremacist capitalist system. The contentions which arose in various points of these women's journeys highlight the diversity of political thought and organising frameworks present in the Black movement. However, despite the challenges encountered, their struggles continued. Their stories provide us with important lessons on the need for constant perseverance, reflection and renewal.

NOTES

1. Elouise Edwards, speech at the dedication of the Kath Locke Centre, 30 January 2001, Ahmed Iqbal Ullah Race Relations Resource Centre, Manchester: MAN/GE.1/EDW.
2. Ibid.
3. Beverley Bryan, Stella Dadzie and Suzanne Scafe, *The Heart of the Race: Black Women's Lives in Britain* (London: Virago Press, 1985), p. 2.
4. George Bankes, 'Exploring Africa in Manchester', *Journal of Museum Ethnography*, 13 (March 2001), p. 22.
5. The available information regarding Alfred Lawrence's arrival to Britain is derived from Kath Locke and Coca Clarke's accounts of their father's life. See Kath Locke, 'Photograph of Universal Coloured People's Association (UCPA) Demonstration' (1968), Ahmed Iqbal Ullah Race Relations Resource Centre: GB3228.7/3/40; see also Coca Clarke, 'Roots Family History Project', interviewed by Sarah Porter, (1982), transcript pp. 1–2, Ahmed Iqbal Ullah Race Relations Resource Centre: GBB3228.7/1/9.

6. Coca Clarke, transcript p. 4.
7. Ibid.
8. Coca Clarke, 'The Legacy of Black Power in Moss Side: Activist Coca Clarke Tells Her Story', interviewed by *The Meteor* (2 September 2018), part one, https://soundcloud.com/user-990460881/20180710-coca-on-black-power-section-03 (accessed 19 January 2023).
9. Kath Locke, interviewed by Paul Okojie (Manchester, 1992), transcript p. 1, Ahmed Iqbal Ullah Race Relations Resource Centre: MAN/GE.1/OKO.
10. Ibid., p. 14.
11. Ibid., p. 14.
12. For accounts of Black people's contributions and experiences in the CPGB post-World War II, see Hakim Adi, 'West Africans and the Communist Party in the 1950s', in G. Andrews, N. Fishman and K. Morgan (eds), *Opening the Books: Essays on the Social and Cultural History of the British Communist Party* (London: Pluto Press, 1995), pp. 176–94; see also Trevor Carter, *Shattering Illusions: West Indians in British Politics* (London: Lawrence & Wishart, 1987); Evan Smith, '"Class before Race": British Communism and the Place of Empire in Post-war Race Relations', *Science & Society*, 72/ 4 (October 2008), pp. 455–81.
13. Coca Clarke, transcript p. 20.
14. Kath Locke, transcript pp. 5–6.
15. Peter Fryer, *Staying Power: The History of Black People in Britain* (London: Pluto Press, 1984), p. 353.
16. Coca Clarke, transcript p. 20.
17. Hakim Adi and Marika Sherwood, *The 1945 Manchester Pan-African Congress Revisited* (London: New Beacon Books, 1995), p. 98.
18. Kath Locke, transcript p. 19.
19. Coca Clarke, transcript pp. 8–9.
20. Ibid., pp. 33–4.
21. For more on Stokely Carmichael, the Dialectics of Liberation Conference and the United Coloured People's Association's emergence, see Rosie Wild, '"Black Was the Colour of Our Fight': Black Power in Britain, 1955–1976', University of Sheffield (2008), pp. 65–115; see also Robin Bunce and Paul Field, 'Obi B. Egbuna, C. L. R. James and the Birth of Black Power in Britain: Black Radicalism in Britain 1967–72', *Twentieth Century British History*, 22/3 (2011), pp. 391–414.
22. Laurence Brown and Niall Cunningham, 'The Inner Geographies of a Migrant Gateway: Mapping the Built Environment and the Dynamics of Caribbean Mobility in Manchester, 1951–2011', *Social Science History*, 40/1 (Spring 2016), pp. 93–120.
23. Kerry Pimblott, 'Manchester Community Histories in the Shadow of Urban Regeneration' (19 May 2020), https://gfsc.studio/2020/05/19/

manchester-community-histories-urban-regeneration.html#fn:migrant (accessed 19 January 2023).

24. Diane Watt, interviewed by the author (remote, 26 June 2020), transcript p. 6.
25. Kath Locke, *Blacks Britannica* (1978), directed by David Koff.
26. For more information on the effects suffered by Black owner-occupiers in Moss Side, see Diana Watt and Adele D. Jones, *Catching Hell and Doing Well: Black Women in the UK – the Abasindi Cooperative* (London: Institute of Education Press, 2015), p. 19.
27. Ron Phillips, *Blacks Britannica* (1978), directed by David Koff.
28. Kath Locke, transcript p. 20.
29. Coca Clarke, transcript p. 39.
30. Ibid., p. 40.
31. Elouise Edwards, 'I Never Wanted to Come at All', p. 2, Ahmed Iqbal Ullah Race Relations Resource Centre: GB3228.5/2/1.
32. Ibid.
33. For more information on the early life and migration to Britain of Ruby Inniss, see Ruby Inniss, 'Roots Family History Project', interviewed by Louise Hooker (1983); see also NHS London, 'Four Generations, One Family, One NHS' (21 June 2019), https://nhsenglandldn.medium.com/four-generations-one-family-one-nhs-df7cd66d2dca (accessed 19 January 2023).
34. Elouise Edwards, speech at the dedication of the Kath Locke Centre.
35. UCPA, 'The Exposure and Expulsion of a Con (Ron Phillips) by UCPA', May 1970, available at the Institute of Race Relations.
36. For a history of the BUFP, and summary of its political principles, see Harry Goulbourne, 'Africa and the Caribbean in Caribbean Consciousness and Action in Britain', *The David Nicholls Memorial Lectures: David Nicholls Memorial Trust*, No. 2 (Oxford: University of Oxford, 2000), pp. 113–64.
37. Harry Goulbourne, in conversation with the author (23 April 2020).
38. Kanto Labinjoh, 'Moss Side – Deprived, Capitalist and Racist', *Black Voice* (Autumn/September 1970).
39. Ibid.
40. Elouise Edwards, transcript p. 2.
41. 'Roots Five Years on', pamphlet, p. 3, Ahmed Iqbal Ullah Race Relations Resource Centre: GB3228.6.
42. For more information on the Supplementary School Movement, see Jessica Gerrard, *Radical Childhoods: Schooling and the Struggle for Social Change* (Manchester: Manchester University Press, 2014), pp. 117–81.
43. Kath Locke, 'Historic Evidence of Contributions of African People to the Advancement of Life in Manchester and Britain as a Whole', p. 2, Ahmed Iqbal Ullah Race Relations Resource Centre: GB3228.5/3/34.

44. Elouise Edwards, 'The Roots Family History Project' (1982), transcript p. 2.
45. Kath Locke, interviewed by Paul Okojie, transcript p. 17.
46. Elouise Edwards, 'Heart of the Race Oral History Project', Black Cultural Archives: ORAL1/13.
47. Diane Watt, interviewed for the 'Women of the Soil' project, https://firstcutmedia.com/heritage-digital-archive/black-womens-activism/ (accessed 19 January 2023).
48. Diane Watt, interviewed by the author (remote, 18 May 2021), transcript p. 3.
49. Coca Clarke, 'The Legacy of Black Power in Moss Side'.
50. Vince Wilkinson, 'Celebrating the Life of Nana Bonsu 1930–2003', Nana Bonsu Oral History Project, https://nanabonsu.com/media-archive/celebrating-nana-bonsu/ (accessed 19 January 2023).
51. Photograph: Official opening of the Manchester Black Women's Co-operative in 1974, available at Greater Manchester Record Office, Ref: 1741/11.
52. Diane Watt, 'Silent Warriors: The Women of the Abasindi Cooperative', p. 2, Ahmed Iqbal Ullah Race Relations Resource Centre: GB3228.8/14.
53. Diane Watt, interviewed for the 'Women of the Soil' project, https://firstcutmedia.com/heritage-digital-archive/black-womens-activism/ (accessed 19 January 2023).
54. Claudius Adisa Steven, 'The Evolution of Ideas and Practices among African-Centred Organisations in the UK, 1975–2015', in Hakim Adi (ed.), *Black British History: New Perspectives from Roman Times to the Present Day* (London: Zed books, 2019), pp. 144–61.
55. Diane Watt, interviewed by the author (remote, via Zoom: 18 May 2021), transcript p. 1.
56. 'Statement of the Manchester Black Women's Co-operative', George Padmore Institute (GPI): BPM3/2/3/1.
57. Ibid.
58. Manchester Black Women's Co-operative, 'Position Paper: Part One', p. 1, GPI: BPM3/2/3/1.
59. Diane Watt, interviewed by the author (remote, via Zoom: 18 May 2021), transcript p. 1.
60. Manchester Black Women's Co-operative, 'Statement of the Manchester Black Women's Co-operative', GPI: BPM3/2/3/1.
61. Watt, 'Silent Warriors', pp. 2–3.
62. Watt and Jones, *Catching Hell and Doing Well.*

8

How West Indian Students and Migrants Cooperated in Fighting Racialised Injustices in Britain 1950s–1970s

Claudia Tomlinson

The idea of a West Indian identity in Britain was only emerging in the 1950s and 1960s. During this period, its emergence was driven by two main factors. Firstly, the movement of students from the region to the newly established University of the West Indies in Jamaica, which opened in 1948. The university brought together young people and academics from across the region, and it became a driver for intellectual 'West Indianism' from the 1950s. There was an increase in higher educational opportunities for students from the region, previously dependent on going to Britain for a university education which was economically unachievable for the majority. There was also rapid development of political thought, and an imperative to move the West Indies away from pursuing the economic and political priorities of Britain. More attention was given to objectives connected to the agency and sovereignty of nations to enable them to pursue their own economic and political objectives. Connected to this factor was the plan to build a single economic and political confederation of nations in the region, known as the West Indies Federation. Federation was never established for the West Indies, but it was an important strategic objective that was pursued until the middle of the 1960s, fostering a quest for unity between those in the region.

The second factor driving the emergence of a West Indian identity during this period was the movement of people from the region to Western countries including Britain. They were described as West Indians, and for the first time they met and joined with others from the region. Increasingly they came to be viewed, and to view themselves as a single cultural group. They were the target of the predominant racialised anti-Blackness culture in Britain that saw them subjected to barriers in employment, housing, social and leisure facilities and being subject to overt attacks. In addition, these public attitudes were reinforced by institutions, and organisations. It was also reflected in British politics as all mainstream parties supported, to varying degrees, the 'moral panic' at the migration of West Indians and other racialised groups to the country. The subsequent introduction of immigration legislation formed part of the dominant theme of anti-Blackness in Britain. These were the forces that provided the backdrop for resistance from West Indian organisations, and their supporters in Britain.

It is argued that this new West Indian identity posed ideological and political problems for Britain. It adopted a divisive and contradictory response to West Indianism in Britain. The new settlers, the immigrant workers, were part of its history of colonisation that it could not shed, but did not want to be confronted with in its own land. It dealt with their experience in racist terms. The West Indian students, in contrast, were perceived by some West Indian working migrants as receiving special treatment. With the colonised countries in the region approaching independence, Britain recognised that there was a need to consider the education of the leaders of the new, independent West Indies. These elite students therefore represented this future. It was important for Britain to forge advantageous new relationships with the administrations in the region.[1] However racialisation interfered with these efforts and the elite West Indian students often shared the same fate as the workers, in universities and housing.

This chapter offers an examination of the nature and extent of West Indian cooperation to overcome the common struggles against racialised injustices during the 1950s and 1960s. The narration of this history is hampered by the underdevelopment of research in this area, and the disappearance or destruction of the records of the West Indian Students' Union and Centre.[2]

THE BACKGROUND OF WEST INDIAN STUDENTS IN HIGHER EDUCATION IN BRITAIN

Black students from the West Indies have a very long history of travelling to Britain for a university education. Their numbers increased during the interwar period, and again after World War II. Scholarships were the main source of funding and young people had the opportunity to sit exams for Island scholarships to British universities. It was largely the children of middle-class parents in the West Indies who had these opportunities as secondary education was fee-paying in most of the region, and it was those in the prestigious schools in the Caribbean who predominantly sat these exams. Children from poorer families were needed to work and to contribute to the household income. Children from wealthy families could also afford to independently fund their studies in Britain and formed part of the contingent of university students.[3]

The welfare of West Indian students, and indeed all students from British colonies during this period, was largely under the auspices of a number of unofficial voluntary agencies. For example, Aggrey House, a hostel and club, was opened in 1934 in London by a charity supported financially by African and West Indian colonial administrations and under the auspices of the Colonial Office.[4] From the 1950s and later, there was increased recognition of the changing relations between Britain and its former colonies as they approached independence from Britain.[5] Accommodation and social support for the students was prioritised, and a number of hostels and clubs were available, mostly in the London area. For a period following World War II, the Colonial Office assumed responsibility for student welfare until 1950 when this responsibility was passed to the British Council. Colonial student accommodation continued to be one of the main welfare needs of students, and several hostels were established. Hans Crescent opened in London in 1950 for colonial students and provided accommodation for many West Indian students arriving from overseas. Criticised for its operational strategy, Hans Crescent was the site of sit-ins and agitation by the students who found the terms and running of the hostel inadequate.[6] The focus on meeting the accommodation needs of growing numbers of colonial students in

Britain during this period was therefore met with varying degrees of success.

Many of the hostels doubled up as social clubs providing talks, debates, speakers, as well as sporting and cultural activities including dances. Student unions were an important aspect of student organisation and provided opportunities for those interested in leadership roles in the independence governments of the West Indian nations or the emerging West Indies Federation. The West Indian Students' Union (WISU) was established in London, 1945, and many who eventually became West Indian government ministers or officials were those who held official roles in WISU. WISU's objectives changed over time as a consequence of the new political consciousness in the West Indies. The Union would provide a space for West Indians to start to move away from a purely localised identity as Jamaicans or Trinidadians, and develop a sense of a unity for the benefit of the region in the future.[7] The aims and objectives of WISU's first meeting therefore included as its primary aim to foster 'fellowship between West Indian Students in the UK'.[8] In addition to promoting the welfare of West Indian Students in London, the Union also aimed to 'stimulate interest in the cultural, political and economic development of the West Indies'.[9] It saw its role as making links and cooperating with organisations in Britain with similar objectives. WISU operated without a permanent base until 1955 when the West Indian Students' Centre opened.

The opening of the West Indian Students' Centre by Princess Margaret featured in a British Pathé film. It was based in south Kensington, a wealthy and leafy suburb of central London, with extensive social facilities including a library, a billiards room, a lounge, a writing room, a television room and a games room, as well as a canteen and dining room, providing subsidised West Indian meals.[10] The film featured the princess' speech about a warm welcome for the West Indian visitors, the hope that the lavish club would ameliorate loneliness and help prepare the students for their future roles. The students in the film were beautifully dressed, smiling and happy and there was a display of traditional West Indian artefacts for the princess to admire. It was estimated that there were over 2,000 West Indian students in Britain at the time of the opening of the Centre.[11]

THE EXPERIENCE OF WEST INDIAN WORKERS IN BRITAIN

West Indian immigrants viewing the British Pathé film and reading newspapers about the Centre would have compared their own condition very unfavourably with that of the students. Within days of the docking of the *Empire Windrush* in 1948, eleven Labour MPs wrote to Clement Attlee, the Labour Prime Minister, to take action to reverse Black immigration as an 'influx of coloured people domiciled here is likely to impair the harmony, strength and cohesion of our public and social life and to cause discord and unhappiness among all concerned'.[12] A strong colour bar was in place that restricted and blocked access by Black people to employment, housing, leisure and entertainment facilities. The 1962 poem by Wole Soyinka, *Telephone Conversation* provides a good description of the often-farcical attempts by landlords and landladies to block prospective Black renters who telephoned to enquire about rental properties.[13] The portrayal in the British media of arrivals from the West Indies in the late 1940s and the 1950s was overwhelmingly negative. West Indian workers and settlers were viewed as presenting a moral and cultural threat to the British way of life.[14]

The passage of the 1948 Commonwealth Act conferred British nationality on citizens of the United Kingdom and Colonies, so those travelling from the West Indies at the end of the 1940s and the 1950s were doing so as British citizens. Perceived support by the British public for strengthened anti-immigration legislation prompted the Labour Party, as well as the political right, to also consider the introduction of such controls. This resulted in the gradual reversal of most of the provisions of the 1948 Act.[15] The Immigration Acts of 1962, 1968 and 1971 gradually restricted the rights of Commonwealth immigrants to settle in Britain. Those with a parent or grandparent born in the UK, or who were British citizens were given new immigration rights. This development privileged white immigrants over Black immigrants, as the former were more likely to have a parent or grandparent born in Britain. The 1971 Act included provision for 'voluntary' repatriation of immigrants in a clear rejection of their status as settled Britons.[16] The 1971 Act therefore made Black immigrants second-class citizens with lesser rights to British citizenship and designated them outsiders with different identities.

DEBATES AND DIVERGENCE

The programme of activities for the students at the West Indian Students' Centre made it one of the most important arenas in Britain for Black intellectual thought, and Black political organising. The Fourteenth Annual Report by the Board of Governors revealed that between 1967 and 1968, C.L.R James, the Trinidadian-born historian, gave four talks to the students on 'History of the West Indies', 'The Situation in Nigeria', 'Africa's Contribution to Culture' and the 'Arusha Declaration'.[17] During the same period, the Centre hosted talks by James Baldwin, the American author, Cheddi Jagan, the Guyanese President, Obi Egbuna, the Nigerian author, and leader of the Universal Coloured People's Association (UCPA), Oscar Abrams, member of the Campaign Against Racial Discrimination (CARD), and a founder of the Keskidee Centre, and Dick Gregory, US civil rights activist and comedian. The report also highlighted the strong activity by West Indian Artists at the West Indian Students' Centre. There were talks from Ram John Holder, the Guyanese actor, on 'West Indian Theatre', a talk by George Lamming, the eminent Caribbean writer from Barbados, from John La Rose, the Trinidadian-born publisher and activist, E. Braithwaite, the educator and writer, and Jeremy Verity, the Jamaican broadcaster, on 'Communications Media in and to the West Indies'.

Between 1968 and 1970, the programme of speakers included Michael Manley, vice-president of the Peoples National Party of Jamaica, on 'the Relevance of Black Power to Jamaica', C.L.R. James on 'Problems Confronting Black and White American races,' and a joint speech from Eric Williams, the Trinidadian Prime Minister, Cosmo Pieterse, the South African writer and educator, and student union officials Gary Burton and Ansel Wong on 'The W.I.S.U. and the International Black Struggle'. Caribbean reformer, publisher and political activist Jessica Huntley also gave a talk, entitled 'Our Black Women Speak'.[18]

One of the most important events was in 1968 when Stokely Carmichael spoke at the Centre. In his view the 'educational system which black people received in England and in the West Indies, those dominated by the West and black people in the United States – as a matter of fact most of the education, formal education – is racist'.[19] This talk was evidence that the students had privileged access to the global leaders in Black liberation. Such leaders educated the students and raised their consciousness of global injustices against Black people. West Indian immigrants who were at the Centre as guests of members, or who were prominent members of the West Indian immigrant community also heard Carmichael speak. But restricted entry criteria for the West Indian Students' Centre meant that access to such speakers as Carmichael was not open to the majority of West Indian immigrants in Britain.

Carmichael advised the students to be alert to their privileged position and 'to then be able to give them back to your younger black brothers and sisters wherever you go'. He called for students to move away from an individualistic perspective on viewing education as solely for their personal benefit, as something that would propel their careers and improve their lives but as a responsibility to share with those in the wider Black community.

CONTROLLING ACCESS TO THE WEST INDIAN STUDENTS' CENTRE

Given its unique status in Britain, the West Indian Students' Centre had a wider appeal than its intended users. It quickly drew the attention of the West Indian immigrant community who started to frequent it. The Board of Governors appointed a Sub-Committee in 1969 to consider the question of membership of the Students' Centre. It met on two occasions, without the nominated student representatives, and concluded that in future it would 'ensure its use was essentially for West Indian students and their friends, and not for other persons merely because they are of West Indian origin'.[20] It went further to enshrine this in the membership rule book.

There was consequently tension between management of the West Indian Students' Centre, and the West Indian Students' Union (WISU) with the latter forming a closer connection with the Black immigrant community in Britain. In fact, the Warden of the Centre blamed the Union for the emergent situation from 1968 when there was more use of the Centre by non-students. He investigated this situation on behalf of the Board of Governors and concluded that 'the influx of non-members really began in the early part of 1968 when the Friday evening programmes were organised by Mr Comrie and non-students were encouraged to attend.'[21] Locksley Comrie was a member of the Centre's House Committee. Hyman reported that the majority of non-members attended meetings only, and that half of those making general use of the Centre were non-students, the majority of whom were not signed in as guests of members and thus, Hyman said, 'they are clearly present in breach of the Rules.'

A letter from WISU Executive members Jack Hines, Ansel Wong and Gary Burton, in 1970, to the Board of Governors made a case for the establishment 'as a matter of the greatest practical urgency for Black people in London, the setting up at the Centre, of an independent telephone service to help Black victims of racist violence both from civilians and police.'[22] This request demonstrated WISU's concern for what was happening to West Indian immigrants in Britain; one that was not necessarily shared by all Board members. WISU argued that West Indian immigrants faced a fight for survival, as they were regularly the target of police brutality and from the white British population. WISU argued that this service was needed because 'we face threats of mass repatriation and deprivation of access to social relief; we face a host community that cannot be expected to provide protection in the present climate: at any rate, from our own experience, we cannot expect them to protect us.'[23] WISU summarised the position of Black people in Britain at this time as 'politically, economically, and socially vulnerable. It has no effective agencies of internal communication, no central institutions to which reference can be made in this time of general crisis or at times of acute crisis.'[24] Although this request was considered by the Board of Governors, and received some support, the service was not formally established.[25]

In due course, the President of WISU received a letter from the Board of Governors threatening removal of the Union's privileged access to the Centre citing an allegation that 'the West Indian

Students Union has declared and has put into effect a policy of admitting members who are not students, and that these members are making use of the Centre's facilities without membership'.[26] The President of WISU was reminded that the Union had been given a rent-free office and the right to co-opt a member onto the Board of Governors and warned that 'the Union should continue to be a student organisation, and that the privilege would be subject to review if there were any fundamental changes in the nature of the Union'. The Union's unequivocable support for West Indian immigrants extended to providing its services, and privileges to this section of the community. There is no available evidence to suggest that the Union complied with this request or on how the matter was resolved. It is unlikely that the Board of Governors had the power to expel the Union as acknowledged by Bryan King in a letter to Lionel Luckhoo, then High Commissioner: 'it must not be forgotten that its existence depends on its close working association with the West Indian Students Union, for which it was originally founded to provide a home. Co-operation with student representatives is essential.'[27] WISU's power therefore appeared superior to that of the Board of Governors which failed in its threat to oust the Union from the Centre.

COOPERATION AND CONSENSUS

In some quarters, there was growing resentment by the Black immigrants towards the West Indian Students' Centre. The Centre management feared that elements of the Black community were threatening to burn down the Centre: 'The immigrant community are the personal friends of the type of students who are at present willing to use the Centre … They resent the privileged treatment given to students and the subsidised meals given to them. They cannot be kept out because members are entitled to bring their friends in.'[28] Access to safe, culturally friendly and intellectually nurturing spaces such as the Centre was very limited in 1950s and 1960s Britain due to racialised access to social and leisure spaces such as pubs and clubs.

By the late 1960s and the early 1970s, some West Indian activists became more vocal in their support for broadening the use of the West Indian Students' Centre. Lord David Pitt, the Grenada-born doctor, Labour Party politician and campaigner against racial equality, wrote a letter to Bryan King recommending that broadening the use of the Centre for all West Indians would be ideal. Pitt recommended that 'the general view is that the Centre is very important for the culture and well-being of West Indians in London and should develop as such'. This view was supported by John La Rose, who was invited to become a co-opted member of the Board of Governors. John La Rose (1927–2006), was a Trinidadian poet, publisher and leading activist against racialised injustices in Britain. He had been in Britain since the early 1960s, and was a respected member of the West Indian intellectual community. He wrote to the Chair of the Board of Governors stating that 'I believe that the whole structure of the Centre ought to be reconsidered in the light of the new situation arising with the presence of West Indian citizens and their children in Britain, and the affinity which we feel for all black people because of the common predicament in this society.'[29] Through his activism for improved rights of Black parents, and for the education of Black children, he was acutely aware of the needs of the West Indian immigrants. Jessica Huntley (1927–2013), the Guyanese-born former political activist and reformer, and leading publisher of radical Black literature, was an influential presence in the West Indian Students' Centre from the early 1960s. She mentored the students, and promoted West Indianism and resistance against racialised injustices.[30] This was through her work with WISU's newsletter, giving and chairing talks, and supporting the cultural and political activities of the Centre.

During the 1960s and 1970s, the West Indian Students' Centre hosted a number of organisations that resulted in the bridging of the gap between the students and the Black immigrant community. These organisations and groups brought together various prominent West Indian intellectuals and radical politicians who had migrated to Britain for a combination of political and economic reasons. Many became involved in the Centre and became actively involved in the issues affecting student activism, and the West Indian immigrants. This provided students with greater opportunities to understand and become involved in the politics of domestic Black immigrants.

One of the most prominent of these organisations, the West Indian Standing Conference, was established in 1958 following the Notting Hill riots, and the growing assaults on the freedom and rights of Black people in Britain. It operated as a membership organisation for other affiliated organisations and for individual members. It met on a monthly basis, the first Sunday of every month, at the West Indian Students' Centre, however it was working towards establishing its own separate centre. It aimed to establish a Caribbean Youth League as part of the West Indian Standing Conference, and a Labour officer with special responsibilities for workers and employment in Britain. Its overarching aim was 'to co-operate with other immigrant organisations in Britain at local or national level where our common interests require this co-operation'.[31] It also aimed to 'strive for the social, political, economic and cultural unity of West Indians and their children in Britain by all available means'.[32] The Constitution described the purpose of the West Indian Standing Conference, 'we West Indians in Britain are determined to preserve in WISC that spirit of Caribbean unity and unification even going beyond the dissolved federation in spite of the present political evolution in the territories of the Caribbean'.[33]

Enoch Powell's 'River of Blood' speech in 1968 was seen as an incitement to violent assaults on Black people. This led to the strengthening of action taken to defend the Black communities in Britain, and Jeff Crawford, Secretary of the West Indian Standing Conference, provided advice:

> In my opinion, the point has now been reached where it is imperative that every black person in this country prepare himself for the inevitable offensive ... the black community must prepare for its counter-offensive by arming itself, not only spiritually, emotionally and mentally, but above all, physically. There is no law which absolutely forbids a man from defending his life, the life of his family or his property from attack.[34]

The West Indian Students' Centre's hosting of the Standing Conference provided demonstrable evidence of the student community's increasing sympathy and support for immigrants. Richard Small, an Executive member of the student union and then a law student recalled how he 'was particularly interested in the immigrant community, their organisational work and so on. So, I was a regular attender of the West Indian Standing Conference which had its monthly meeting in the Students' Centre, one Sunday each month they would meet.'[35] Therefore, Small provides one example of how students bridged the two communities as he 'was active in the immigrant community and was seeking to build links between the student community and the immigrant community'.[36] His involvement was not the approach adopted by all students, as Small recalled 'the snobbishness and social distance that existed between the students and the migrant community was something that literally had to be broken down. Among the students there was an exclusiveness about whether or not non-students should be allowed in the building and that kind of nonsense.'[37]

The West Indian Standing Conference published several far-reaching documents including the pamphlet *Nigger-Hunting in England?* by Joseph Hunte in 1966. Hunte, then chairman of the West Indian Standing Conference, conducted a survey to investigate complaints of brutality and targeting by police of Black immigrants in Lambeth. He wrote that 'complaints seem to suggest that policemen are, like other members of the host community, averse to members of the coloured population of this country'.[38] He argued that the focus of police activity was on the house parties held by Black people in the area, with frequent raids to break up the parties, confiscate food and alcohol and arrest guests with the aim of investigating alleged offences including the unlawful sale of alcohol. The expression 'nigger-hunting' was in common use by the police in London, Hunte's research suggested, to describe the objective of some police officers to specifically seek out Black people to arrest. Hunte suggested several remedies to this situation including improving the education and training of police officers. A senior police liaison officer role with special responsibility for liaison with Black people was established, alongside other measures such as the introduction of Black police officers, visits by British police to the West Indies to learn and understand the culture and background of Black immigrants, and educational films to be shown to police.

Another important report published by the West Indian Standing Conference was *The Unsquare Deal*, a campaign against London Transport's discriminatory treatment of Black workers. The campaign argued that 'London Transport Board with the full knowledge and tacit support of the trade unions concerned, particularly the Transport and General Workers Union refuses to promote black busmen to the post of bus inspector.'[39] The West Indian Standing Conference had requested statistics from London Transport but admitted that 'the failure to produce statistics and the failure to produce one black bus inspector in our view substantiates a case of discrimination practiced by the London Transport Board and the very attitudes of the Unions condone this practice.'[40] The West Indian Standing Conference also played a significant role in the campaigns for race equality laws in Britain. Its publication *Play the Black Man; Britain's Race Laws* addressed the deficiencies of the amendments of the Race Relations Act.[41]

The West Indian Student Union newsletter, *Bumbo*, increasingly had articles of importance to the immigrant community and was an effective way to inform students of the priorities of Black immigrants. An example is a notice from the South East London Parent's Association, which also described itself as the Black People's Association, 'formed for the purpose of assisting black people in all spheres, from the provision of nursery education to the welfare of the aged.'[42] The notice was an appeal for financial donations and for new members. The aims of the organisation were to provide assistance to Black people of all ages. Its programme included education for Black children, the establishment of 24-hour informal childcare, including during school holidays. It also called for legal advice for Black immigrants. Overall, it called for unity: 'We provide the opportunity for Black people to work together as a team in remedying their problems' and pledged that 'the only qualification for membership is being Black.'[43]

The Centre also moved towards providing educational services for Black children, young people and adults, becoming a Centre where the West Indian immigrant community could benefit from the education facilities available to the students. It established a 'School for Black Youth' which became the C.L.R. James School. The syllabus included academic subjects such as Maths, English,

French, Spanish and History. The non-academic offer included Black Music covering 'Slavery to Be-Bop', 'History of the Steel-band Music', and 'The development of Contemporary Jamaican music' taught by Ansel Wong and other students. The non-academic programme also included Black Literature taught by Ansel Wong, Andrew Salkey, C.L.R. James, George Lamming and other students. The syllabus included Black Art taught by Aubrey Williams and Errol Lloyd, 'An education for the Black Mind' by Augustine John (Gus John), and 'the importance of maths and science in the development of the Third World', by Ewart Thomas. The politics section of the programme was covered by C.L.R. James, Cris Le Maitre, Andrew Salkey and several students including Jack Hines. A session entitled 'Know Your Rights' was delivered by Rudy Narayan and Cris Le Maitre.[44]

The West Indian Students Centre, intended as a social club for students from the Caribbean to reduce loneliness and isolation grew to represent much more. Its programme of activities included internationally renowned Black leaders from the Caribbean region, and radical Black activists as speakers at the Centre. Its recognition as a safe Black space for socialising and being in the company of other West Indians in Britain was highly valued by others than students, at a time when Black people experienced a strong colour bar that reinforced their isolation. They called for more support for the Black immigrants in deprived areas, and less for students perceived as unfairly benefitting from the resources provided by West Indian leaders By the late 1960s this change was evident. The West Indian Students' Centre's hosting of groups, organisations and programmes included a focus on the rights and interests of the West Indian immigrant community. The Centre evolved into a hub not only for students from the Caribbean, but for all who needed it. Thus, the level of cooperation among sections of West Indians can be evaluated as enabling efficient resistance against racialised injustices.

NOTES

1. J.M. Lee, 'Commonwealth Students in the United Kingdom, 1940–1960: Student Welfare and World Status', *Minerva*, 44/1 (2006), pp. 1–24 (p. 1).

2. David Clover, 'Dispersed or Destroyed: Archives, the West Indian Students' Union, and Public Memory', *The Society for Caribbean Studies Annual Conference Papers*, 6 (2005), p. 2.
3. Lloyd Braithwaite, *Colonial West Indian Students in Britain* (Barbados: The University of the West Indies Press), pp. 6–21.
4. Ibid., p. 4.
5. Lee, 'Commonwealth Students in the United Kingdom', p. 1.
6. Ibid., p. 11.
7. Braithwaite, *Colonial West Indian Students in Britain*, p. 113.
8. Ibid., p. 134.
9. Ibid., p. 134.
10. 'Princess Margaret Opens Centre for West Indian Students; a Need for Knowledge in the Commonwealth'. *The West London Observer*, 3 June 1955, p. 6.
11. Ibid.
12. Bob Carter, Clive Harris and Shirley Joshi, 'The 1951–1955 Conservative Government and the Racialisation of Black Immigration', *Centre for Research in Ethnic Relations*, Policy Papers in Ethnic Relations No. 11 (Warwick: Centre for Research in Ethnic Relations; University of Warwick, 1987), p. 13.
13. Wole Soyinka, 'Telephone Conversation', in *Modern Poetry from Africa* (Harmondsworth: Penguin Books, 1963), pp. 144–5.
14. Kennetta Hammond Perry, *London Is the Place for Me: Black Britons, Citizenship, and the Politics of Race* (New York: Oxford University Press, 2015), pp. 71–8.
15. M.D.A. Freeman and Sarah Spencer, 'Immigration Control, Black Workers and the Economy', *British Journal of Law and Society*, 6/1 (1973), p. 53.
16. Ibid.
17. B.E. King, 'West Indian Student Centre. Fourteenth Annual Report by the Board of Governors, 1969, George Padmore Institute (GPI), GB 2904 WIS/1.
18. V.L. Page, 'West Indian Students Centre. Fifteenth Annual Report by the Board of Governors, 1970, George Padmore Institute (GPI), GB 2904 WIS/3.
19. Transcript of a talk given by Stokely Carmichael at the West Indian Students Centre, *NEXUS The West Indian Students Union Newsletter*, Vol. 2, March 1968, Black Cultural Archives (BCA), Papers of Ansel Wong, WONG/1/5, pp. 5–7.
20. 'Minutes of Meetings of the Sub-Committee Appointed by the Board to Review Qualifications for Membership and the Use of the Centre, Held on Tuesday 15 April and Tuesday 6 May 1969', 1969, George Padmore Institute (GPI), GB 2904 WIS/11.

21. W.K. Hynam, 'Note on the Use of the Centre by Non-Members', 1969, George Padmore Institute (GPI) GB 2904 WIS/1.
22. Jack Hines, Ansel Wong and Gary Burton, 'Letter from Members of the Executive of West Indian Students Union to the Board of Governors, George Padmore Institute (GPI), GB 2904 WIS/4.
23. Ibid.
24. Ibid.
25. Ansel Wong, personal communication (email), 9 December 2021.
26. 'Letter from the Board of Governors of the West Indian Students Centre to the President of the West Indian Students Union', 1969, George Padmore Institute (GPI), GB 2904 WIS/4.
27. Bryan King, 'Letter to Lionel Luckhoo from the Chair of the Board of Governors, West Indian Students Centre', 1969, George Padmore Institute (GPI), GB 2904 WIS/4.
28. Ibid.
29. John La Rose, 'Letter from John La Rose to Bryan King, Chairman of the Board of Governors of the West Indian Students Centre', 1969, George Padmore Institute (GPI), GB 2904 WIS/4.
30. Ansel Wong interviewed by Claudia Tomlinson, 17 June 2020.
31. 'West Indian Standing Conference, Draft of Revised Constitution', Undated, c. 1970, George Padmore Institute (GPI), GB 2904 WIS/3: Statements, Reports and Constitution 1967–1970.
32. Ibid.
33. Ibid.
34. Jeff Crawford, 'Text of Statement Issued by Mr Jeff Crawford at Bramshill House Police College', December 1968 (London: West Indian Standing Conference, 1968), WISC/PRO/1, George Padmore Institute.
35. Richard Small, interview with Claudia Tomlinson, University of Chichester PhD research, 1 August 2020.
36. Ibid.
37. Ibid.
38. Joseph A. Hunte, *Nigger Hunting in England?* (London: West Indian Standing Conference, 1966), p. 1.
39. Ibid.
40. Ibid.
41. *Play the Black Man: Britain's Race Laws* (London: The West Indian Standing Conference, 1970).
42. *Bumbo, Newsletter of the West Indian Students' Union*, September 1969, p. 15, Black Cultural Archives, WONG/1/1.
43. Ibid.
44. 'West Indian Students Centre School for Black Youths Provisional Syllabus', 1969, George Padmore Institute (GPI), GB 2904/WIS.

9

'The Black Power Desk': The Response of the State to the British Black Power Movement

Perry Blankson

Stood atop a small stepladder and dressed smartly in a blazer, tie and cream-coloured trousers, a confident and charismatic orator addressed a small crowd at Speakers' Corner in London's Hyde Park:

> There are many white people who are terribly worried about what black power means, but for those of you who have not the slightest idea let me tell you what it means. It means the destruction of the white man's society ...[1]

His style of oration was didactic yet humorous, and he took great pleasure in verbally sparring with onlooking hecklers who took offence to his particularly 'controversial' statements. However, hecklers were not the only spectators taking note of his more inflammatory declarations. Embedded amongst the spectators were two Metropolitan Police Special Branch officers, diligently recording his declarations.

The speaker in question was Roy Sawh of the Universal Coloured People's Association (UCPA) and the content of his speeches would be used in court to prosecute him under section 6(1) of the 1965 Race Relations Act: 'incitement to racial hatred'. The Special Branch officers present were Detective Sergeant Francke and Detective Sergeant G. Battye, who were able to mingle amongst the diverse Hyde Park crowd. The record indicates that Sawh and his contacts were very much aware that their activism had attracted the attention of the Metropolitan Police:

> Some of you who have seen what has happened to Michael 'X' when he was arrested, by now must know many speakers, including myself, are apt to be very soon getting a visit from the police telling us that we have contravened section 1(b) of the Race Relations Act, an act that was made by white people without asking black people.[2]

Utilising open files available at the National Archives, as well as those released by Freedom of Information requests (courtesy of Eveline Lubbers, Rosie Wild, Robin Bunce and Paul Field), I will explore the multifaceted reaction of the British state to the fledgling domestic Black Power movement.

BLACK POWER IN BRITAIN

While there has been debate as to the origins of Black Power in Britain, some scholars argue that the genesis of the British Black Power movement can be found at the Dialectics of Liberation conference in July 1967 and the arrival in Britain of prominent Black Power advocate Stokely Carmichael (later Kwame Ture). A Trinidadian by birth, Carmichael was largely responsible for popularising the term 'Black Power' upon his release from prison in 1966, and his radical, uncompromising stance and oratory had raised serious concerns for the British state about the threat he posed to the status quo.[3]

Carmichael's presence in Britain prompted an immediate response. Following his influential speech at the Dialectics of Liberation conference, he was visited by Special Branch officers and soon after left the country.[4] While there are no public files revealing the extent of Special Branch surveillance during his visit to Britain, the arrival of officers at his secret address would lead one to infer that Carmichael had been under surveillance since his arrival. The visit from Special Branch officers was enough to persuade Carmichael to break off his further planned engagements, and upon his departure he was prohibited from re-entering Britain, by order of

Home Secretary Roy Jenkins.[5] From these measures alone we can see that the British state took the threat of Black Power incredibly seriously.

Despite Carmichael's removal from Britain his has been seen by some as having an immediate radicalising effect in Britain:

> Within a week of Carmichael's Roundhouse speech the United Coloured People's Association (UCPA) had expelled its white members and adopted the ideology of Black Power; and, within a month, Michael X, who quickly became the media face of Black Power in Britain, was arrested for inciting racial hatred. Finally, by the middle of 1969 the British Black Panthers was created. In short, Carmichael's visit led to the formation of an indigenous Black Power movement.[6]

While Carmichael's visit did contribute to the galvinisation of the Black Power movement in Britain, it is not entirely accurate to say that it led to its formation. The first organisation in Britain that could be said to represent Black Power was the Racial Awareness Action Society (RAAS), formed by Michael de Freitas (aka Michael X) and Roy Sawh in 1965.[7] Carmichael himself was conscious of existing 'Black Power formations' that had 'begun to emerge' in Britain, indicating that his trip had the purpose of building connections with a Black Power movement already in existence.[8]

Though Carmichael's visit gave impetus to Black Power in Britain, the movement itself, and many of its key figures, developed from the earlier Pan-African and anticolonial movements of the 1940s and 1950s. Through understanding the continuity of personnel from Pan-African to Black Power organising, we can also examine the continuity of surveillance by the British state. Obi Egbuna was one such individual that found his origins in the Pan-African movement.[9] Egbuna was a prominent member of the Committee of African Organizations (CAO), which itself grew out of the West African Students Union (WASU) established in 1925.[10] The CAO, an outwardly Pan-African organisation, can be viewed as a bridge between the 'pre-history' of Pan-Africanism and the rise of Black Power in Britain. This is perfectly encapsulated through their role in organising the visit of Malcolm X to

Britain in 1965 where a young Michael de Freitas, heavily influenced by the visit, would soon become Michael X and establish the aforementioned RAAS.[11]

Surveillance of prominent Pan-African organisers in Britain by the state was extensive. High-profile Pan-Africanists such as future Ghanaian president Kwame Nkrumah and Trinidadian anticolonial organiser George Padmore found themselves under heavy surveillance from MI5, the Colonial Office and Special Branch – with the state continuing into the late 1960s and 1970s to carry out surveillance on the Black Power movement in Britain.[12]

THE MANGROVE NINE

The British Black Power movement gained significant national attention during the trial of nine Black British activists who became known as the Mangrove Nine – named after the restaurant in Notting Hill which was subject to repeated police harassment. Established by Trinidadian-born Frank Critchlow, the Mangrove restaurant would become a hub of Black radicalism in Britain, and as such was raided by police six times between January 1969 and July 1970, on the pretence of searching for illegal drugs.[13] Despite the firm anti-drug stance of Critchlow and no illegal substances being found during any of the raids, local Constable Frank Pulley maintained that the restaurant was a 'den of iniquity' which harboured 'pimps, prostitutes and criminals'.[14]

Frequent harassment by the police (often under similar pretences of possession of illicit substances) to disrupt and demoralise activists was an example of one of the responses of the British state to radical Black Power organisations. As well as this, a racialised notion of inherent criminality in the Black British community was often deployed in the press (such as in the example of Constable Pulley) to discredit British Black Power movements in the eyes of the wider public. In the example of the Mangrove, these tactics would backfire significantly. The ensuing trial took on a national profile, boosting the profile of the British Black Power movement while also vindicating their actions – the trial would see the first acknowledgement by the courts of racial hatred informing the actions of the Metropolitan Police.[15]

THE INFORMATION RESEARCH DEPARTMENT

One of the most important Foreign and Commonwealth Office (FCO) files available in the archives is dated 1970, and consists of an assessment of the state of Black Power in Britain. It is worth noting that the report is an updated version of a Joint Intelligence Committee (JIC) report on Black Power published in 1968.[16] The involvement of the JIC – the body responsible for coordination between Britain's intelligence services – is indicative of how seriously the British state took the threat of Black Power. This file is also our first introduction to the Information Research Department (IRD), the clandestine Cold War propaganda arm of the British state, established with the task of countering Communism and anticolonial agitation, collecting subversive materials for study and disseminating anti-Communist propaganda.[17]

The key information from this report includes a list of early British Black Power organisations, as well as prominent individuals active within them. Among these individuals are not just Obi Egbuna and Roy Sawh but Jagmohan Joshi. Joshsi was the Maoist secretary of the Indian Workers Association (IWA), which agitated on behalf of Commonwealth arrivals from India. The IRD report quotes Joshi's aims as:

> ... uniting the black peoples of Great Britain, helping to fight against British imperialism here and abroad. Our work is not intended to exclude the white working class, the most advanced sections of which, for example, the new Communist Party of Great Britain, Marxist Leninist (CPGB-ML) (*sic*), are with us.

Joshi and the IWA provide us with a clear example of how 'political Blackness' encapsulated South Asians as 'Black' in the struggle against racism in Britain during the early stages of the Black Power movement. Moreover, his Maoist ideology (highlighted within the IRD report) and association with the CPGB-ML was a major cause for concern for the anti-Communist IRD. In the list of Black Power affiliated organisations being monitored by the IRD is the Black People's Alliance (BPA), a coalition of 'immigrant' organisations established in 1968, with Joshi as one of its founding members.

The IRD was keenly aware that ideological differences were rife in the BPA, noting that 'soon after it was founded, moderate groups on its periphery began to drop away'.[18]

The IRD report also contains a section on 'Foreign Influence on Black Power in Britain', attributing the rise in prominence of British Black Power to individuals such as Malcolm X, who was identified as being responsible for the rise to prominence of Michael de Freitas. Also noted by the IRD as a 'foreign influence' on British Black power is founding member of the American Black Panther Party (BPP), Bobby Seale. Seale was monitored during his visit to Britain in 1969, and the IRD concluded that 'his presence had little immediate effect, but encouraged the small Black Panther Movement which had already been set up in London'.[19] The IRD would be much more heavily involved in the response of the British state to the Black Power movement in the Caribbean but their involvement in a domestic context provides us with valuable conclusions. Firstly, the state deemed British Black Power enough of a threat to warrant IRD involvement, and further, what motivated the state's reaction was not just fear of 'racialism' but fear of Communist subversion. The ever-looming 'Red Menace' and Cold War context of the period cannot be understated when examining the response of the state to domestic Black Power organising, as fear surrounding the influence of the Soviet Union persisted across domestic and international environments. 'Trotskyists and Maoists' are also included in the list of 'foreign influences' on Black Power, among them Paul Boutelle, 'an American Trotskyist and a member of the Socialist Workers' Party which has tried to ally itself to the American Black Power Movement'.[20] The link between Boutelle and British Black Power is not explicit, with the IRD observing that during his visit to Hyde Park (a known hotspot for Black Power activists) in June 1968, 'he urged that black people everywhere should arm themselves'.[21]

The IRD summarised that 'American influences have largely worked on West Indians in Britain, while Maoists (and Trotskyists) have largely worked on Asians'.[22] This summary omits the mention of Africans, which is puzzling as the Nigerian Obi Egbuna was one of the leading Black Power activists. Furthermore, the African connection to British Black Power is ignored entirely, and there is no mention of the links between Pan-Africanism and Black Power. Interestingly, included in the report is the Campaign Against Racial Discrimination (CARD), which was not explicitly in support of Black Power, but their mere proximity was enough for the state to deem them as a potential threat. CARD was assessed by the IRD as 'predominantly middle class and essentially moderate in tone', however, its London branches are identified as potentially being 'dominated by the pro-Chinese London Workers' Association'.[23] No evidence is provided to support this claim, and no verifiable source material on the London Workers' Association was available in the National Archives or in the archives of the *Daily Telegraph*, which is referenced by the IRD here. The inclusion of the CARD amongst Black Power organisations demonstrates that the reaction of the British state to the growing domestic Black Power movement was one of significant over-reaction, in that organisations with only tangential links to Black Power were deemed worthy of surveillance.

The summary of the state of Black Power in Britain in 1970 concluded that 'the various groups and leaders show little capacity for co-operation, but occasionally outside influences temporarily unite the coloured communities'.[24] However, prominent Black Power organisations such as the Black Unity and Freedom Party (BUFP) and the Black Liberation Front (BLF) (established in 1970 and 1971, respectively) are not included in the report. Notwithstanding these limitations, this IRD report is a valuable source of information, with its final conclusion being particularly illuminating:

> Black Power, however sporadic its manifestations, or few its followers, must be regarded as a threat to the comparative harmony which has, with a few exceptions, long characterised race relations in Britain.[25]

A cursory look at some examples in the history of 'race relations' in Britain shows this justification to be false. Rather than 'harmony', as the IRD claim, the late 1950s through to the 1960s were characterised by the kind of fraught 'race relations' that made Britain a fertile breeding ground for Black Power. Fresh in living memory were the 1958 Notting Hill 'race riots' where the Black population of Notting Hill were subject to racialised terror from organised white mobs. The ferocity of this organised white terror would again be placed in the national spotlight during the General Election of 1964. Instead of London, however, the spotlight was placed on the Midlands, where the Conservative Party ran open segregationist Peter Griffiths on the slogan 'if you want a n***** for a neighbour, vote Labour'. So vicious was the racism experienced by the African, Caribbean and South Asian residents of Smethwick that it prompted the revolutionary Malcolm X to visit in solidarity.[26] In fact, Malcolm X was invited to Smethwick by the then-general secretary of the IWA, Avtar Singh Jouhl. It was during this visit that Malcolm X also visited London at the behest of the CAO in February 1965. Three years later, Conservative MP Enoch Powell made his infamous 'Rivers of Blood' speech, predicting that 'in 15 or 20 years' time the black man will have the whip hand over the white man' if immigration was not curtailed.[27] Reference to 'comparative harmony' by the IRD is made all the more contradictory as their report on Black Power in Britain recognises that the Black People's Alliance arose 'as a result of the unease felt in the various coloured communities following Mr Enoch Powell's controversial speeches on the racial situation in Britain'.[28]

In the false reality established by the IRD, it was not the racial terror of white civilian mobs, the frequent harassment by the police or discrimination in housing, employment, immigration, education and daily life that was responsible for racial disharmony in Britain, but the Black Power organisations that arose to fight these issues. With this justification established, action had to be taken to target Black Power membership and disrupt its organisations.

THE BLACK POWER DESK

The reaction of the British state to Black Power manifested in many different forms. Among these was the establishment of a Black Power Desk dedicated to the surveillance of prominent organisations and individuals associated with Black Power. According to Bunce,

> The Black Power Desk was established in 1967 by order of Roy Jenkins, then Home Secretary. Based in New Scotland Yard, it was staffed by as many as six officers. It was one of a number of such desks, alongside others keeping tabs on the IRA, Trotskyites or Marxists.[29]

Bunce also revealed that the desk played a key role in securing the conviction of Obi Egbuna in December 1968 for 'incitement to murder police officers'.[30] It can be observed that resources allocated to the desk followed the fluctuating profile of the Black Power movement, as it expanded vastly in the build-up to the trial of the Mangrove Nine in 1970.

There has been debate as to whether or not the Black Power Desk was an MI5 or Special Branch unit, with the key evidence for the former being found in a memo sent to a Home Office civil servant by the name of D.H.J. Hilary. The sender, whose name is redacted, briefly noted that 'you may like to note that I have taken over the Black Power desk from [redacted]'.[31] While the pertinent information is redacted, Lubbers notes that this brief letter was included in the file index as 'Correspondence with Box 500'. The Post Office Box for MI5, the security service is also colloquially referred to as Box 500, or 'The Box' in government circles, indicating that around the time of 31 December 1971 (the date on the file), the Black Power Desk was possibly under the direction of an MI5 official. On balance, it appears that the Black Power Desk was a cooperative effort, with Special Branch gathering intelligence 'with an eye to public order and policing, while MI5 would concentrate on subversion and international aspects; in practice the work would overlap'.[32]

Evidence available in the National Archives indicates that the state was fully aware of the socio-economic conditions that allowed Black Power to take root, and a crackdown on its leaders alone would not be enough to stamp it out. One section of a report into Black Power noted:

> One of the most serious problems of race relations in Britain is the possibility that coloured school-leavers may not be able to get the jobs to fit their aspirations and qualifications. If this

> happens they may turn to more aggressive methods of securing their rights and thus become vulnerable to the views of agitators and extremists.[33]

Reference to 'agitators and extremists' was synonymous with Black Power. So, what measures did the state take to improve these conditions? The 1965 Race Relations Act (viewed by the state as a key weapon in the fight against 'racialism') was overseen by a Race Relations Board, which had its size increased in 1968. While the practical outcome saw a disproportionate prosecution of Black agitators (relative to their percentage of the population), in the eyes of the state, targeting these subversive elements was a prerequisite to preventing civil unrest. Additionally, the report notes that the National Committee for Commonwealth Immigrants was made into a statutory body and renamed the Community Relations Commission, with the responsibility for advising the government 'on matters involving race relations'.[34] Importantly, the 1968 Urban Programme, which granted national and local funds to community groups, has been highlighted by Wild as particularly significant. While Black Power in Britain may be popularly associated with climactic demonstrations and rousing speeches, much of the emphasis within Black Power organisations was on community activism, self-help and social welfare programmes. With full knowledge of this, the British government utilised the Urban Programme at a local level to target Black Power-led community organisation.

The state made a gesture at addressing inequalities within the education system, noting that 'official policy is to provide extra teachers and equipment in areas where the teaching of English to immigrant pupils is a problem'.[35] These measures relating to education are incredibly vague, and any effectiveness of these provisions did little to combat the institutionalised racism within the British education system. For example, in 1971, according to a Parliamentary Select Committee, over 5,000 'immigrant' children were placed into 'special schools' for the 'educationally subnormal', with Caribbean children comprising 70 per cent of these children.[36] Where the state intervention did succeed was in fracturing the movement, as the 1968 Urban Programme soon saw

Black Power activists being unable to compete with the funding offered to community projects by the government, splitting the movement between those who opted for or rejected government funding. While the true ramifications would not be visible until later in the 1970s, providing some Black Power grassroots organisers with 'urban aid' and driving a wedge in the movement was a 'soft' response of the state that saw some success. As former BLF leader Tony Soares explained in an interview with Wild:

> The government started a lot of programmes that were intended to buy out the [Black Power] leadership. By the early 1970s it became all grants and Urban Aid [*sic*] … A lot of money was going in, employing people, channelling them into community work and taking them away from political work. They all got caught up in some kind of project or the other because there was money on a scale they'd never seen before.[37]

Legislation and the criminal justice system were core to the response of the British state to Black Power agitation, but it was not always successful. The 1965 Race Relations Act, which introduced the crime of incitement to racial hatred to British statute books, was used to criminalise and target provocative Black Power speakers. According to Wild, while the Act was purportedly drawn up with the intention of combatting racial discrimination against minorities, 'nearly 50 per cent of the defendants in incitement to racial hatred trials were black' – it was even suggested that Carmichael be prosecuted for incitement, however, this idea was dropped when he was banned from re-entering the country.[38] The downside was that the state ran the risk of having high-profile cases boost the profile of Black Power in Britain. While the trial of Michael X was significant, a better example would be the trial of the Mangrove Nine, which received national attention. So, while the criminal justice system was key to harassing, disrupting and targeting the leaders of Black Power, if specific cases were allowed to receive national attention, it could backfire spectacularly for the state.

Crucially, the state was not inflexible in the methods it used to crack down on domestic Black Power. The surge in the popularity of figures such as Michael X and Roy Sawh following their arrests for incitement of racial hatred caused a brief reconsideration of policy regarding the arrest of prominent Black Power leaders, as explained by Wild:

> [After the release of Michael X] Black Power activists usually spent months on remand awaiting trial for offences that, upon conviction, rarely resulted in custodial sentences. The most effective punishment in terms of social control was the suspended custodial sentence, which meant that the convicted person was left with the threat of prison ... should they be arrested again.[39]

As previously mentioned, the Black Power Desk was able to facilitate the conviction of British Black Panther leader Obi Egbuna in July 1968. Crucially, Egbuna was given a suspended three-year sentence, the terms of which prohibited him from partaking in any subversive political activity.[40] This suspended sentence had the desired effect of silencing Egbuna without necessarily providing him the martyrdom of imprisonment, such as after he was arrested and jailed in 1965. His successor, the Trinidadian Altheia Jones-LeCointe, would later be a part of the Mangrove Nine. The flexibility of the state did not mean they were averse to using the full force of the law to attack the Black Power movement. Formerly known to police, Black Liberation Front leader Tony Soares was tried in 1973 for a litany of serious charges including 'incitement to murder, arson, bomb making and possessing firearms'.[41] This was after the BLF's *Grassroots* newspaper reprinted instructions from the US *Black Panther* newspaper on how to make a Molotov cocktail.

The harassment, intimidation and prosecution by the state did not end there. On the evening of 16 March 1972, following a meeting discussing Soares' defence fund, Winston Trew, Sterling Christie, George Griffiths and Constantine 'Omar' Boucher were attacked and arrested by undercover transport police. All four men arrested were members of the Fasimbas, originally the 500-strong youth wing of the South East London Parents Organisation (SELPO), but later subsumed by the BLF in late 1972. Such a 'coincidence' led those involved, namely, Trew, to suspect Special Branch surveillance, although unsurprisingly no evidence exists in the National Archives to verify their suspicions.[42] The four defendants would become known as the Oval Four, and it would not be until December 2019 (and later March 2020) that their convictions were overturned, due in large part to the corruption of the leading arresting officer, Detective Sergeant Derek Ridgewell.[43] In a similar vein, 'sus laws' – provisions which allowed the police to stop and search individuals deemed suspicious – were liberally used by the Metropolitan Police throughout the 1970s to target Black Power activists and the Black community at large.

In terms of physical monitoring of 'subversive groups', an interesting observation can be made when the surveillance of Black Power groups is compared to their contemporaries. According to the Undercover Policing Inquiry, between 1967 and 1972 there were approximately 18 undercover officers embedded within 'subversive' organisations ranging from the Vietnam Solidarity Campaign to the Socialist Workers' Party, but only a single officer – designated HN 345 or 'Peter Fredericks' – had infiltrated an organisation associated with Black Power on behalf of the Special Demonstration Squad (SDS).[44] The organisation infiltrated by Fredericks was not revealed by the inquiry, his deployment instead being listed under the umbrella term 'Black Power movement'.[45] This evidence begs the question: why was Black Power, having been assessed as a threat by the IRD, not infiltrated by the SDS on a level similar to its contemporary 'subversive' organisations? One explanation could be the relatively small size and community-based orientation of Black Power groups, making outsiders more easily visible. As well as this, organisations such as LeCointe's Black Panther Movement were highly secretive and carefully screened new recruits. A likely explanation, and one offered by Eveline Lubbers and Rosie Wild, is the institutional racism of the Metropolitan Police. They explain:

> Blending into a multi-racial crowd of onlookers or demonstrators was one way of gathering information, infiltrating Black Power groups, however, proved almost impossible. This was because the Metropolitan Police, having spent years actively preventing black people from joining the force, found itself with no black officers available to go undercover in the Black Power movement.[46]

Here Lubbers and Wild make reference to a Metropolitan Police report carried out from 1958 to 1968, which notes that 'we [the Metropolitan Police] are not yet prepared to recruit coloured men, although the time may not be so far distant when we shall be unable to turn down well-qualified men who have been born and educated in this country'.[47]

In the place of undercover officers, then, were informants. Use of informants was a crucial part of the response of the state to Black Power, and the lifeblood of Special Branch intelligence gathering. Documents digitised by the *Special Branch Files Project* make frequent reference to 'reliable information' (implied to have been gathered from informants) and Black Power activists themselves were near certain that informants were responsible for feeding information to the authorities. Lubbers and Wild point to notes concerning the Mangrove Nine trial, which makes reference to 'information from secret and delicate sources', further indicating use of informants.[48]

In light of the evidence available, we can conclusively argue that the British state viewed domestic Black Power as a significant threat. The measures they took against Black Power were varied, and flexible. 'Hard' measures saw prominent Black Power organisers such as Roy Sawh and his UCPA harassed by Special Branch and the Metropolitan Police, raided in their homes, or meeting places, and prosecuted under the 1965 Race Relations Act. Agents of the state were also not averse to openly attacking Black Power activists in the street, such as in the case of the Oval Four. It must be understood that in some cases, such as that of Michael X and the Mangrove Nine, prosecution by the state could have the undesired effect of boosting the profile of Black Power. However, it is also important to understand that the state was limited by its own practice of pervasive institutional racism, preventing the Metropolitan Police from embedding undercover officers into Black Power organisations and increasing their reliance on informants.

Despite this limitation, intelligence continued to be collected on individuals and organisations associated with Black Power and was facilitated through the establishment of a Black Power Desk by the Home Secretary, which was potentially a joint Special Branch-MI5 operation. In terms of the 'softer' tools the state used to challenge domestic Black Power, the response centred around surveillance via Special Branch, the Black Power Desk and through use of informants. In addition to the collection of 'subversive' materials, the state was able to use grants to drive a wedge between Black Power activists internally, as well as attempting to cut them off from the communities in which they organised. The state response to Black Power was nothing new, but rather a continuation of state policy towards 'subversive' anticolonial movements, such as the Pan-African movement. Understanding this, we can see that the state took careful note of the birth of Black Power in Britain, and ensured a concerted effort towards facilitating its downfall.

NOTES

1. 'Transcript of shorthand notes taken by Det. Sgt. Battye, Special Branch, part of a speech made by Roy Sawh at a meeting held under the auspices of the Universal Coloured People's Association at Speakers' Corner, Hyde Park, W.1, 13 August, 1967' (Digitised files courtesy of Rosie Wild and Eveline Lubbers, *Special Branch Files.*
2. Ibid.
3. Stokely Carmichael, *Ready for Revolution: The Life and Struggles of Stokely Carmichael (Kwame Ture)* (New York: Scribner, 2005).
4. Robin Bunce and Paul Field, Obi B. 'Egbuna, C. L. R. James and the Birth of Black Power in Britain: Black Radicalism in Britain 1967–72', *Twentieth Century British History*, 22/3 (2011), pp. 391–414.
5. Ibid., p. 392.
6. Ibid.
7. Hakim Adi, *Pan Africanism: A History* (London: Bloomsbury Academic, 2018), p. 179.
8. Carmichael, *Ready for Revolution*, p. 572.
9. Obi B. Egbuna, *Destroy This Temple: The Voice of Black Power in Britain* (London: Marrow, 1971), p. 17.
10. Adi, *Pan-Africanism*, p. 178.
11. Ibid.
12. See Marika Sherwood, *Kwame Nkrumah and the Dawn of the Cold War: The West African National Secretariat, 1945–48* (London: Pluto Press, 2019).
13. Diane Taylor, '"It Was Like a Family": Remembering the Mangrove, Notting Hill's Caribbean Haven', *The Observer*, 15 September 2018.
14. Rob Waters, *Thinking Black: Britain, 1964–1985* (Oakland, CA: University of California Press, 2019), p. 99.
15. Robin Bunce and Paul Field, 'Mangrove Nine: The Court Challenge against Police Racism in Notting Hill', *Guardian*, 29 November 2010.

16. TNA, CAB 158/68, Joint Intelligence Committee: Black Power, 28 February 1968.
17. Hugh Wilford, 'The Information Research Department: Britain's Secret Cold War Weapon Revealed', *Review of International Studies*, 24/3 (1998), pp. 353–69.
18. TNA, FCO 95/792, Briefing Paper: Black Power, 'The Black Power Movement in Britain', 1 January–31 December 1970, p. 5.
19. TNA, FCO 95/792, 'Black Power in Britain: Foreign Influences on Black Power', p. 3.
20. Ibid.
21. Ibid.
22. Ibid.
23. Ibid.
24. Ibid.
25. TNA, FCO 95/792, 'Black Power in Britain: Conclusions'.
26. Perry Blankson, 'When Malcolm X Came to the West Midlands', *Tribune*, 10 March 2022, https://tribunemag.co.uk/2022/03/malcolm-x-smethwick-peter-griffiths-racism-1965 (accessed 6 May 2022).
27. Enoch Powell, *Freedom and Reality* (Kingswood: Elliot Right Way Books, 1969), p. 282.
28. TNA, FCO 95/792, 'The Black Power Movement in Britain', p. 5.
29. *BBC History Extra*, '"Guerrilla" and the Real History of British Black Power', 13 April 2017.
30. Ibid.
31. TNA, HO 325/143, 'Relationships between the Police and Immigrants: Black Power Movement; Demonstration and March in Notting Hill, London', August 1970.
32. Eveline Lubbers, 'Black Power–4. The Black Power Desk', *The Special Branch Files*, 17 September 2019, http://specialbranchfiles.uk/black-power-4-black-power-desk/ (accessed 6 May 2022).
33. TNA, FCO 95/792, 'The Black Power Movement in Britain', p. 2.
34. Ibid., p. 1.
35. Rosie Wild, *'Black Was the Colour of Our Fight': Black Power in Britain, 1955–1976* (PhD thesis, University of Sheffield, 2008), p. 164.
36. Nah E. Dove, 'The Emergence of Black Supplementary Schools: Resistance to Racism in the United Kingdom', *Urban Education*, 27/4 (1993), pp. 430–47.
37. Rosie Wild Interview with Tony Soares, 2004, cited in Wild, *'Black Was the Colour of Our Fight'*, p. 173.
38. Ibid., p. 176.
39. Ibid., p. 163.
40. TNA, MEPO/11409, 'Benedict Obi Egbuna, Peter Martin and Gideon Ketueni T. Dolo Charged with Uttering and Writing Threats to Kill Police Officers at Hyde Park, W2', 1968.

41. Rosie Wild, 'Black Power – 1. Overview', *Special Branch Files Project*, 17 September 2019, http://specialbranchfiles.uk/2174-2/ (accessed 6 May 2022).
42. Rosie Wild and Eveline Lubbers, 'Black Power – 2. Main Groups', *Special Branch Files Project*, 17 September 2019; ibid.
43. Lizzie Dearden, 'Oval Four: Black Man Framed by Corrupt Police Officer at London Tube Station Cleared 48 Years Later', *Independent*, 24 March 2020.
44. 'HN 345', 'Undercover Policing Inquiry', www.ucpi.org.uk/individuals/hn-345/ (accessed 6 May 2022).
45. Ibid.
46. Rosie Wild and Eveline Lubbers, 'Black Power – 3. Special Branch Files in Context', *The Special Branch Files*, 17 September 2019, http://specialbranchfiles.uk/2174-2/ (accessed 6 May 2022).
47. TNA, MEPO 2/9859, 'Police Liaison with the West Indian Community in London. Account of the Metropolitan Police's Attempts to Improve Relations with the West Indian Community through Liaison with the West Indian Standing Conference. Examples of Accusations against the Police and Notes on Meetings between Police and Community Representatives'.
48. HO 325/143, 'Letter to from [redacted] to Mr Hilary', 31 December 1971.

10

Black Power in Britain and the Caribbean: Establishing Connections, 1968–73

Elanor Kramer-Taylor

On 9 August 1970, at about 4:45 pm, Margaret O'Connell of 172 Portnall Road, West London, looked out of her window and saw 'a large crowd of coloured people shouting and gesticulating'. According to O'Connell, these people were carrying signs which read, 'Hands off Black People' and 'People's Power'.[1] But in addition to the signs, she may have also seen men and women wearing black berets and with their fists raised. How this protest on 9 August 1970 ended has, in recent years, become increasingly acknowledged in the British public sphere. The Mangrove Nine Trial, held at the Old Bailey the following year, captured national and international attention and has come to represent the long-standing battle between non-white communities in Britain and the police.[2] This moment, moreover, which is often understood to be the 'high watermark' of the British Black Power movement has also come to symbolise a larger shift in the political rhetoric and ideology of many of Britain's ethnic minority communities in the late 1960s.[3] The notion of 'Black Power', which travelled across the Atlantic from the US, stimulated radical movements amongst migrant and non-white communities in Britain. Visits to Britain by figures such as Malcolm X and Stokely Carmichael in the mid-1960s have particularly been identified as notable turning points.[4] Their message of Black liberation resonated with Britain's Black and Asian populations as a variety of citizenship laws, coupled with economic exclusion and state oppression, stimulated socio-economic discontent and led to a proliferation of groups advocating for 'Black Power' between 1965 and the early 1970s.[5]

There is little doubt that Black radical movements in the US influenced the rise of Black Power groups in Britain; a fact that has been well documented by a number of historians, such as Ann-Marie Angelo, Rob Waters and Rosalind Wild.[6] But we should, as Waters has emphasised, be wary of centring the US as the primary international influence on the entire British Black Power movement. The Black radicalism that emerged in Britain was formed in relation to a myriad of global influences. In particular, with many British Black radicals hailing from formerly colonised countries, the continuation of global decolonisation struggles should be foregrounded when considering the motives and concerns of this movement. As Wild has demonstrated, liberation movements in Angola and Mozambique and fights against apartheid in South Africa were headline news for Black Power groups in Britain.[7] Moreover, the Anglophone Caribbean, itself in the midst of what Richard Drayton has labelled a 'secondary decolonisation', witnessed the emergence of its own Black Power movement.[8] Between 1968 and the early 1970s, political and cultural groups calling for Black Power proliferated in many Caribbean territories. Crises erupted such as the Rodney Riots in Kingston in October 1968 and the 'February Revolution' in Trinidad in 1970. The February Revolution specifically, which over a period of three months saw large numbers of the young, unemployed and poor march the streets of Trinidad and Tobago, clash with police and demand 'Black Power', occurred only months before the Mangrove Nine March in London.[9]

Despite the temporal parallels between Black Power in Britain and the Caribbean, and the large Caribbean membership of British Black Power groups, scholars have rarely traced the connections between the two movements.[10] W.C. Johnson's research on the links between the National United Freedom Fighters (NUFF) insurgency in Trinidad in 1973 and Black groups in Britain is one of the only works to illustrate the significance of Black radical politics in the Caribbean for activists in Britain.[11] Rob Waters, in his book *Thinking Black: Britain, 1964–1985*, has also emphasised the relevance of moments like the Rodney Riots for British Black Power, noting that after 1968 'the American focus of Black politics was increasingly challenged by political developments in the Caribbean.'[12] Indeed, the presence of the Caribbean in the activities of British Black Power groups becomes especially explicit after 1968. The statement of the Action Group for the Defence of the Mangrove Nine, for example, which outlined the purpose of their infamous protest in August 1970, notes that copies of the statement were sent to the British Home Office and Prime Minister, but also to the High Commissioners of Jamaica, Trinidad, Guyana and Barbados.[13]

The Mangrove Nine March itself was in response to the continuous raids on Trinidadian Frank Crichlow's restaurant, while almost all the nine arrested and tried at the Old Bailey were born in the Caribbean.[14] Altheia Jones-LeCointe, prominent defendant in the trial, had moved to Britain from Trinidad only years before.[15] Another defendant, Darcus Howe, was in Trinidad in the months before the Mangrove Nine March, engaged in the political activity that led to the February uprisings there.[16] And, as Howe himself noted years later, 'the power of demonstrations' he had witnessed in Trinidad helped inspire the subsequent Mangrove Nine protests.[17] Thus, one can see that the Caribbean and its politics echoed in minds and activities of British Black Power advocates. This chapter explores this Caribbean presence further, presenting early-stage research that is part of a larger project examining the transnational connections between West Indian activists in Britain and the Caribbean as the region moved through the long process of decolonisation. While this chapter does not purport that Caribbean Black Power was *the* key influence on Black Power in Britain, it traces the intimate connections that existed between Black Power advocates in the two locations, and highlights the extent to which British Black Power groups were actively engaged with the parallel movement underway in the Caribbean.

BRITISH AND CARIBBEAN BLACK POWER: SOME HISTORICAL CONTEXT

As Kate Quinn has noted, the Black Power movement in the Caribbean was best defined by its highly variable character. Different groups, both within and between territories, had varying motivations, ideological tenets, material concerns and methods of activism. Their main consistency lay in their impetus: a 'crisis of failed expectations'.[18] For many in the Anglophone Caribbean, the region's post-independence reality had brought with it many disappointments and much disillusionment. Social and economic inequality, high unemployment, entrenched racial hierarchy and state oppression remained widespread. In the late 1960s, Black Power, broadly the reallocation of political, economic and cultural power into the hands of the majority Black working classes, emerged as the only route to upending the status quo.[19] Student groups at the University of the West Indies and new political groups such as National Joint Action Committee (NJAC) and the Antigua Caribbean Liberation Movement (ACLM), as well as emerging publications such as *Abeng* and *Moko*, all developed radical critiques of their local governments that expressed a mixture of race and class discontents, while also maintaining solidarity with international liberation movements. Although the rhetoric utilised by many of these groups held close similarities with those in the US, it had deep roots in the Caribbean itself. In Jamaica in particular, ideologies such as Garveyism and Rastafarianism, with their centralisation of Blackness and adherence to pan-Africanist values, had been present since at the least the 1930s.[20] By the late 1960s, these deep-rooted ideologies entangled with long-held economic discontents, the disappointment of independence, and global movements calling for Third World liberation and Black Power to result in multiple uprisings across the region. The Rodney Riots in Kingston in 1968 signalled the first eruption.[21] But by the following year, the first regional Black Power conference had been held in Bermuda.[22] And by 1970, Trinidad teetered on the brink of revolution.

Similar to Caribbean Black Power, the British movement was grounded in contemporary, local concerns but also deep historical traditions. Although there is not the space to explore all of this rich history here, Black activism in Britain can be dated back at least to abolitionist figures such as Olaudah Equiano and traced through to the nineteenth and twentieth centuries, encompassing foundational moments such as the Pan-African Conference in London in 1900, as well as interwar anticolonialist figures such as George

Padmore and organisations such as International African Service Bureau (IASB).[23] This activism, although physically located in Britain, was always in tune with global issues, whether that be slavery in the Americas or the Italian invasion of Ethiopia. Thus, as C.L.R. James noted in 1967 following the infamous visit to Britain by Stokely Carmichael: 'too many people see Black Power and its advocates as some sort of portent, a sudden apparition ....'[24] The expressions of global solidarity that were central to British Black Power should therefore be seen in the longer lineage of transnational Black politics and activism. But further, the figure of C.L.R. James, the Trinidadian Marxist and thinker, reflecting on British Black Power in 1967, in many ways illustrates how the unique local histories of British and Caribbean Black Power also had a shared lineage; a diasporic connection which, as we will see, drew these two movements together.

RESPONSES OF BRITISH BLACK POWER TO THE RISE OF CARIBBEAN BLACK POWER

On 15 August 1968, a group of 'Jamaicans in exile' organised a demonstration outside the Jamaican High Commissioner's office in London.[25] The reason for their demonstration: the Jamaican government's ban on the writings of Stokely Carmichael, Malcolm X and Elijah Muhammad. On the day of the protest, a petition that had been signed by a mixture of Caribbean activist and Black radical groups, including the West Indian Standing Conference (WISC), the Caribbean Artists Movement (CAM), Racial Adjustment Action Society (RAAS) and the Black Power Movement (BPM), was handed directly to the High Commissioner. For these protesters, the Jamaican government was attempting to silence 'two of the most powerful and articulate spokesmen for the freedom and dignity of the Black Man'. 'We DEMAND the lifting of these orders!', they declared.[26] But this ban was merely indicative of what was soon to come. Only two months later, in October 1968, the Jamaican government issued another ban. This time on an individual: Walter Rodney, the Guyanese historian and professor at the University of the West Indies, was prohibited from re-entering Jamaica following his participation in the Black Writers Congress in Montreal, Canada. The resulting 'Rodney Riots' erupted on the university campus in Kingston and snowballed into a wider indictment of the Jamaican government.[27]

Unsurprisingly, those in Britain with close links to the Caribbean were often the first to receive news of uprisings in the region. In a letter to Edward Kamau Brathwaite, John La Rose recounted how, in October 1968, he had been on his way to deliver a talk in Nottingham when he had received a phone call from a friend alerting him to the Rodney Riots. 'When I got to Nottingham that night' he said, 'I dedicated my talk ... to those who had fallen in Kingston. None of the Jamaicans or other West Indians knew or had heard.' In the following days, he recalled, 'a meeting was held at the WI Students' Centre to consider what might be done. The most important thing was to find a way to telegraph our sympathy and solidarity and to make Jamaicans in Britain aware of what was happening.'[28] Ensuring the wider Black and Caribbean communities were aware of the crises underway in the Caribbean became an essential and immediate response amongst Black Power advocates in Britain. This desire to draw attention to Caribbean news was largely due to the belief that the British press and Caribbean governments were actively suppressing information revealing the extent of the West Indies' instability. British Black radical groups such as the Black Eagles, for example, claimed that the Jamaican government was 'trying to make out that the Black masses of Jamaica, who were previously happy ... were being stirred up by an evil and wicked young man, Dr. Walter Rodney'. 'How true is this?', they asked, 'Let us look at the facts ...'[29] Such a determination to present 'the facts' was also expressed by *The Black Ram*, who explained: 'We feel ... we must present as much as possible how life is with them and their strivings ...'[30]

With the suspicion that news from the Caribbean was being actively repressed, circulating and distributing information became a crucial response for Black Power advocates in Britain, with the Black radical press acting as an important vehicle for bringing 'public attention' to Caribbean Black Power. Caribbean affairs were recounted in the newsletters and pamphlets of many Black Power groups, such as the Black Regional Action Movement (BRAM), the Black Panthers, *Harambee*, the Black Liberation Front (BLF), and another pamphlet called *Black Dimension*, whose editor was Darcus Howe.[31] Of course, moments of large significance were reported in detail, with the majority covering the Rodney Riots and the February Revolution.[32] The death of Beverley Jones, member of NUFF and sister to Altheia Jones-LeCointe, at the hands of Trinidadian police in 1973 was also well covered, with the Panther's newspaper, *Freedom News*, printing her image on the front cover.[33] But other seemingly smaller events and news items were so well reported that a review of publications from this period provides a vivid history of the consistent turmoil and protest underway in the Caribbean. *Freedom News* and *Grassroots*, published by the BLF, reported on everything from elections in Jamaica and workers strikers in Trinidad, to the struggles against Eric Gairy in Grenada.[34] Many of these groups also articulated a deep disillusionment and malaise with the region's political institutions.

Local leaders were discussed in especially critical terms, accused of being corrupt actors who were actively exploiting the West Indian people. *Bumbo*, a newsletter published by members of the West Indian Students' Union (WISU), framed the uprisings of the late 1960s as a result of the 'betrayal and sell-outs by so-called nationalist leaders'.[35] By the early 1970s, the Panthers had labelled Eric Williams 'the Caribbean's most hated tyrant'.[36] Alongside circulating news in the press, groups such as the British Black Panthers organised a number of public solidarity meetings to publicise the unrest in the West Indies and to ensure support for activists there continued even after moments of protest had subsided. According to Panther documentation, a 'Freedom meeting' was held in 1971 'to support [*sic*] struggle of suffering Black people in Trinidad & Tobago'.[37] By September 1973, the Panthers had launched a 'campaign for the release of all political prisoners of the Caribbean ... to bring to public attention' to the government oppression of activists there.[38] As the West Indian political landscape roiled, Black Power advocates in Britain revealed a deep concern for the region and appointed themselves as truth-tellers exposing the reality about events as they unfolded.

As well as becoming a key news source on Caribbean Black Power, Black radicals in Britain analysed Caribbean society and provided a commentary on the meaning of current Black Power uprisings for the region's future. This is especially notable amongst pamphlets published by more radical segments of the WISU who in some newsletters dedicated several pages to issues in Caribbean society in general, and the goals of Caribbean Black Power in particular. For them, the region's instability lay in the large socio-economic disparity between a small group of local elites and the majority working classes who often lacked access to decent employment and reasonable living conditions. Such economic issues had been further compounded by the profound racial stratification of Caribbean society. A newsletter, *Struggle*, summarised these problems which for them lay at the heart of events such as the February Revolution:

> … in an island such as Ja [*sic*]. Where the population is 97% African … a small clique of white, fair skins and Afro-Saxons control the economy, act as overseers for the absentee masters in the metropolitan countries (AmeriKKKa, U.K. and Canada) …[39]

For groups such as the Panthers, the presence of American and British military interests in the region and the role they played in repressing Caribbean freedom struggles was also important to highlight. They framed the February Revolution, for example, in the context of previous 'popular uprisings against oppressive regimes in … British Honduras, Gautemala [*sic*], Curacoa [*sic*], Burmuda [*sic*], Dominican Republic, St. Vincent, Grenada' which had 'been suppressed by British-American imperialists ….'[40] Similar to their peers in the Caribbean, Black radicals in Britain contextualised contemporary social and economic issues within the long history of Caribbean colonisation and exploitation. The Rodney Riots, the February Revolution, and the plethora of workers' strikes that erupted throughout this period were all perceived as attempts to extricate the region and its people from foreign control and its historical legacies. As a pamphlet published by Black Unity and Freedom Party (BUFP) stated: 'Black people in the Caribbean are no longer prepared to tolerate the oppressive and degrading system which has dominated our lives and denied us our humanity for five centuries.'[41]

While news of Caribbean unrest was amplified through public meetings and through the Black radical press, there were also moments where protest and demonstration were deemed as the crucial course of action. During the Rodney Riots, two large protests were held in London; the first outside the Jamaican High Commissioner's office, the second outside the Commissioner's home.[42] These protests sometimes resulted in serious consequences for the demonstrators: 13 people were arrested at the first of these two protests, and at the second John La Rose, Richard Small and Chris Le Maitre, another Trinidadian radical, were all arrested and subsequently tried in court.[43] In April 1970, the Black Panthers organised a protest in Hyde Park to demonstrate against the presence of American and British ships in Caribbean waters during the uprisings in Trinidad. Here, 20 people were reportedly arrested.[44] Finally, after the death of Beverley Jones in 1973, another demonstration was organised outside the Trinidadian embassy.[45]

Lastly, there were also attempts to provide material support for Caribbean activists. Black groups in Britain established relief funds for the legal defence of those detained during demonstrations in the Caribbean. For example, the WISU set up a 'Trinidad detainee relief' fund following the February Revolution and held a dance at the West Indian Students' Centre to raise money. In 1973, the Black Workers Movement (BWM), formerly the British Black Panthers, also organised a 'fund raising dance' for 'the defence fund of Andrea Jacob' who had been arrested in uprisings in Trinidad that year. And in December that same year, they reported that they had sent '£200 towards the defence fund of political prisoners in Trinidad'.[46]

It is clear that Caribbean Black Power became an important locus of support and solidarity for Black Power advocates in Britain. From the late 1960s, Black radicals in Britain organised public information meetings and protests, and published articles, all with the express purpose of drawing attention to Caribbean Black Power. Such solidarity was not only a response to instances of acute political crisis, such as the February Revolution, but was long-lasting and consistent throughout the whole period. Groups like the Black Panthers strove to generate continuous support for Caribbean activists, while members of the WISU remained engaged in Caribbean politics more broadly and at times positioned themselves as commentators on West Indian society.

TRACING TRANSNATIONAL CONNECTIONS BETWEEN BRITISH AND CARIBBEAN BLACK POWER

To understand why Black Power advocates in Britain produced such a marked response to unrest in the Caribbean, one must understand the historical transnational connections between the two movements and locations. As has already been noted, Black activism in Britain had always been transnational in structure, connected to global networks of activists striving to overturn systems of oppression, including slavery and imperialism, and the resulting racial inequality. The preservation of these networks relied on several modes of transnational communication, including private correspondence and a burgeoning, transnational press.[47] By the second half of the twentieth century, these communication routes were little changed and enabled the British Black Power movement to, as scholars like Waters and John Narayan have discussed, remain international in its activism, and to respond strongly to a range of global political moments and movements.[48] As Black Power arose in the Caribbean, British Black Power advocates, in particular those with familial or kinship ties to the Caribbean, maintained connections with the region, regularly corresponding with friends and family throughout the period, and receiving news and information on Black Power uprisings. These networks were essential to sharing news throughout the African and Caribbean diaspora in Britain and enabling the quick and consistent acts of solidarity and support we saw in the first section.

According to La Rose, news of the Rodney Riots arrived in Britain so thick and fast that 'he had since bathed in waterfalls of words about Jamaica from private letters to public documents'.[49] In the 1960s, members of CAM such as Edward Kamau Brathwaite and Gordon Roehler had moved to the Caribbean and subsequently lived through the era of Black Power, during which their correspondence with La Rose and other members of CAM provided a vivid picture of the realities on the ground in the West Indies. Brathwaite, during the Rodney Riots, wrote to La Rose and his wife, Sarah: 'We still hangin' on here, praise God; but things bad; they really bad …'[50] While in a letter sent to La Rose during the February Revolution, Rohlehr revealed that '… everyone is in hibernation (including myself, who have been threatened with violence, whose name is supposed to be on the police list)'.[51]

As friends and family members shared updates via private correspondence, political newsletters and pamphlets also made their way across the Atlantic. Caribbean magazines such as *Moko* and *Abeng* were circulated in Britain and in turn, British Black Power pamphlets were sent to the Caribbean; Brathwaite, for example, wrote to La Rose asking him to send more copies of *The Black Liberator*, a magazine published by members of the BUFP.[52] Evidence also suggests that a range of individuals in Britain and the Caribbean engaged with these materials. In 1969, *Abeng* published a letter it had received from a Black man in Britain, who claimed he had 'been reading ABENG for some time with great interest …', but, he stated, it was 'about time that you publish some of the brothers work here in BABYLONIAN England'.[53] Only a month later, *Abeng* had published an article by Andrew Salkey, another member of CAM based in Britain.[54] These exchanges provide a sense that at the very least Black Power advocates in Britain and the Caribbean were aware of and engaged with each other's causes. But, moreover, they indicate that transatlantic networks of communication played a key role in the dissemination of news and opinions about the Caribbean in Britain.

If the circulation of Caribbean and Black British publications enabled Black Power advocates in Britain to remain connected to the Caribbean, the physical transatlantic movement of people also played an important role. When able to afford it, both the wider British Caribbean community and West Indian activists travelled to the Caribbean to visit friends and family, or to attend specific events. With the region in turmoil so frequently in this period, often on their return to Britain these travellers would bring news of what they had witnessed in the 'mother country'.[55] La Rose, for example, was in Trinidad just weeks before the February Revolution and, once back in Britain, shared recollections of what he had witnessed to an audience at the West Indian Students' Centre.[56] Others brought back news of Caribbean society in general, with some accounts subsequently published in Black newsletters in Britain. Often these articles documented what was understood to be the degradation of Caribbean society. A pamphlet called *Unite*, published by the Youth Forces for National Liberation (YFNL), ran an article entitled: 'A Shocking and Disgraceful State of Affairs – Says Jamaican after a Visit to the Homeland'.[57] A similar article was also published in *Harambee* where the author explained: 'On recently visiting Jamaica, I observed some of the reasons for mass discontent … Things are so bad amongst the poor … SOMETHING MUST BE DONE!'[58] Articles such as these allowed activists in Britain to understand the discontents that propelled the Black Power movement in the Caribbean and pushed some to advocate for change within Caribbean society, arguably enhancing Black British support for the region's Black Power movements.

In fact, receiving such news from the Caribbean provided the Black radical press in Britain with the opportunity to encourage the Black community to partake in acts of solidarity with Caribbean Black Power. In 1971, a pamphlet published in conjunction with the National Conference on the Rights of Black People in Britain ran an article entitled 'We Live in the Caribbean in Ferment: The Carnival is over'. The article, after discussing the recent February Revolution, argued that a revolution in the Caribbean was imminent and thus, 'Black people in Britain have got to decide NOW what we are going to do, when the confrontation comes. We cannot afford to sit back and allow the imperialists to get away with any invasion of our countries …'[59] Even during the Rodney Riots, *The Black Ram* went so far as to call on Jamaicans living 'abroad' to 'go and strengthen the rank-and-file of the movements at home'.[60] In these instances the transnational circulation of news regarding Caribbean Black Power, whether via personal correspondence or through the radical Black press, directly stimulated expressions of solidarity and foregrounded the notion that the Black community in Britain should contribute to it directly.

The awareness Black activists in Britain had of Caribbean Black Power, and their clear desire to support the movement, may have also been compounded by the visits of several Caribbean radicals and revolutionaries to Britain in this era. Such individuals shared news from the West Indies and attempted to generate support for their causes by delivering talks to the Black community at venues like the West Indian Students' Centre. The Students' Centre had historically acted as a hub for visiting West Indian politicians and activists, and in the era of Black Power it played a similar role, providing space for radicals from the Caribbean to discuss their activism with British Black Power advocates. In July 1969, at the monthly general meeting of the WISC, the executive committee heard 'first hand reports on the present political and economic situation in Jamaica and Trinidad ...'. According to the meeting's schedule, the 'Jamaican situation' was discussed by none other than Trevor Munro, lecturer at the University of the West Indies and editor of *Abeng*. While 'the Trinidad situation' was 'dealt with personally by one of the accused men at present in this country for a short stay'.[61] Only a month later, Roosevelt Brown visited the Students' Centre after he had organised the first Caribbean Black Power conference in Bermuda. This meeting was chaired by C.L.R. James and provided Brown with a platform to discuss the outcomes of the Bermuda conference.[62] In 1973, Maurice Bishop reportedly travelled to Britain from Grenada to rally support for the New Jewel Movement and against Eric Gairy's government. In his wake, an organisation was set up called 'Cause for Concern', which worked to publicise the plight of Grenadians amongst their British peers.[63]

It is in these often very personal and sometimes physical connections that we can see how and why there was such consistent concern and solidarity articulated by British Black Power advocates for their peers in the Caribbean. Information was shared through personal correspondence or pamphlets and newsletters while the physical movement of people between the two locations meant that both Britain and the Caribbean, and venues such as the Students' Centre in London, became spaces where the British and Caribbean Black Power movements met, became entangled and generated mutual solidarity.

From the late 1960s to the early 1970s, Black radicals in Britain showed significant solidarity with their peers in the Caribbean Black Power movement; they held protests, organised public meetings, and published numerous reports and articles on Caribbean affairs. Communication networks between Britain and the

Caribbean were essential for keeping those in Britain up to date with Caribbean politics; through personal correspondence, the circulation of newspapers and pamphlets, and physical movement of people across the Atlantic, West Indians in Britain were highly aware of the repression and turmoil underway in the Caribbean as calls for Black Power arose.

Examining such transnational dynamics, as well as how they were formed and maintained, enhances our understanding of the political activism within Britain's Black community in this era. By acknowledging the temporal parallels between British and Caribbean Black Power, and by tracing their transnational connections, we can see more clearly how events outside of American Black Power or British racism were important stimuli for the anticolonial and global concerns of British Black Power groups. Moreover, what this research also reveals, leaving room for further exploration, is the role of personal relationships in driving much of this activism and solidarity.

NOTES

1. The National Archives, London, Metropolitan Police Papers, MEPO 31/21, 'Black Power' demonstration: original statements and newspaper cuttings. Photographs from the file show people with signs, some with their fists raised and one person with a beret. O'Connell's statement is in the same file.
2. Rob Waters, *Thinking Black: Britain, 1964–1985* (Oakland, CA: University of California Press, 2019), p.101.
3. Ibid., p. 93.
4. Ibid., p. 27; John Narayan, 'British Black Power: The Anti-imperialism of Political Blackness and the Problem of Nativist Socialism', *The Sociological Review*, 67 (2019), pp. 945–67, 948.
5. Kennetta Hammond Perry, *London Is the Place for Me: Black Britons, Citizenship and the Politics of Race* (New York: Oxford University Press, 2016), pp. 58–61; ibid., p. 946.
6. *Rosalind Wild, 'Black Was the Colour of Our Fight": Black Power in Britain, 1955–1976* (University of Sheffield, DPhil thesis, 2008), p. 68; Waters, *Thinking Black*, pp. 15–16; Anne-Marie Angelo, 'The Black Panthers in London, 1967–1972: Diasporic Struggle Navigates the Black Atlantic', *Radical History Review*, 103 (2009), pp. 17–35, 20.
7. Waters, *Thinking Black*, p. 15; Wild, 'Black Was the Colour of Our Fight', p. 7.

8. Richard Drayton, 'Secondary Decolonisation: The Black Power Movement in Barbados, c.1970', in Kate Quinn (ed.), *Black Power in the Caribbean* (Gainesville, FL: Florida University Press, 2014), p. 118.
9. W. Chris Johnson, 'Guerrilla Ganja Gun Girls: Policing Black Revolutionaries from Notting Hill to Laventille', *Gender & History*, 26 (2014), pp. 661–787.
10. Many groups associated with the Black Power movement in Britain were led by West Indians or had prominent Caribbean members: for example, Michael de Freitas, leader of RAAS, Altheia Jones-LeCointe, eventual leader of the British Black Panthers, and Darcus Howe, leader of the Black Eagles, were all Trinidadian; Jan Carew and Roy Sawh, also co-founders of RAAS, were from Guyana; the list of other influential West Indians in British Black radical circles is too many to name here but includes John La Rose, Ansel Wong, Andrew Salkey, Richard Small, Edward Kamau Brathwaite, Jessica and Eric Huntley, and Locksley Comrie. Waters, *Thinking Black*, p. 21.
11. Waters, *Thinking Black*, p. 674.
12. Ibid., p. 47.
13. MEPO 31/21, 'Black Power' demonstration: original statements and newspaper cuttings.
14. For details of who were the Mangrove Nine, and details of Howe's visit to Trinidad, see Robin Bunce and Paul Fields, *Darcus Howe: A Political Biography* (London: Bloomsbury Academic, 2014), ch. 10.
15. Narayan, 'British Black Power', p. 951.
16. Bunce and Fields, *Darcus Howe*, pp. 70–83.
17. 'Nelson Mandela, CLR James and the Brixton Radicals: How South Africa Inspired South London', *Red Pepper*, 6 December 2013, www.redpepper.org.uk/nelson-mandela-clr-james-and-the-brixton-radicals-how-south-africa-inspired-south-london/ (accessed 17 September 2021).
18. Kate Quinn, 'Introduction', in Kate Quinn (ed.), *Black Power in the Caribbean* (Gainesville, FL: Florida University Press, 2014), p. 3.
19. Ibid., p. 3.
20. Rupert Lewis, 'Jamaican Black Power in the 1960s', in Kate Quinn (ed.), *Black Power in the Caribbean* (Gainesville, FL: University of Florida Press, 2014), pp. 55–8.
21. Ibid., pp. 55–61.
22. Quinn, 'Introduction', p. 42.
23. For details on Equiano, see Hakim Adi, *Pan-Africanism: A History* (London: Bloomsbury Academic, 2018), p. 7; discussion of Padmore and the IASB can be found in Marc Matera, *Black London: The Imperial Metropolis and Decolonisation in the Twentieth Century* (Oakland, CA: University of California Press, 2015), pp. 82–5.
24. C.L.R James, "Black Power", 1967, www.marxists.org/archive/james-clr/works/1967/black-power.html (accessed 30 September 2021).

25. George Padmore Institute (hereafter: GPI), JLR/3/1/33, 'Protest – Expression Not Repression'.
26. GPI, JLR/3/1/33, Petition Handed to the Jamaican High Commissioner, 15 August 1968.
27. Lewis, 'Jamaican Black Power in the 1960s', pp. 55–61.
28. GPI, LRA 01/143/4, La Rose to Brathwaite, 18 December 1968.
29. Black Cultural Archives (hereafter: BCA), WONG/7/30, Black Eagles newsletter, October 1968?
30. BCA, WONG/7/41, *The Black Ram*, 1/1, 15 December 1968.
31. BCA, WONG/7/45, *Black Dimension*, 1/2, March 1969.
32. BCA, WONG/7/30, Black Eagles newsletter, c. October 1968; BCA, WONG/7/41, *The Black Ram*, 1/1, 15 December 1968; article on the February Rrevolution: GPI, NEW/17/32/3, *Black Peoples News Service*, May 1970; WONG/1/9, *Struggle*, c. 1970.
33. GPI, NEW/17/20, *Freedom News*, 22 September 1973; according to W.C. Johnson, this was also reported in *Race Today*. Johnson, 'Guerrilla Ganja Gun Girls, p. 679.
34. See GPI, NEW/17/11, *Freedom News*, 4 March 1972; GPI, NEW/17/15, *Freedom News*, 1 June 1973; GPI, NEW/17/15, *Freedom News*, 1 June 1973; BCA, NEW/9/10 (2/3), *Grassroots*, 3/3 (n.d.); BCA, NEW/9/10 (2/2), *Grassroots*, 3,/2 (n.d.).
35. BCA, WONG/1/1, *Bumbo* (1969?), p. 18.
36. GPI, NEW/17/21, *Freedom News*, 30 June 1973.
37. GPI, JLR/3/1/5, 'Freedom Meeting' Poster, Sunday 21 November 1971.
38. GPI, NEW/17/20, *Freedom News*, 22 September 1973.
39. BCA, WONG/1/9, *Struggle*, c. 1970.
40. GPI, JLR/3/1/5 Black Panther Movement poster, Sunday 26 April, c.1970; Angelo, 'The Black Panthers in London', p. 28.
41. BCA, WONG/3/7, National Conference on the Rights of Black People in Britain, Special Conference Issue, 22– 23 May 1971.
42. BCA, WONG/7/41, *The Black Ram*, 1/1, 15 December 1968.
43. Ibid.
44. GPI, JLR/2/1/5, Black Peoples Legal Aid and Defence Fund.
45. GPI, NEW/17/21 *Freedom News*, 30 June 1973.
46. BCA, WONG/7/12, *Freedom Fighter*, c. December 1973.
47. Work on Black internationalism in Britain includes, Matera, *Black London*, ch. 1–2; Minkah Makalani, *In the Cause of Freedom: Radical Black Internationalism from Harlem to London, 1917–1939* (Chapel Hill, NC: University of North Carolina Press, 2011), ch. 7; Imaobong D. Umoren, *Race Women Internationalists: Activist-Intellectuals and Global Freedom Struggles* (Oakland, CA: University of California Press, 2018), ch. 1; Priyamvada Gopal, *Insurgent Empire: Anticolonial Resistance and British Dissent* (New York: Verso, 2019), ch. 6–8.
48. Waters, *Thinking Black*, p. 36; Narayan, 'British Black Power', p. 953.

49. GPI, LRA 01/143/4, La Rose to Brathwaite, 18 December 1968.
50. GPI, LRA 01/143/4, Brathwaite to John and Sarah La Rose, 31 October 1968.
51. Ibid.
52. La Rose mentions copies of *Moko* Rohlehr had sent to him, GPI, LRA/01/0684/02, La Rose to Rohlehr, 5 June 1969; Look Lai mentions sending copies of newspapers to La Rose, GPI, LRA/01/0485, Wally Look Lai to John La Rose, 23 July 1969; LRA 01/143/4 Brathwaite to La Rose, 12 August 1972.
53. 'Black British', *Abeng*, 1/25, 19 July 1969, https://dloc.com/UF00100338/00026/allvolumes (accessed 26 September 2021).
54. Andrew Salkey, 'A Revolutionary Black Community', *Abeng*, 1/27, 2 August 1969, https://dloc.com/UF00100338/00026/allvolumes (accessed 26 September 2021).
55. GPI, LRA/01/0143/04, La Rose to Brathwaite, 5 February 1970; GPI, LRA/01/0143/04, La Rose to Brathwaite, 24 October 1971.
56. GPI, JLR/2/5/4, 'Warden's Report for Month of March 1970', West Indian Students' Centre, 9 April 1970.
57. BCA, WONG/7/11, *Unite: Youth Forces for National Liberation*, 3 December 1968.
58. GPI, JLR/3/1/25, *Harambee*, n.d.
59. BCA, WONG/3/7, National Conference on the Rights of Black People in Britain, Special Conference Issue, 22–23 May 1971.
60. BCA, WONG/7/41, *The Black Ram*, 1/1, 15 December 1968.
61. GPI, JLR/3/1/33, Letter from Secretary of the West Indian Standing Conference (London), 1 July 1969.
62. GPI, JLR/2/5/4, Poster from West Indian Students' Centre (1969?); WONG/1/1, *Bumbo*, September 1969.
63. GPI, NEW/17/15, *Freedom News*, 1 June 1973.

11

'The Enemy in Our Midst': Caribbean Women and the Protection of Community in Leeds

Olivia Wyatt

The multi-ethnic Chapeltown News Collective was situated in the inner-city suburb of Chapeltown in Leeds, and its monthly publication – *Chapeltown News* – reported stories for its working-class readership. Throughout its five-year history, the newspaper became embroiled in disputes between radicals and locals who held relatively moderate political views. In their August 1974 edition, the collective published a letter from Lornette Weekes that concluded with the following remarks:

> Black people here are well aware of slavery and all the tortures that went with it, but this is the 20th century when we as young people are trying to build a better and more tolerable society. Over the past few months a few radicals have managed to get too near the printing press of the *Chapeltown News*, and have published articles that are often farcical or distorted. It is time that the paper returned to its original ideals, when it was a useful media for passing on information about the community, instead of the opinions of a few.[1]

Weekes had grown up in Chapeltown and she wrote to the collective to express her disappointment at a letter that they published. In that letter Imruh Bakari – a member of the radical arts group UHURU Arts – criticised an educational student exchange that had been organised between a school in Chapeltown and another in St Kitts. Bakari had argued that the Caribbean children were deliberately kept from 'the Black community', concluding that: 'It is important that Black people both here and in the West Indies are aware of these types of conspiracies by individuals who claim to be working in the interests of good race relations, but are in fact nurturing the lies that enslaved our people for 400 years.'[2] Weekes' response illustrated the frustration of some Caribbean residents with the radical elements of activism in their neighbourhood – elements which they believed had the potential to hold the community back.[3] Her emphasis on the twentieth century and the need for a 'more [tolerant] society' reflects the sentiment held by some Black Britons: that radical activists were preoccupied with the historical suffering of Black people and disinterested in cooperation. Bakari's letter, however, captures the frustration of some activists with their neighbours' reluctance to condemn the racist state that oppressed them.

The focus of Weekes' letter on children and young people reflected the importance of the youth to community activists. Young people were vulnerable and held the future of the community; therefore, the most vehement disputes stemmed from conflicting ideas about the needs of this demographic. As the gendering of Caribbean communities ensured that women were often responsible for children, the concentration on young people encouraged some Caribbean women to involve themselves in local activism, many of whom rejected mainstream politics. According to the authors of *The Heart of the Race*, education was 'a burning issue' for Caribbean women as they witnessed how education provided subjects with better prospects within the colonial Caribbean; therefore, many women who settled in the impoverished area of Chapeltown pursued better educational opportunities for the children growing up there.[4] It is, therefore, fitting that this dispute over the priorities for Black children, captured in *Chapeltown News*, occurred between Weekes, a woman, and Bakari, a radical man. The embracement of radicalism was often perceived as a male endeavour despite the monumental contributions of women to Black radical thought; therefore, most (but not all) radicals in Chapeltown appear to have been men. Rather than render the radical activity of women obscure, however, I argue that this focus on men enabled radical Black women to evade the scrutiny of the state.[5]

Throughout this chapter, 'radicalism' describes the politics of activists who sought thorough change rather than reform through state institutions; whereas 'militancy' indicates the preference for forceful methods, whether that be strikes or violent protests, not all forms of militancy are violent. The term 'conservative' loosely describes the traditional values of order and stability held by some Caribbean residents within Chapeltown – values that can be traced to the old colonial elite.[6] As we shall see, the use of militant tactics by some younger people challenged what one activist described as their elders' 'law-abiding' nature. It is important to remember that in reality these categories were fluid and activists rarely applied these labels to themselves, but it is helpful to distinguish between the types of activism within the neighbourhood. The 1970s was an era of great political activity and ordinary people were forced to defend their rights in a multitude of ways.

Locating the position of Caribbean women within radical actions in Chapeltown during the 1970s, I analyse women's attempts to protect a Caribbean community through the provision of assistance to children and young people, and it reveals the varying degrees to which women utilised radicalism to achieve their goals. Charting the development of political organisations and the ways in which activists worked together to involve the community, before analysing how such unity fell apart due to political differences, I utilise new oral histories alongside archival evidence to represent the voices that are missing from narratives of Black British resistance.

THE ORIGINS OF A CARIBBEAN COMMUNITY IN CHAPELTOWN

The poor infrastructure, limited job opportunities and low standards of living encouraged an estimated 280,000 Caribbean migrants to relocate to Britain between 1951 and 1961.[7] The older Chapeltown residents that I interviewed had travelled as children; therefore, their recollections of migration contradict the official narrative that celebrates the arrival of 'the Windrush generation'.[8]

This sentiment is captured by Nia Ward, who relocated to Chapeltown in the late 1950s:

> It is interesting that you use the word move. We were children so it was not a question of *we* move ... We did as we were told and we were told that we were going to England ... I don't really know how we managed to survive that experience, being away from our parents, and we were in no man's land for 6 weeks ... So yeah I don't really look back on those days with fond memories.[9]

Many migrants followed the promise of work to industrial cities, and the increasing number of vacant properties alongside the proximity of major factories encouraged migrants to settle in Chapeltown.[10] Kittitians and Nevisians in particular were drawn to the suburb because migrants tended to settle in the areas that associates mentioned or recommended; therefore, migrants who had belonged to different social circles now lived alongside each other. An example is the relationship between Gertrude Paul, who was educated alongside future politicians at an elite grammar school, and Lucina Dore Hendrickson, a young mother of humbler beginnings.[11] Hendrickson's son, Claude, explained that despite her background: 'Mrs Gertrude Paul had a soft spot for my mum. I don't know why, but she did. And that soft spot for my mum came onto me. So I have fond memories of Gertrude Paul – very strict lady, but had her house always open for me.'[12] Caribbean migrants settled alongside their Polish, Irish, South Asian and African counterparts in Chapeltown, however, they also established their own organisations to cultivate a sense of community premised on Caribbean traditions.

During the 1970s many Caribbean people in Chapeltown began to engage with the principles of Black Power – a revolutionary movement that emerged in the US but included transnational influences and implications due to its diasporic, socialist and anti-imperial origins. The idea of political Blackness was central to British Black Power's conceptualisation of community; it proposed that 'real' community was composed of those who were racially oppressed and required the use of leftist principles to end (racial) capitalism.[13] As explained by the director of the Institute of Race

Relations, Ambalavaner Sivanandan: 'Black is the colour of our politics, not the colour of our skins.'[14] This appropriation of community influenced some Chapeltown-based activists such as Dawn Cameron (the daughter of Clinton Cameron – a founder of *Chapeltown News*), who helped organise the Sahara Black Women's Refuge which grouped people of African and Asian descent in its definition of Blackness.[15] However, many activists in Chapeltown rejected this definition because they sought a community that centred their Caribbean cultures. In his upcoming publication Max Farrar pondered whether London-based Black Power activists 'LeCointe, Howe, Beese and the other Panthers weren't sufficiently African-centred for the Brotherhood' – a Black Power organisation in Chapeltown.[16] By documenting the involvement of women in the protection of a Caribbean community within a multicultural locality, we can develop our understanding of the limits of political Blackness – limits which led Winston James to observe that: 'There is a tendency among black radicals of both Asian and African descent to sweep this problem under the carpet.'[17]

THE DEVELOPMENT OF CARIBBEAN ACTIVIST ORGANISATIONS IN CHAPELTOWN

Although Chapeltown hosted numerous organisations, I begin with the United Caribbean Association (UCA) because it became the main organisation in which Caribbean settled migrants voiced their grievances. In his 1988 observation of the politics of Black youth workers, Farrar commented: 'The campaigning general organisations of the 1970s (such as the Indian Workers Association and the United Caribbean Association) have exhausted their historic role, but no new general organisation has yet emerged which can provide a framework in which the new political tendency can be developed.'[18] This comment hints at UCA's shift from radicalism – a shift that can be traced to the struggles of the organisation since its inception. Radical activists such as Arthur France, Errol James and George Archibald founded the UCA in 1964 to tackle the injustices faced by Caribbean migrants. Gertrude Paul and Eulalie Procope had established the African, Caribbean and Asian Organisation (ACAO) to bring Commonwealth migrants together through dances and other social activities, however, France believed that the ACAO lacked the political framework required to challenge racism.[19]

The UCA eventually surpassed the ACAO as they began to organise more popular dances, leading Paul and Procope to join the new organisation. France expressed the need 'to do better' than the ACAO to raise funds, however, the potential impact of their political differences on the nature of their competition cannot be ignored. France's words suggest that he perceived the ACAO as a threat because it could receive more support than the UCA: 'We had to chop the ground from under Mrs Procope and them.' Calvin Beech – a radical newcomer who became the chair of the UCA in 1972 – initially rejected Paul's offer to organise dances for the UCA because 'their political differences were already clear to him', according to Farrar. The founders, therefore, believed it was necessary for the UCA to become the main organisation for Caribbean migrants because it could assume a leadership role within the community – a community which France believed must be politically aware and 'had to do much more than socialise'.[20]

Alongside its pursuit of injustices, however, the UCA launched events that were tailored to the Caribbean heritage of its members, such as dominoes evenings and calypso nights – the organisation needed to maintain cultural traditions and provide entertainment to appeal to the masses. While the UCA did not formally align itself with Black Power, leading members formed links with the Black Panther Movement and organised anti-racist demonstrations in which they invited prominent Black Power activists Darcus Howe and Altheia Jones-LeCointe in 1971.[21] The inner core of the UCA were noticeably all men, reflecting the exclusion of women from radical activity; however, some women began to assume official positions over the years, and Paul was the secretary by 1972. Nevertheless, the radical activity of the organisation began to decline throughout the 1970s because fewer of its members agreed with the tone established by its founders, and Beech resigned as chair in 1975.

While Paul and Procope were wary of radicalism, there were female radicals who organised away from the male inner core of the UCA. Veryl Harriott and her husband George, Trevor Wynter,

Mr and Mrs Cruise and other Caribbean migrants founded the West Indian Afro Brotherhood (WIAB) in 1971 because they believed – like the founders of the UCA seven years prior – that the current organisation was not radical enough. France and Beech struggled to understand the reasons behind the formation of the WIAB, however, the two organisations seemed to work together on occasions.[22] For example, they jointly sent a telegram to Trinidad demanding the release of revolutionary Jennifer Jones – the sister of Jones-LeCointe – in 1973.[23] A commentator labelled the WIAB as 'the largest black militant organisation in Leeds' in 1972.[24] Its early publications reveal the group's Marxist leanings, with frequent references to Black Power and African Marxist liberation movements. In his book on Chapeltown, Farrar observed: 'It is an indication of the gender-power relations of the time that this small organisation of radical young people named itself a Brotherhood, despite the presence of articulate and influential young women in its ranks.'[25] Not only does the name of the WIAB indicate such relations, it also demonstrates the common association of manhood with radicalism – an association exemplified by the masculine iconography of underground militant groups like the Black Liberation Army in the US.[26]

While Beech admitted that the WIAB 'were more militant than us', some of the younger members split from the organisation in 1972 because they believed it did not go far enough.[27] In a poem she authored in memory of her grandfather, Trevor Wynter, Khadijah Ibrahiim wrote: 'elders watered the branches so Uhuru could grow in Violet [Fayola] Hendrickson, Annette Liburd and Imru Caesar [Imruh Bakari], who created with artistic freedom and no apologies'.[28] Her use of 'no apologies' captures the vehemence of UHURU's activism because the organisation was not afraid to be critical. The Swahili words 'uhuru' and 'harambee' translate as 'freedom' and 'working together', respectively, and UHURU Arts and the Harambee Collective (UHURU) evolved in conjunction with one another in 1972. Both were splinter groups of younger women and men that seem to have merged, and their names illustrate the dissemination of the Afrocentric belief in practicing traditional African values. The political emphasis of these organisations, however, ensured that they shared a socialist Pan-African vision for the African diaspora; therefore, they used Afrocentric imagery and expressions to achieve their aim. UHURU Arts was a radical arts group and the Harambee Collective distributed the local newsletter *Lookya!* to 'inform people, the community, about what was going on', according to UHURU member Fayola Hendrickson.[29] In an attempt to radicalise the community, the newsletter informed locals that 'the immediate threat to the Black Community is the present development and extension of the Capitalist Society in which we live', and that the solution was 'to put Black Power in its correct perspective as the resistance of Black People against Racism, Oppression and Exploitation'.[30]

RADICAL ATTEMPTS TO IMPROVE EDUCATION AND CHILDCARE PROVISIONS

Members of the UCA, the WIAB and UHURU helped orchestrate the Studley Grange playgroup takeover of 1972 and the Cowper Street school strike of 1973 – campaigns that borrowed the rhetoric of militants to challenge the racist and paternalistic powers overseeing provisions for the children of Chapeltown. Caribbean women took the lead in both instances despite appealing for support from other working-class families in the neighbourhood. What is of interest, however, is the participation of older women in these radical activities; the conditions and ideas forced upon the children convinced them of the need for militant action within the moment. Many women had limited time for activism because they worked long hours due to their financial difficulties as migrants, yet it was traditionally considered the responsibility of 'The intelligent mother' to 'use all her faculties if her child is to develop its full potentials', as reflected in a document prepared by Annette Liburd in 1973.[31] Therefore, the association of women with the maternal encouraged several women of different political dispositions to campaign together for the welfare of the children in the community.

Black women involved themselves in the Chapeltown Parents and Friends Association (CPFA), which was formed to challenge racism and paternalism within the Studley Grange playgroup committee. Caribbean mothers initiated the playgroup in 1963/1965, but white professionals from middle-class areas dominated the committee by November 1972.[32] According to the coverage provided by *Chapeltown News*, public demands for greater diversity within the committee were countered with warnings that funds would be cut if 'responsible people' were not in control.[33] Infuriated by the implication that Black people were irresponsible, locals accused the committee of displaying a 'paternalistic attitude'. The CPFA, spearheaded by Veryl Harriott, was created to address this issue, and the organisation assumed a militant tone due to its leader's membership of the WIAB. A document published by the CPFA named 'WHITE POWER STRUGGLE FOR CONTROL OF MULTI-RACIAL PLAY CENTRE' criticised 'white liberals' and conveyed the revolutionary sentiment of Black Power: 'control of a country, a school or, as in this case, a children's centre, has got to be TAKEN'.[34] The document persuaded a crowd of Black parents to interrupt a meeting at the playgroup on 24 November, and Harriott criticised the committee for 'muzzl[ing] the power of the people'.[35] A new committee was eventually elected, with Harriott as its chairperson and Lucilda Wynter, the wife of another founder of the WIAB, listed as 'the Organiser'.[36]

The Chapeltown Parents Action Group (CPAG), formed in June 1973 by parents concerned about the conditions of the local Cowper Street school, also engaged in radicalism under the influence of members of the UCA and UHURU. In 1971, the UCA, with support from the WIAB, had established a supplementary school to undermine the curriculum's negative portrayal of Black people.[37] These types of schools centred the Black Power principles of self-determination and Pan-African education, and their success proved that state classrooms were damaging to Black children.[38] A new study by Bernard Coard – *How the West Indian Child Is Made Educationally Sub-normal in the British School System* (1971) – also revealed the high rates at which Caribbean children were being labelled as educationally subnormal, and Gertrude Paul, now a teacher at Cowper Street school, complained that the headteacher made racist remarks about the pupils.[39]

These developments inspired Calvin Beech and Arthur France of the UCA to create the CPAG, but according to Farrar's upcoming publication, they positioned Black mothers as the driving forces of the organisation. Beech and France declared that they wanted the organisation to be associated with kinship instead of radicalism, as this would help the organisation garner support within the community and evade the scrutiny of the state.[40] UHURU member Fayola Hendrickson recalled that it was Beech and France who encouraged her to become the secretary of the CPAG, and they also ensured that mothers at the school – highly respected within the neighbourhood – took up leadership roles.[41] Odessa Stoute was a married Barbadian mother of lower middle-class origins who chaired the CPAG, and like most migrants at the time, she would not have identified herself as militant; however, reflecting on her involvement in 1992, she recognised that Black people needed 'to be seen and heard'.[42] Under the leadership of Stoute and the influence of radicals within the UCA and UHURU, the CPAG organised a strike for 25 June in which nearly all of the Black parents withdrew their children from Cowper Street school and protested outside of its gates. The strike was unprecedented in Leeds and a rare occurrence in British education; the Education Department declared that they would make significant concessions only two days later, which included replacing the headteacher. In a letter that was later published in *Chapeltown News*, John La Rose, on behalf of the Black Parents' Movement that he founded, argued that 'This victory was an example to us all.'[43] The CPAG, therefore, may have inspired the Black Parents' Movement which was formed two years after the strike – an example of the overlooked ways in which the activities of peripheral areas shaped anti-racist activism in London.

The strike exemplifies the militancy that 'just ordinary housewives' – according to Beech – engaged in, with the encouragement of radicals like Hendrickson, Beech and France.[44] Black Power was frequently referenced at the meetings of the CPFA and the CPAG, and the local Community Relations Council (CRC) expressed concerns that supporters of the strike expected to receive funds from organisations in the US. Notes made during an interview for *Chapeltown News* report that a representative of the CRC feared that Beech and France were connected to Black Power activists in St Kitts and wanted 'to return home as heroes'.[45] The preoccupation of the CRC with the radical activities of men connected to the

CPAG is another example of the gendering of Black radicalism, yet it also suggests that women who practised radical politics were less visible to the state. Harriott and Hendrickson were members of the WIAB and UHURU, respectively, and the two women circulated anti-capitalist material, yet they were perceived as less of a threat by the CRC despite being leader and secretary of the CPFA and the CPAG. Therefore, the decision to place women at the forefront of these campaigns appears to have been fruitful because their conduct went relatively unchecked. Under Harriott's leadership, the CPFA persuaded ordinary Black parents to occupy a building and demand the replacement of the paternalistic Studley Grange committee, and women who usually opposed the rebellious values associated with militancy were willing to orchestrate and support a strike for the betterment of the community.

There was a line, however, which conservative Caribbean women drew when they involved themselves in radical activity. The minutes of the CPAG's meetings note that Stoute declared that 'we are [only] talking about a bad school' when Imruh Bakari proposed applying Black Power principles to 'all of life', which suggests that many women within the CPAG perceived their engagement in militancy as temporary.[46] They agreed with militants in this instance, but they did not wholly support radical politics; therefore, the political tensions between activists could not be papered over for long. For example, Eulalie Procope, as an assistant community relations officer at the CRC and a member of the UCA, voiced concerns over the action against the school. During the Chapeltown News Collective's interview with the CRC, she reportedly agreed that the racist headteacher should resign but believed that 'many parents approach him wrongly'.[47] These disagreements over what constituted inappropriate action eventually led radicals to use the pages of *Chapeltown News* to publicly denounce 'another enemy ... within the community'.[48]

THE NEW OUTSIDER: *CHAPELTOWN NEWS* AND THE CRITIQUE OF THE UCA

There was widespread backing for the Studley Grange playgroup takeover of 1972 and the Cowper Street school strike of 1973, however, the bonfire night incident of 1975 exposed the limits of support for militants. The incident occurred when hundreds of young people attacked undercover police on the streets of Chapeltown. The police had broken a prearranged agreement to limit their surveillance of Black youngsters during the bonfire celebrations following a minor incident the previous year. Eleven Black boys and a white man were selected and trialled as scapegoats; however, a defence committee organised representation for the youngsters – representation that included anti-racist barrister Rudy Narayan.[49]

The defence committee was mainly composed of women from the UCA and UHURU who had participated in the playgroup takeover and the school strike, such as Gertrude Paul, Fayola Hendrickson, Nia Ward and Annette Liburd; however, the committee struggled to garner support because many of their older Caribbean neighbours disapproved of the use of violence. As Hendrickson explained: 'The older generation were law-abiding, coming out of the harsh lives that they lived in the Caribbean ... We were more outspoken than our parents. So there may have been some who would not give their support to the young people because they would see it as unruly behaviour.'[50] For example, the UCA proclaimed their sympathy towards those arrested, but they added that they 'regret[ted] the unfortunate incidents on Bonfire Night', whereas the Chapeltown News collective sought to rationalise the violence.[51]

Nonetheless, many people celebrated when most of the defendants were acquitted on 11 July 1976 in a trial that *Chapeltown News* labelled 'a victory for all'.[52] However, some Caribbean residents had criticised the involvement of *Chapeltown News* because the issue concerned Black youngsters and most of the collective was white and middle class. Icilma Browne complained to *Race Today* in London that the Chapeltown News Collective were 'opportunists who do not encourage blacks, youth or otherwise to participate in their activities' because they believed they needed 'to look after black people's affairs for them'.[53] After the trial, Narayan also declared that he wanted 'to see a black community that's independent of white ... newspapers'.[54] Subsequently the editors of *Chapeltown News*, including Farrar, handed the newspaper to UHURU – 'young blacks ... capable of becoming an authentic militant leadership' according to Farrar in a letter he wrote to *Race Today*.[55] The founder of UHURU – Imruh Bakari – had relocated to London but Liburd and Hendrickson continued as members. Contrary to Robin Bunce and Paul Field's claim that UHURU worked alongside Farrar to produce *Chapeltown News*, it was crucial that Farrar and his colleagues resigned for Liburd, Hendrickson and their colleagues to join the collective.[56] While Narayan hoped that Black ownership of the newspaper would unite the community, the newspaper became an important medium for local power politics and the contestation of community.

From 1977, the new editors used *Chapeltown News* to challenge the UCA. The UCA had become noticeably less radical as it began to cultivate greater resources for the community and celebrate the culture and resilience of Black Britons. The departure of Calvin Beech in 1975 'due to pressure from within', according to *Chapeltown News*, reflected the new membership of the UCA.[57] The deradicalisation of the UCA is also exemplified by the appointment of Gertrude Paul as chair and Eulalie Procope as secretary: two women who voiced their disapproval of militancy. Criticism of the UCA was deemed necessary because UHURU feared that the UCA was taking control of resources that were intended for the entire community, to the exclusion of youthful associations. Paul was the recipient of most of this criticism because the collective argued that 'since the new chairman was elected all the organisation stood for has been abandoned'.[58] The editors also published letters anonymously written by 'The Hawk' which criticised Paul and the UCA; the first letter, published in January, described Paul's leadership of the UCA supplementary school as 'dictatorial'. Paul had become the first Black headteacher in Leeds in 1976, and her radical contemporaries believed that her position within the state was incompatible with her control of the supplementary school. 'The Hawk' argued that her decision to deradicalise – or 'dilute' – the school was 'traitorous'.[59]

In the February edition, UHURU argued that the UCA's 'pursuit of its rigid capitalistic policies' inadvertently harmed the community: 'They are sadly that group of Blacks with a totally colonialistic mentality, lacking in political ideology and therefore ill equipped to aid the struggle. They serve only to suffocate progress and more fatally to delay our deliverance from the architects of oppression.'[60] The expression of sadness not only captures the dismay of many younger radicals when their neighbours opposed their politics, it also reflects how these activists believed that UCA members were afflicted with an illness – a 'colonialistic mentality' – due to their cooperation with the authorities (the 'colonisers'). Whereas older activists like Paul believed that such cooperation was vital for the community's survival, as captured in the words of Arthur France: 'The youngsters had to realise that they have to work within a certain system, within parameters.'[61]

Throughout the rest of 1977, the editors outlined the ways in which they believed that the 'colonialistic mentality' of the UCA could damage the community, particularly its youth. In the June editorial titled 'The Enemy in Our Midst', they argued for the removal of the UCA as 'community leaders': 'another enemy comes to light within the community itself. The fact that this new enemy is identical in colour does not alter our position.' Many activists had campaigned in the defence of a Caribbean community in Chapeltown, however, UHURU's criticism of their (once) allies for using 'the people in this community as instruments for achieving their personal ambitions' demonstrates that activists were aware of the flaws in organising around their ethnic identity.[62] Radicals realised that they were at odds with other activists despite growing up together in the same neighbourhood and sharing an ethnicity.[63]

The Chapeltown News Collective expanded on their positioning of the UCA as the 'instruments of the ... Authorities' to argue that Paul's agreement with the CRC to hold a contained bonfire celebration at the Chapeltown community centre was an attempt 'to keep Black youths off the streets' following the previous incident.[64] The accusation was strengthened by the instruction which Paul directed at young people leaving the celebrations: '[do not] congregate on the street corners – go straight home.'[65] The collective labelled the bonfire of 1976 as 'a defeat for the community' and called on Black people in Chapeltown to go 'back to the streets' in 1977. While older members within the UCA preferred to cooperate with the state, the younger and radical UHURU argued that 'if we are attacked then we are left with no alternative but to DEFEND OURSELVES.'[66] The UCA preferred to keep the youngsters away from police patrols, whereas UHURU believed that they should walk those streets like any other.

The Race Today Collective – a Black Power organisation composed of activists such as Leila Hassan and Darcus Howe – appears to have encouraged the Chapeltown News Collective to oppose another 'jailhouse bonfire'. They interviewed local youngsters and concluded that the residents had been subjected to an 'imprisoned bonfire' in the November 1976 edition of their publication *Race Today*; they additionally claimed that 'the mood of defeat even spread to the militant *Chapeltown News*' because 'there was no leadership, none at all, to which [the youth] could turn'.[67] Howe was also friends with Liburd – he wept at her passing in 2006 and described her as an 'uncompromising ... unsung heroine'.[68] Therefore, the criticism of the UCA that appeared in *Chapeltown News* from January 1977 was arguably inspired by the writings of the Race Today Collective. UHURU, adhering to Farrar's belief in their 'authentic militant leadership', stepped forward to confront the activists they had once worked alongside – individuals presented as exploitative 'race relations activists' by *Race Today*.

Nonetheless, the *Race Today* article only acted as a catalyst for the attack on the UCA if it had any bearing on the Chapeltown News Collective. UHURU had implored conservatives within their community to abandon their views since the group's formation in 1972, and the criticism of the UCA, and of Paul in particular, was specific to their experiences.[69] However, my interviews revealed that others within the community felt that members of the collective had been manipulated by those who disapproved of Paul's change in status – individuals who may have written the letters of 'The Hawk'.[70] Paul's daughter, Heather, also recalled feeling 'angry at the time', and she was surprised to read such criticism in *Chapeltown News* because her mother had previously taken care of Liburd and helped her become one of the first Black teachers in Leeds.[71] Therefore, it seems likely that the new Chapeltown News Collective required a greater impetus to criticise a community leader they previously respected and worked alongside. Heather's confusion at Liburd's criticism of her mother, alongside fears that the collective may had been misled, reminds us to interrogate our written sources and the ways in which they were produced – processes of production that are less visible within the archive. Although, to argue that the editors of *Chapeltown News* were simply used as tools by others would overlook their commitment to radicalism, as well as Farrar's belief that UHURU could be genuine militant leaders of the Black youth. Regardless of where the criticism stemmed from, it is evident that the unity between radical and relatively moderate activists began to fragment in the wake of the violent bonfire incident in November 1975.

The diverging path of the UCA, alongside the influence of other activists and publications, encouraged UHURU to use *Chapeltown News* to argue that Paul's cooperation with the racist state transformed the UCA into an internal enemy. Rather than ascertain the extent to which the actions of UHURU and the UCA were justified, I outlined how these disputes emerged when activists acted according to their different ideas of protecting the community. During our conversations, Hendrickson revealed the impact of her untreated trauma on her feelings towards others – a realisation she arrived at after years of self-reflection. The distressing experience of migration, the dislocation of resettlement and the alienating consequences of racism are often overlooked as contributing factors to the behaviour of traumatised Caribbean migrants and their descendants.[72] Reflecting on her role in the criticism of Paul and her peers over 40 years later, Hendrickson observed: 'I see them as teething concerns of a community in its infancy. Naturally growth and development over the years have given insight and the ability to demonstrate a more united approach.'[73]

The disagreement between Lornette Weekes and Imruh Bakari over the student exchange in 1974 was one of many quarrels between radicals and non-radicals that emerged in *Chapeltown News*. Radicals realised that those they sought to protect, who they had respected and worked alongside, were at odds with the ideologies that shaped their desires for the community. In seeking to protect the community they identified another 'enemy' among them: the community leaders who cooperated with the state and could be manipulated by the authorities.

While a limited number became committed campaigners, women were central to the disputes between activists and the decline of radicalism from the mid-1970s. The focus on children and education attracted women, many of whom were mothers, to the Studley Grange playgroup takeover and the Cowper Street school strike. Gertrude Paul, as a respectable older activist, sought to improve the community's relationship with the state, whereas two young female militants, Annette Liburd and Fayola Hendrickson, worked alongside other UHURU activists to edit *Chapeltown News*. Despite being women within an environment dominated by men, Liburd and Hendrickson thrived within UHURU; their success was not only due to their proven ability and commitment to the radical tradition through their involvement in the school strike and the defence committee of the Bonfire Twelve, it was also shaped by the inability of the state to recognise their potential as community activists. As a result, they continued to be active into the early 1990s and are widely regarded as founders of UHURU despite Hendrickson's clarification that Imruh Bakari established the organisation.

By complicating common pictures of activism, the findings from this case study exemplify why historians of Black British history must produce more local studies. Concentrating solely on activists can overlook the ways in which participation in radical activities was fluid, as relatively conservative individuals occasionally engaged in militant activities that would have been avoided had they not been launched in the name of the community and its children. The processes that led Caribbean women to support militancy within one moment, and reject it during another, develop our understanding of the permeation of radical thinking within peripheral localities during the Black Power movement. The prominence of conservative values within Chapeltown also nuances recent scholarship that concentrates on Black British radicalism – a concentration that can create the false impression that the majority of Black Britons were militant during the 1970s.

The stories revealed in this chapter demonstrate that the collection of new oral histories is important because, unlike sources that are frozen in time, these testimonies reveal new possibilities, such as allowing us to learn about the power dynamics behind the production of sources like community newspapers. When writing the histories of communities that have been marginalised and misrepresented, the ability to ask our historical subjects for their truths should be treasured.

NOTES

1. 'St. Kitt's Exchange', published letter sent to the collective, *Chapeltown News*, August 1974, p. 5.
2. 'Exchange "biased"', published letter sent to the collective, *Chapeltown News*, July 1974, p. 2.
3. The Caribbean is made up of various ethnic groups including Indo-Caribbean people and Sino-Caribbean people, however, I use the term 'Caribbean' to refer to African Caribbean people in Britain throughout this chapter.
4. Beverley Bryan, Stella Dadzie and Suzanne Scafe, *The Heart of the Race: Black women's Lives in Britain* (London: Virago Press, 1986), p. 59.
5. Many thanks to Fayola Hendrickson and Kate Dossett for helping me develop this concept.
6. For more information about conservative Caribbean cultures, see Paul Sutton, 'Politics in the Commonwealth Caribbean: The Post-Colonial Experience', *European Review of Latin American and Caribbean Studies*, 51 (1991), p. 53; Anthony Maingot, *The United States and the Caribbean: Challenges of an Asymmetrical Relationship* (Boulder, CO: Westview Press, 1994), p. 120.
7. Kevin Searle, 'Before Notting Hill: The Causeway Green "riots" of 1949', in Hakim Adi (eds.), *Black British History: New Perspectives* (London: Zed Books, 2019), p. 90; C. Richardson, 'Caribbean Migrations 1838–1985', in Franklin W. Bonham and C. Richardson (eds), *The Modern Caribbean* (Chapel Hill, NC: University of North Carolina Press, 1989), p. 216.
8. I further interrogate this idea in my discussion of Kennetta Perry and Jade Bentil's talks: Olivia Wyatt, 'The Art of Narration: Memory, Voices and Archival Deadening in the Reconstruction of Black British History', *History Matters*, 1/3 (2021), pp. 19–26.
9. Nia Ward, interview conducted by the author, Leeds, 4 November 2019.
10. Max Farrar, *The Struggle for 'Community' in a British Multi-ethnic Inner-city Area* (New York: Edwin Mellen Press, 2002), p. 13.
11. Heather Paul, interview conducted by the author, Leeds, 14 February 2020.
12. Claude Hendrickson, interview conducted by the author, Leeds, 14 March 2020.
13. For more information on political Blackness, see Rob Waters, *Thinking Black: Britain, 1964–1985* (Oakland, CA: University of California Press, 2019); John Narayan, 'British Black Power: The Anti-imperialism of Political Blackness and the Problem of Nativist Socialism', *The Sociological Review*, 67/5 (2019), pp. 945–67.
14. Jenny Bourne, 'When Black Was a Political Colour: A Guide to the Literature', *Race & Class*, 58 (2016), p. 130.

15. Dawn Cameron, interview conducted by the author, Leeds, 6 July 2021.
16. Max Farrar, *Arthur France's Biography* (working title, currently unpublished), p. 81. For further examples of the differences between political Blackness and African-centric Black organisations in other localities, see Kieran Connell, *Black Handsworth: Race in 1980s Britain* (Oakland, CA: University of California Press, 2019) and Ferdinand Dennis, *Behind the Frontlines: Journey into Afro-Britain* (London: Gollancz, 1988).
17. Winston James, 'Migration, Racism and Identity Formation: The Caribbean Experience in Britain', in Winston James and Clive Harris (eds), *Inside Babylon: The Caribbean Diaspora in Britain* (London: Verso, 1993), p. 267.
18. Max Farrar, 'The Politics of Black Youth Workers in Leeds', *Critical Social Policy*, 8 (1988), p. 113.
19. Farrar, *France's Biography*, pp. 72–3.
20. Ibid.
21. 'Lookya!', September 1973, WYL5041/41/4, WYAS1006, West Yorkshire Archive Service, Leeds.
22. Farrar, *France's Biography*, p. 79.
23. 'Lookya!', September 1973, WYL5041/41/4.
24. Snippet of article 'Blacks Occupy – Defy "Revolutionary"' by Red Mole Reporter, 27 November 1972, WYL5041/41/1, WYAS1006, West Yorkshire Archive Service, Leeds.
25. Farrar, *The Struggle for 'Community' in a British Multi-ethnic Inner-city Area*, p. 171.
26. For more information on the Black Liberation Army, see William Rosenau, '"Our Backs Are against the Wall": The Black Liberation Army and Domestic Terrorism in 1970s America', *Studies in Conflict & Terrorism*, 36 (2013), pp. 176–92.
27. Farrar, *France's Biography*, p. 73.
28. Khadijah Ibrahiim, *Another Crossing* (Leeds: Peepal Tree Press, 2014), p. 49.
29. Fayola (Violet) Hendrickson, interview by the author, Leeds, 27 January 2020.
30. 'Lookya!', 1/5, 6 October 1972, WYL5041/41/4, WYAS1006, West Yorkshire Archive Service, Leeds.
31. Document titled 'EDUCATION: PRE SCHOOL' written by 'Annette Francis' for 'U.C.A. and Parents Meeting', dated 10 June 1973, WYL5041/41/4, WYAS1006, West Yorkshire Archive Service, Leeds.
32. Sources provide different start dates for the organisation, see document titled 'WHITE POWER STRUGGLE FOR CONTROL OF MULTI-RACIAL PLAY CENTRE', distribution dated as 22 November 1972, WYL5041/41/1, WYAS1006, West Yorkshire Archive Service, Leeds; Susan Pitter, *Eulogy* (Leeds: Jamaica Society Leeds, 2019), p. 41.

33. 'Warden at the Centre of Studley Grange Row', *Chapeltown News*, Octover 1972, p. 1.
34. 'WHITE POWER STRUGGLE FOR CONTROL OF MULTI-RACIAL PLAY CENTRE', 22 November 1972, WYL5041/41/1.
35. Notes titled 'STUDLEY GRANGE AGM', dated 24 November 1972, WYL5041/41/1, WYAS1006, West Yorkshire Archive Service, Leeds.
36. 'Studley Grange', *Chapeltown News*, June 1973, p. 3.
37. 'The Voice of Young Chapeltown: Saturday Self-education School', *Chapeltown News*, July 1974, p. 4.
38. Kehinde Andrews, 'Toward a Black Radical Independent Education: Black Radicalism, Independence and the Supplementary School Movement', *The Journal of Negro Education*, 83 (2014), pp. 8–11.
39. Bernard Coard, *How the West Indian Child Is Made Educationally Subnormal in the British School System: The Scandal of the Black Child in Schools in Britain* (London: New Beacon Books, 1971); Hendrickson, interview by the author, 27 January 2020.
40. Farrar, *France's Biography*, p. 50.
41. Hendrickson, interview by the author, 27 January 2020.
42. Chapeltown Black Women Writers' Group, *When Our Ship Comes in: Black Women Talk* (Yorkshire Art Circus, 1992), p. 30.
43. 'Black Parents' Movement: How We Organise', *Chapeltown News*, February 1976, pp. 3–4.
44. Notes titled 'CPAG Mtg', dated 24 June 1973, WYL5041/41/4, WYAS1006, West Yorkshire Archive Service, Leeds.
45. Notes from meeting with the Community Relations Council titled 'Cowper St Strike', dated 19 June 1973, WYL5041/41/4, WYAS1006, West Yorkshire Archive Service, Leeds.
46. 'CPAG Mtg', dated 24 June 1973, WYL5041/41/4.
47. 'Cowper St Strike', dated 19 June 1973, WYL5041/41/4.
48. 'The Enemy in Our Midst', editorial, *Chapeltown News*, June 1977, p. 2.
49. 'Verdicts a Victory', *Chapeltown News*, August 1976, p. 4.
50. Hendrickson, interview by the author, 27 January 2020.
51. 'U.C.A. Speaks out', *Chapeltown News*, November 1975, p. 4.
52. 'Verdicts a Victory', *Chapeltown News*, p. 1.
53. 'India: Tyranny and Resistance', *Race Today*, January 1976, pp. 42–3.
54. 'Verdicts a Victory', p. 7.
55. 'Elections in India: The Ballot and the Bullet. Carnival '77: The Threat Is from within', *Race Today*, February 1977, p. 2.
56. Robin Bunce and Paul Field, *Renegade: The Life and Times of Darcus Howe* (London: Bloomsbury, 2017), p. 259.
57. 'UCA – Whose Interest Do They Serve?' editorial, *Chapeltown News*, June 1977, p. 6.
58. Ibid.

59. 'The HAWK Strikes: U.C.A School Accused of Losing Direction & Vigour', published letter to the collective, *Chapeltown News*, January 1977, p. 8.
60. 'Our Building Not UCA Headquarters', editorial, *Chapeltown News*, February 1977, p. 2.
61. Arthur France quoted from an interview conducted by Max Farrar, in Farrar, *Arthur France's Biography*, p. 84.
62. 'The Enemy in Our Midst', *Chapeltown News*, p. 2.
63. These discussions became increasingly prominent, see Arun Kundnani, 'The Death of Multiculturalism', *Race & Class*, 43 (2002), pp. 67–72.
64. Ibid.; 'No Jail House Bonfire', editorial, *Chapeltown News*, September–October 1977, p. 2.
65. 'Bonfire Night', editorial, *Chapeltown News*, November 1976, p. 1.
66. 'No Jail House Bonfire', *Chapeltown News*, September–October 1977, pp. 2–3.
67. 'We Are in the Majority at Fords. Elections in Trinidad and Tobago. The Bonus Struggle in India', *Race Today*, November 1976, pp. 221–2.
68. Darcus Howe, 'Urban life – Darcus Howe Pays Tribute to an Unsung Heroine', republished in 'Sorrel and Black Cake: A Windrush Story', www.mylearning.org/stories/sorrel-black-cake-a-windrush-story/1121 (accessed 13 September 2021).
69. See 'The Voice of Young Chapeltown', *Chapeltown News*, p. 4.
70. These have not been cited as per the expressed wishes of the interviewees.
71. Paul, interview conducted by the author, 14 February 2020.
72. Institutionalised inequalities and experiences of racism have ensured that as of 2017, Black women constitute the group most likely to suffer from a mental disorder and Black men are ten times more likely to experience a psychotic disorder. See Institute of Race Relations, 'Health and Mental Health Statistics', https://irr.org.uk/research/statistics/health/ (accessed 3 February 2022).
73. Hendrickson, interview by the author, 27 January 2020. She suggests the following YouTube videos/playlists for those interested to know more about trauma: Dr Jewel Pookrum's *The Residue of Slavery* and Dr Amos Wilson's *A False Reality and The Educated Individual.*

12

Moving through Britain with Rastafari Women: Resistance and Unity in Babylon

Aleema Gray

Rastafari is a socio-spiritual movement that has formed part of the revolutionary cultural and political offshoots of Pan-Africanism. Since the emergence of the Rastafari, the movement has been entangled in the colonial landscapes of Britain and the possibilities of Africa. The origins of the movement can be found in Jamaica following the coronation of Haile Selassie I and Empress Mennen in 1930. During his coronation, Haile Selassie acquired the title 'Kings of Kings, Lords of Lords, Conquering lion of the tribe of Judah'. Seeing this as a prophetic moment, early adherents of the movement interpreted the crowning of a Black king and queen as a direct critique of British colonial rule, and the beginning of a new way to interpret the world outside of a Eurocentric gaze and thus, adopted the name 'Ras Tafari' – the pre-regnal title of Haile Selassie I.

Nearly a hundred years since the movement took hold in Jamaica, the experiences of Rastafari women remain largely unknown. At the forefront of many of the conflicting discussions on gender has been a preoccupation with examining whether Rastafari is a source of empowerment. While Obiagele Lake explores the tensions between subordination in the midst of liberation, Julia Subury reminds us to be critical of our search to portray Black women in a positive light. 'The desire to portray Black women in a positive light', she notes, 'leads potentially to silencing those aspects of Black women's organising which have been less than positive or outright destructive. The idealisation ultimately is of little benefit to Black women because it dulls ability to think critically about our actions.'[1]

The ability to document a history of Rastafari that doesn't reinforce epistemic violence or erasure demands putting forward a story that helps, as opposed to a story that hurts. This call adopts what Jalani Niiaah has recently referred to as 'sensitive scholarship'. Sensitive scholarship, as defined by Niiaah, represents a largely indigenous or local in spirit approach, 'rendered through the creative imagination with a kindred spirit congealed over time and cognition of the experience, in expressing and interpreting cultural reality'.[2] This not only involves re-reading the written literature of the movement within the context of its time, but also demands thinking through a history of the movement that is 'sensitive' to the struggle.

Written from the positionality of someone born *within* a Rastafari tradition between Jamaica and Britain, I am less concerned with demarcating what it means to be a Rastafari woman, and instead, am interested in thinking through how Rastafari ideals survived and manifested themselves amongst Black women in Britain. Britain provides an important site to not only examine the growth of the movement, but also Rastafari's organisational sentiments that reckoned with history.

MOVING *WITH* RASTAFARI WOMEN

> People want to say Rasta religion, but there is a Rastafari experience. The nucleus of this experience is Haile Selassie. This is what is confusing to sociologists, historians and anthropologists studying Rasta. They get it wrong because they are looking for a pattern to study … It is an experience that cannot be studied in the same way we study other religions.[3]

Scholarship on the Rastafari movement has undergone radical shifts in focus and style since the 1960s, largely reflecting the changing milieu in British race relations, as well as developments in anticolonial research, Black internationalism and Pan-African debates in the Caribbean. Early work on the movement situated

Rastafari within the context of Caribbean revivalism and labelled them as forming part of what Patrick Lee Fermor described as 'pseudo-Ethiopian' with destitute messianic flags of the Lion of Judah.[4] While Ethiopianism sits at the core of Rastafari's world-views, their positive evaluation of Africa and their criticism of the British Crown connected the movement to wider geographies of Black resistance and anticolonialism. By 1962, the Commonwealth population in Britain had increased from 2,000 in 1948 to 140,000. With large portions of Caribbean migrants venturing to Britain, they became the face of a declining Empire. The children of these migrants found themselves existing on the margins of Blackness and Britishness, and thus, by the 1970s were drawn closer to the revolutionary praxis found in Rastafari. Rastafari adopted a new expression in Britain; one which weaved the popular expression of Black Power of the 1960s with a reality of 'living in Babylon'. As argued by Stuart Hall, the Rastafari movement 'saved second-generation young Black people in British society'. It gave them a distinct identity with a historical gaze that broke through Eurocentric knowledge.

However, despite Rastafari's cultural appeal, the experiences of women have gleaned little academic attention. The lack of reliable data on the movement has reinforced their invisibility. In a report in 1976, Rastafari was said to have gained over 5,000 members. What remains unclear in several census reports, however, is how many members of the movement identified as women. For many, the idea that some women could find meaning in the teachings of H.I.M. Haile Selassie and Empress Menen seemed unfathomable. For others, the Rasta woman could only be seen through the lens of the Rasta-man. In this perspective, while they formed an important thread in preserving the royal lineage of the movement, women were secondary when it came to theological matters.

The absence of Rastafari women's voices reflects a broader assumption that their experiences were merely an extension of the Rasta-man. While such assumptions were put forward within Rastafari reasoning circles where men were seen as the 'head' and woman as the 'tail', they have been particularly reinforced among scholars who have either inadequately engaged with sufficient methods of researching Rastafari gendered relations or have centred their work on androcentric accounts of the movement's emergence in Jamaica.[5]

In Britain, this challenge has been reinforced by academic studies on the movement written by white sociologists who sought to examine the 'Rasta Rude Boy' as part of the problem of the inner city. *Rastaman*, the first book dedicated in its entirety to examining the emergence of the Rastafari movement in Britain, was written by Ernest Cashmore in response to the problems emerging out of Handsworth summarised in John Brown's report, *Shades of Grey*. Unlike Brown, Cashmore's major claims were that he had listened to the Rastafari brothers, uncovered new grounds, and wrote a book that was very much *for* them.[6] Yet, the title alone articulated a view that women were not an integral part of the movement. The majority of Cashmore's participants were Rastafari young men and thus reinforced an understanding of the movement as solely linked to masculinity. While he argued that Rastafari represented the desire for Black migrants to break away from a hostile world and find mutual support and encouragement from their Black community, the framework Cashmore drew on observed Rastafari as a trend among West Indian youth, who began forming the prototype of Black gangs.[7] While Black youth invariably took part in a culture of street crime, for Cashmore, it was the Rastas who transformed West Indian groups into the prototype Black gang. As he noted, 'gangs became the breeding ground for cultural forms'.[8]

Cashmore's work set the tone for a number of sensational pieces labelling the Rasta as a 'drug mafia' and 'lost tribe on a warpath'. Portrayals of fraught police relations and the 'Rasta Rude boy' promoted a number of hysterical essays depicting scandalous slurs of 'youth in crisis', 'Babylon falling' and 'Handsworth revolution' all under the banner of youth subcultures which examined a peculiar alliance between the Punk and the Rasta.[9] Aside from removing a representation of Rastafari as producers of knowledge forms, the literature reinforced an inherent masculinism within the movement which silenced the experiences of women. Often overlooked, for example, were the experiences of Rasta girls. Though rarely depicted within the scholarship, Rastafari girlhood has characterised the photography captured by Derek Bishton and Brian Homer as part of the self-portrait project in Handsworth in response to the tensions between Black youth and the police in 1978. The photograph of everyday life in Handsworth challenges depictions that have been at the forefront of Rastafari culture – sound systems, confrontations with Babylon, gang culture – to capture less idealised spheres of Rastafari life – community, friendship and play. At the forefront of the photograph, for example, are Rastafari girls dressed in what was seen as modern Rastafari attire; long skirts, tights and head ties. Their male counterparts appear to be shuffling behind them, which suggests less prevailing interpretations of Rastafari gendered dynamics where women were rarely seen. These girls were, as the image suggests, reclaiming their position and their right to be seen and their right to be in the frame.

For many girls growing up in Britain in the 1970s, Rastafari was a righteous act of self-love. As described by Barbara Hannah Makeda Blake, 'It was the start of a process of becoming Black that had begun as a reaction to racism.'[10] Blake, who became the first Black journalist to appear on British television in the 1960s, decided to 'opt out' of English society and moved towards 'trodding' the path of Rastafari in the early 1970s. She arrived in England enthusiastic to be a part of European cultural norms but was soon faced with the harsh reality of racism. Disillusioned with working in the corporate world, she returned to Jamaica after being hired to work on Chris Blackwell's 1971 film, *The Harder They Come*. The combination of racism combined with the teachings she received in Jamaica produced for Blake a 'new life'. This transition, as she describes, was an active way of pursuing Black political and economic practices with spiritual goals.

Like many Black women who arrived in Britain, Blake transformed herself from a devoted Black Englishwoman wishing her skin was white, into a Rasta woman, growing out her perm and loving her Black skin. This declaration of self-love was reinforced by the subgenre of reggae music, Lovers' Rock, that developed out of the experiences of 'growing up and out of Britain'. During a period where Black experiences had been seen in terms of criminality, the genre put forward what Lisa Palmer has argued as the 'ethic of loving blackness'. For women, this became a radical act.[11] Highly influenced by Jamaica's Rock Steady period, Lovers' Rock was characterised by its slowed tempo and romantic lyrics and stood in contrast to the masculine and militant representations in reggae music. The genre emerged following Louisa Mark's 1975 track, 'Caught You in a Lie', but gained significant prominence in 1979 when Janet Kay released 'Silly Games'. Written by Dennis Bovell, who coined the term 'Lovers' Rock', 'Silly Games' reached number two in the UK charts. The song became a declaration of Black love and coincided with the coming of age of Rastafari women. Songs such as Carol Thompson's 'Simply in Love with You' and Sheila Hylton's 'The Bed's Too Big without You', blended America R&B genres with roots reggae to secure a wider commercial audience. Aside from allowing women to profess their love for the unlawful dread, it allowed them to unapologetically express and embrace their sexuality within a Black womanist realm. Singers such as Judy Mowatt became foundational in articulating what it meant to be a Rastafari woman. Her Grammy nominated album entitled *Black Women* can be examined as the soundtrack of the Rastafari women's movement. Songs such as 'Sisters Chant' and 'Slave Queen' uncovered the realities of heartache, loneliness, intergenerational trauma and colonial memory. Through her lyrics, she encouraged Black women to 'remove the shackles from your mind', and acknowledged the Black woman as 'trodding one of life's roughest road'.

By the 1980s, many of the young girls pictured in Bishton's photography grew as women and pioneers in their own right. 'By the 1980s, we were coming out and moving upfront', as one sistren explained.[12] This does not limit women's involvement in the movement strictly to the 1980s, but it acknowledges a shift had taken place which saw Rastafari confronting the meaning of heritage. Prior to the 1980s, women were rarely recognised as an integral part of the Rastafari movement because scholars had interpreted its leadership, status, prophecy and healing traditions within a masculine realm. Quite often, such conclusions were based on Western perceptions of gender equality, which silenced the perspectives of Rastafari women, replacing them with lazy clichés depicting the Rastafari man as the archetypal 'Jamaican Rude-boy' and took little regard of how and why women were choosing to become Rasta.

The 1980s thus brought forward more promising attempts to platform Rastafari gendered relations. Carole Yawney, Imani Tafari Ama, Jeanne Christenson and Maureen Rowe took to the cause of exploring the previously overlooked experience of women in Rastafari.[13] Rastafari Womanism – a term coined by Christenson – found new meaning among scholars who sought to present a more nuanced picture of Rastafari gender relations. More emphasis was placed on the methodology of research which acknowledged the need to include more voices and perspectives of the movement from Rasta women and those sensitive to the struggle. Maureen Rowe's influential article on Rastafari women in Jamaica in 1980, for example, argued that the Rastafari women occupied a grey space. For Rowe, the grey space not only emerged through a process of creolisation, which merged national cultural behaviour such as the Rude Boy without any rational explanation, but it also represented an area that could *only* be explained by those inhabiting the grey space – in other words, to understand Rastafari, one needed to listen and include their perspective within their analysis.[14] Carole Yawney's *Rastafarian Sistren by the Rivers of Babylon*, and *Moving with the Dawtas of Rastafari* in 1994, furthered this argument by critiquing the notion of masculine dominance rooted in diasporic religious practices. Yawney contextualised Rowe's assertion that '*only* those who are Rastafari can best explain the position of women within the movement' by considering the role feminist scholars can play in questioning ethnocentrism. Published in 1994, her work documents the processes of change that were weaving Rastafari women together across borders, and connecting them in their *own* form of womanism rooted in the concept of 'livity' – the metaphysical and natural essence of simply being. For Yawney, livity provided a way to speak back to academic research on women, while negotiating her positionality as a white academic.[15]

The idea of moving *with* Rastafari demonstrates three important threads explored throughout this chapter. Firstly, the notion of moving *with* articulates the importance of the personal, that is, to truly understand the emergence of Rastafari womenism in Britain, one needs to situate them as agents of history. This not only involves addressing one's own positionality in relation to such narratives, but also involves entering the private spheres to recover interior archives that have been under-researched in the history of the Rastafari movement in Britain. Carving out a physical space in a hostile city acquired a sense of urgency for women, but such private spaces became an important part of their emergence in Britain as they were often utilised as important locations to wage their own forms of liberation campaigns. It provided them with an energetic Black space of knowledge exchange assembling circles of conviviality, support and organising. Within such circles, a practice of livity had formed. Often referred to as a lived philosophy, livity was more than a way of life; it was a practice of freeing oneself from the shackles of societal expectations, and instead, pursuing an understanding of self within a Devine realm.

Secondly, the idea of moving with Rastafari women acknowledges the fact that unlike other forms of feminist groups, Rastafari women had been defined through movement, or what Monique Bedasse has described as a 'trodding diaspora', where constructions around national boundaries collapse in an insistence on transnational connections across the African diaspora.[16] As explained by the Director of the Empress Menen Foundation, Mama Askale,

> This Britain is the port from which we came. From Africa, you have to come to Britain before you can leave to the Caribbean. Britain is an entry point and a departure point. The foundation of these colonial things from which we found ourselves is Britain. Britain is the Headquarters of colonial powers. Therefore, we can only get back our HQ from Britain. It is a place that says organise and centralise![17]

The spatial complexities articulated in Mama Askale's reasoning offer a new lens of historical enquiry that attends to the ways in which Rastafari women negotiated their placement in Britain. Britain was both an entry point and a departure point. As such, this chapter makes a point to emphasise Rastafari women '*in*' Britain', as opposed to 'British Rastafari women' to make the distinction clear. For most Rastafari women, they could never be British. Their refusal to participate and comply *with* British society and state created a powerful distance, which acknowledges the potential power of ordinary people in producing revolutionary currents.

For some West Indians, coming to England represented a homecoming of an overseas citizenry. For example, drawing on Lord Kitchener's song, 'London Is the Place for Me', Perry demonstrates the ways in which West Indians who came to Britain contested the boundaries of subject-hood and reasserted their right to *be* British.[18] However, such a phenomenon for Rastafari didn't exist. Rastafari refused to identify within the confines of British citizenship. Citizenship for the Rastafari had always been situated within a global complex landscape concerning heritage. Correspondingly, to be British meant rejecting the pain of one's ancestors. It was this sense of ambivalence towards the wider British society that offered women a space to explore a kind of decolonial practice that didn't see Britain or whiteness as its starting point.

And thirdly, women's *move* into Rastafari was interpreted as an ever-enduring cultural and political project. Within this, Rastafari was understood as a Black liberation project with Ethiopia, and more specifically, Haile Selassie I and Empress Menen at its centre. Situated in the heart of the colonial empire, their emergence in Britain was understood as manifest destiny which brought forward a reckoning with history. As explained by Sister Sheba,

> As a Rasta woman in the UK your hurdles were higher than other Black women. You not only had issues with the outside world, you had it within your race because of the colonised way of thinking that was embedded in many of us. I was strengthened by the fact that I felt that I was being true to myself, but also I was striking a blow for my woman ancestors who were forced to be a certain way. Part of the freedom that we had as young Rasta women was the fact that we could be true to our livity in our militant and African clothes rather than being true to what society's expectations of us were.[19]

In embracing Africa, Rastafari allowed women to unapologetically decentre whiteness and form their own decolonial liberation praxis that honoured the role of the Black woman. Rastafari offered women route and root to form new positive identifications with self. As Empress Zauditu explains, 'it was this love of my Black skin that led me to embracing Africa and Rastafari'.[20]

Cultural codes through dress, for example, provided a space to navigate their womanism, while recovering aspects of their ancestral history. While their hair represented their crown, their righteous guerrilla-chic battle dresses and combat jackets stood as a reminder that they could never be a part of *Babylon*. As explained by a sistren featured in a Elmina Davis' documentary film on Rastafari women, 'a woman doesn't just dread ... If a woman puts on her dreads, it is in defiance to what has already been ordained as beautiful, clean and upright.'[21]

OMEGA RISING

The 1980s signalled an important shift in the making of Black British identity. The decade had been characterised by violent confrontations with the state which further reinforced the fragility of Black life in Britain. The first incident took place in St Pauls in Bristol in 1980 following increasing police raids in a Black-owned cafe. In 1981, 13 Black teenagers died in a fire that broke out during a house party in New Cross. Though the cause of the fire remains unknown, it was strongly believed to be racially motivated. The following spring, a spread of riots in Brixton and Tottenham broke out, which led to a reckoning with the meaning of Black British identity. Though the causes of the outbreak of violence fall outside the scope of this chapter, it sets the tone for the kinds of political and cultural responses among Rastafari women. As explained by Sister Askala Miriam:

> We started this in the beginning of 1980 – why? Because we were looking at this and was seeing the decline. We weren't doing anything we were supposed to be doing. Sisters were dying. Youths were dying. Looking at this we thought we have something we could offer ... lets offer it before we destroy ourselves.[22]

The period inspired a reconfiguration of the meaning of heritage. In demonstrating the vulnerability of the state as a central body, the 1980s brought the process of decentring and democratising knowledge. In the same year, the Rastafari International group organised a conference at Brixton Town Hall on 23 July 1981. Attracting over

500 people, the main aim of the conference was to discuss matters relating to repatriation. The conference brought together several Rastafari organisations in Britain including Rastafari Universal Zion (RUZ), Tree of Life (TOL), Rasta Unity (RU) and Mind and Body and Soul (MBS). Representing RUZ, Jah Bones took to the cause of establishing the central mission of the movement. While some argued that repatriation should be the core focus, it was widely accepted that I-nity [unity] should be the spiritual foundations of the movement.[23]

The emphasis on I-nity provided an opportunity for women to reclaim their narrative. Following the conference, the Universal Rastafari Women's Group (URWG) was founded by Wolette Medhin and Sister Liveth Ivory. Wolette Medhin, who arrived in London in 1954 at the age of five, joined the Universal Black Improvement Organisation (UBIO) after she had her first son in 1966, at the age of 17. Founded in 1967 following the onset of the Black Power movement, UBIO was the first Rastafari-led organisation dedicated to discussing matters relating Black history and self-reliance. Based in Notting Hill, they established a UBIO youth wing, which taught lessons on the history of African and self-defence. Medhin's involvement in the UBIO is particularly important in demonstrating how the UBIO provided a space for young women to embrace their Blackness and African heritage as part of a process of redefining womanism. Medhin was one of the first Rasta women to participate extensively in community engagement in Britain. In setting up URWG, she had imagined it would be used as a source to remobilise a type of Rastafari womanism predicated on balance. The idea of balance centred a kind of womanism that looked at the synchronicity between feminine and masculine energies. It focused less on women's roles as separate, but rather as in harmony with her male counterparts.[24] The aims and objectives of URWG harnessed this notion of balance. It represented a sisterhood defined by unity, not uniformity. The organisation provided a space to also discuss pressing matters within the community such as polygamy, contraception and work but within a 'Godly' realm. The spiritual core of their organising must not be overlooked. As sister Claudette remembers,

> Usually Black organisations were led by academics, or intellectuals or activists, who somehow didn't feel safe within the perspective of Rastafari. Many of the Black women's group seemed to be run by students and people who were saying socialism or Marxism. To me none of it made sense, I wanted spiritual balance to resist Babylon.[25]

URWG became a springboard for splinter organisations such as the Tree of Life and Rastafari Advisory Service (RAS). Unlike the Ethiopian World Federation (EWF), which demanded formal membership through the constitution, such organisations embodied an element of openness in that they drew from the principles of self-reliance to support the wider community. As explained by Sister Rasheda, organisations such as Tree of Life, founded by Askala Miriam and the Rastafari Advisory Service (RAS), founded by Sister Liveth, provided a 'beacon of hope during a dreadful time'.[26] Such ambitions particularly resonated with Rastafari women, who would often have to stand as a pillar of strength during the absence of their male counterparts.

RAS's core aim was to provide services that would be of benefit to the Rastafari community. With two full-time members of staff, three part time-staff and volunteers, they provided educational programmes for parents and children, advice on health and well-being, training for unemployed youth and advice on legal matters. Every Wednesday they held an evening legal surgery with solicitors and barristers in attendance for free legal advice.

While RAS aimed at providing legal advice on matters relating to prison sentences, Tree of Life focused on community welfare and played an important role in developing community history projects. By 1981, Tree of Life initiated a fundraising campaign to bring Queen Mother Moore to London. Following the urban unrest in 1981, Tree of Life saw Queen Mother Moore's political activism and campaigns for reparations as an important source of strength for the Rastafari community in Britain. It was during this period that Moore argued for more research and awareness that could honour the African people who perished during slavery. In other words, the past was seen as a reparative tool that could be used to encourage a better sense of belonging and identification.

Inspired by Moore's declaration for more monuments and spaces that acknowledge the contributions of people from the African diaspora, the African People's Historical Monument (APHMF) was founded. The main goal looked at promoting and celebrating positive self-image and historical awareness within the community. APHMF original board members included Sister Askala Miriam and Makeda Coaston, Richie Riley and Habte Levi. Working with Len Garrison, they provided an important wing in the establishment of the Black Cultural Archives (BCA), one of the first funded institutes dedicated to collecting and preserving African and Caribbean heritage in Britain. Spaces such as the BCA were formed with a pride in being 'independent' from mainstream archival institutes and had been informed by and through the African and Caribbean community. As explained by Sister Askala:

> We are political in the sense that we are saying Africans for the Africans at home and abroad. Political because we are confronting the state. Even by the way we dress we are showing that we reject what the white man has always talked about in our politics.[27]

This increase in historical awareness re-energised Rastafari's organisational spirit and created an intellectually vibrant space to debate important strands of Rastafari livity; Pan-Africanism and repatriation, self-sufficiency and the role of women. Often providing the role of advisors and organisers, Rastafari women were at the heart of this shift.

In observing this shift, Yawney argued that the movement had reached 'a kind of critical density' by the 1980s, which accelerated the pace of international networking and consolidation, while bringing much more positive public attention to the movement.[28] In 1986, the second Rastafari international conference, *Rastafari Focus*, was hosted at the Commonwealth Institute. Organised by RAS under the banner Sister Liveth, the conference formed part of a week-long community programming and aimed to redress the damaging stereotypes of Rastafari. Described by Ras Mweya as the 'best coordinator and mediator', Sister Liveth Ivory was in the best position to take on the aims of the conference.[29] For Sister Liveth, the conference provided a timely opportunity to fill the gap in the insufficient information about the movement.

Rastafari Focus was seen as a historical event that connected regional and global networks of Rastafari brethren and sistren. For one, it challenged what had been seen as Rastafari women's disengagement with active strands of the movement. But it also harnessed a central part of Rastafari women livity – knowledge. A quest to glean more knowledge that could account for their experiences in Britain had led to the development of a number of reasoning circles. As explained by Sister Sheba, 'Sisterhood was our therapy and classroom.'[30] The *Wadada Educational Magazine*, for example, was set up in the 1980s to educate the community on the Rastafari livity. Initiated by writer, Sister Rasheda Malcolm, the magazine was different from the works of the *Voice of Rasta* and *JAHUG* as it included contributions from Rastafari sistrens. In a regular series entitled, 'Woman Reasoning', the publication dedicated a specific space to discuss matters concerning Rastafari women including work, lifestyle and polygamy.

By the end of the decade, the idea of sisterhood had found itself in the streams of artistic practices. Sister 'D' Elmina Davis' documentary film *Omega Rising* was released in 1988, which made visible the hidden archives of Rastafari. Sister D was one of the founder members of Ceddo Film workshop – one of several Black collectives set up in the 1980s with support from Channel 4, the Independent Broadcasting Authority, the British Film Institute and the Greater London Authority. Self-taught, she gleaned much of her radical tradition from her experiences working on the 1985 film documenting the Broadwater Farm riots, *The People's Account*. The film was the first to explore the interior histories of Rastafari women in Britain and the Caribbean, and thus made a significant leap in the fact that it created the material and cultural reference points needed to challenge the erasure of the Rastafari embodied experience within our cultural imagination. Prior to this point, Rastafari were merely subjects of Black British film who, while representing a central theme in the making of Black identity in Britain, were rarely behind the lens.

In honouring the 'Godly' realm of 'Alpha and Omega' as seen in the union between Empress Menen and Emperor Haile Selassie

I, Sister D centres the feminine realm of Rastafari in her recognition of 'Omega'. Throughout *Omega Rising*, the voices of Rastafari women take centre stage. Drawing on the Rastafari oral traditions of reasoning to allow each woman to speak on a horizontal platform. Rather than juxtaposing the experiences of the Rasta women against those of their male counterparts, the film records each woman in their environment on their own terms. We see some women defending their right to work or to dress in the way they please, while others are presented as wearing their headwrap and seeing to childcare duties. Though their journey in Rastafari is characterised by differences, they are united under a 'Godly' realm.

Indeed, Sister D was in the best position to document and interpret their experiences and memories; not only because she was working 'within' the community, but also because she had lived out the internal frustrations and celebrations of what it meant to be a Black Rastafari woman. In telling the stories of Rastafari women, and compiling them with archival material, Sister D succeeds in disentangling subjugated knowledges that had been silenced by patriarchy.

Rastafari women carved out their own womanist struggle in Britain. It is important to move beyond a preoccupation with defining what Rastafari woman is, and instead, examine the ways in which they negotiated space and place. Britain must be seen as a radicalising space where Rastafari ideals could flourish; not only because of its spatial and relational significance as the 'HQ of Babylon', but also because it constituted a site that offered a certain *kind* of political agency and autonomy for Rastafari women. The focus on the experiences of Rastafari women in Britain offers a way to explore Rastafari women as agents, as opposed to bystanders, of the movement. Through looking at Rastafari as part of a growing presence in Britain, we are opened up to the different textures of Black experiences during a formative period in the making of Black Britain – anger, displacement, invisibility and unity.

NOTES

1. Julia Sudbury, 'Kinds of Dreams: Black Women's Organisations and the Politics of Transformation', submitted for PhD, University of Warwick, Department of Sociology, April 1997, p. 77.

2. Jalani Niiah, 'Sensitive Scholarship: A Review of Rastafari Literature(S)', *Caribbean Quarterly*, 51 (2005), pp. 11–34 (p. 14).
3. Taken from the Jamaican Rastafari dub poet, Mutabaruka's talk for the University of Amsterdam's theology department, recorded in Michael Barnett, *Rastafari in The New Millennium* (Syracuse, NY: Syracuse University Press, 2014).
4. Patrick Leigh Fermor, *The Travellers Tree; A Journey through the Caribbean Islands* (London: John Murray, 1950).
5. Shamara Wyllie Alhassan, 'This Movement Is Not about Man Alone; Toward a Rastafari Woman's Studies', *IDEAS*, 15 (2020), pp. 8–26.
6. Ernest Cashmore, Ernest, *Rastaman: The Rastafarian Movement In England* (London: Allen and Unwin, 1979).
7. Ibid., p. 20.
8. Ibid., p. 85.
9. Len Garrison, *Black Youth, Rastafarianism and the Identity Crisis in Britain* (ACER Centre, 1980); John Plummer, *Movement of Jah People: Growth of the Rastafarians* (Birmingham: Press Gang, 1978); Dick Hebdige, *Reggae, Rastas and Rudies* (Birmingham: University of Birmingham Press, 1979).
10. Barbara Makeda Hannah Blake, *Growing up Daughter of Jah* (independently published, 2020), p. 35.
11. Lisa Amanda Palmer, '"*LADIES A YOUR TIME NOW!*" Erotic Politics, Lovers' Rock and Resistance in the UK', *African and Black Diaspora: An International Journal*, 4/2 (2011), p. 177.
12. Empress Zauditu, Interview by Aleema Gray, 18 January 2020.
13. See Christensen, Jeanne, *Rastafari Reasoning and the Rasta Woman: Gender Constructions in the Shaping of Rastafari Livity* (Lanham, MD: Lexington Books, 2014); Imani Tafari-Ama, 'Rastawoman as Rebel: Case Studies in Jamaica', in N.S. Murrell, W.D. Spencer and A.A. McFarlane (eds), *Chanting down Babylon: The Rastafari Reader* (Philadelphia, PA: Temple University Press, 1998), pp. 89–106; Carole D. Yawney, 'Moving with the Dawtas of Rastafari: From Myth to Reality', in B.J. Ferguson and T.E. Turner (eds), *Arise Ye Mighty People!: Gender, Class and Race in Popular Struggles* (Trenton, NJ: Africa World Press, 1994), pp. 65–74.
14. Maureen Rowe, 'The Women in Rastafari', *Caribbean Quarterly*, 26/4 (1987), pp. 13–21.
15. Yawney, 'Moving with the Dawtas of Rastafari', pp. 65–73.
16. Monique A. Bedasse, *Jah Kingdom: Rastafarians, Tanzania, and Pan-Africanism in the Age of Decolonization* (Chapel Hill, NC: University of North Carolina Press, 2017), p. 81.
17. Mama Askale, Interview by Aleema Gray, 17 October 2019.
18. Hammond Kenetta Perry, *London Is the Place for Me: Black Britons, Citizenship, and the Politics of Race* (Oxford: University of Oxford Press, 2016). p. 12.

19. Sis Sheba Levi, Interview by Aleema Gray, 11 January 2020.
20. Empress Zauditu, Interview by Aleema Gray, 18 January 2020.
21. *Omega Rising*. Film by Elmina Davis, Ceddo Film Collective (1988).
22. *Race Rhetoric Rastafari*. Film by Makeda Hannah Blake, Jamaica TV Productions (1982).
23. Jah Bones, 'Rasta Evidence to Scarman Inquiry', *Ethiopian World Federation, Voice of Rasta*, 35 (1982), p. 3.
24. See Alhassan, 'This Movement Is Not About Man Alone'.
25. Sister Claudette, Interview by Aleema Gray, in person, 13 September 2019.
26. Sister Rasheda Malcolm, Interview by Aleema Gray, in person, 14 January 2020.
27. Interview featured in the film *Race Rhetoric Rastafari* (1982).
28. Carole Yawney, 'Rasta Mek a Trod. Symbolic Ambiguity in a Globalizing Religion', in B.J. Ferguson and T.E. Turner (eds), *Arise Ye Mighty People! Gender, Class, and Race in Popular Struggles* (Trenton: NJ: Africa World Press, 1994), p. 166.
29. Ras Mweya Masimba, Interview by G. Bonacci, Addis Ababa, 18 August 2003.
30. Sis Sheba Levi, Interview by Aleema Gray, 11 January 2020.

13
The Black Parents' Movement

Hannah Francis

The Black Parents' Movement (BPM) was an exclusively Black-led political organisation that was formed as a response to the aggressive state racism and racial violence inflicted upon Black people in Britain during the 1970s. The organisation first formed in 1975, after a young man of Caribbean heritage, Cliff McDaniel, 'was beaten up by police' just a short distance from his secondary school in North London.[1] Many of the BPM's founding members had children that witnessed this incident, triggering a collaborative effort between Black youth and their parents to tackle Britain's racist police, schools and courts. To advance community interests, the founders drew inspiration from previous independent movements rooted in education and self-help.

Key initiatives such as the Black Education Movement (BEM) and the Black Supplementary School Movement (BSSM) were successful predecessors of the BPM. Founded in Haringey by activists John La Rose and Albertina Sylvester in 1965, the BEM sought to tackle the assumption that school students of Caribbean heritage would 'lower academic standards'.[2] The BEM influenced the establishment of the North London West Indian Association (NLWIA) and the Caribbean Education and Community Workers Association (CECWA). These organisations were made up of Black parents, educators and activists concerned about the state of their children's education and treatment at school. From 1969 to 1970, the BEM launched the Anti-banding campaign, opposing the use of banding against pupils of Caribbean heritage proposed by the Conservative-led council. This meant that 'pupils would be allocated to lower streams and dispersed around the borough' to avoid tainting the academic achievements of their white middle-class peers.[3] These assumptions about intelligence were rooted in a history of racist schooling and stereotypes of Black youth perpetuated by the British media and legislature.

In 1971, Grenadian educationalist and member of the CECWA Bernard Coard's pamphlet *How the West Indian Child Is Made Educationally Subnormal in the British School System* was published by La Rose's publishing house, New Beacon Books. Coard's research identified that 'three-quarters of all the immigrant children in … [educationally subnormal/ESN schools] are West Indian' in Britain.[4] To combat this, the founders of the BEM extended their call to action and opened Saturday schools to interrogate 'the normative mainstream discourse on "race" and education'.[5]

Moreover, with the revival of the 1824 Vagrancy Act during this period, 'the experience of the young at school began to be mirrored on the streets … the young, were virtually assumed to be criminal or potentially criminal by police on the streets'.[6] This Act, also dubbed 'SUS', gave police free reign to stop and search people without proof of their criminality, often resulting in Black youth bearing the brunt of racially motivated police violence. To counter this, alongside the work of the BEM, the Scrap Sus Initiative was formed in the 1970s 'in a Black woman's front room in Deptford' to provide legal support for falsely accused young Black people.[7]

As an extension of the groundwork laid by the campaigns above, the BPM promoted ideas of self-help through education and community alliances. The BPM 'fought many cases … [against] the police using the principles that cases should be organised with not for' young people.[8] Their collaborative efforts on many local and national campaigns sought to maintain the independence of their activity against their main opponent – the British state. Whether against the courts, the police or schools, the BPM campaigned solely in the interests of Black workers, youth, migrants and the unemployed.

While the BPM originated in North London, Black parents had been organising themselves across the country, most actively from 1975 until the mid-1980s. It would be impossible to cover all the national campaigns of the BPM, let alone its interests in global, independent Black movements.

THE INCIDENT

On Thursday 17 April 1975, a well-known student at the George Padmore Supplementary School (GPSS), named Cliff McDaniel, was on his lunch break with his two friends, Chris Adegbite and Keith La Rose. McDaniel and his friends were quickly spotted and apprehended by three police officers. As reported in the May 1975 issue of the Black-led radical magazine *Race Today*:

> They were waving to friends when a police car, driven by PC Ryan David, whose number is Y650, and with two other policemen in it, passed them and turned up the next corner at Interwick Road. Then almost immediately it reversed back to Weston Park and drew up beside the boys. PC Ryan David then provoked an incident.[9]

Despite McDaniel's efforts to mediate the situation, even suggesting the officers search him in his headmaster's office, more police were called, and he was subsequently arrested. McDaniel was charged with 'insulting behaviour and likely to cause a breach of the peace and with assaulting … Ryan David' and further beaten after his arrest.[10] The evident vitriol with which Hornsey police acted was expected. Staff at the Stationers School had known PC Ryan David to have 'abused and punched McDaniel' prior to this incident but reports were not taken seriously.[11] With a local history of Black educationalist organisations campaigning for the nurturing of their children in Haringey schools, it is unsurprising that many concerned Black parents had heard of the incident and took matters into their own hands.

THE BPM

The Black Parents' Movement (BPM) was founded the day of the incident and on Sunday 20 April 1975 many of its founding members who were affiliated with local supplementary schools held their first meeting.[12] There are two pertinent schools to name here: the George Padmore and Albertina Sylvester Supplementary Schools, founded in 1969 by John La Rose and Sylvester herself. Born in Arima, Trinidad and Tobago, La Rose grew to prominence as a teacher, activist and trade unionist. He moved to Britain in the early 1960s and settled in North London. Sylvester arrived in London in 1957 from Grenada and soon after married Albert. According to the George Padmore Institute (GPI), Sylvester 'had met John … through some meetings about the banding … in Haringey … in the late sixties'.[13] As a teacher, matriarch and 'a black working-class woman', Sylvester was a pioneer in the education movement and highlights the presence of women in the establishment of the BPM.[14] Other founding members included Cliff McDaniel's mother Violet and brother Egbert, the Sylvesters, and Roxy Harris who was a qualified schoolteacher of Sierra Leonean descent and began teaching at the George Padmore Supplementary School in 1975 after meeting La Rose.[15] The BPM formed a Steering Committee soon after establishing the organisation, chaired by La Rose, it also included Sylvester, Harris, fellow Black teacher Sebastian Paul, McDaniel's parents Violet and Egbert, founding members of the Race Today Collective Darcus Howe and Leila Hassan, and BPM treasurer Akua Rugg. A monthly membership council was also launched in which £2 fees went towards funding their campaigns.

THE BSM

Soon after the founding of the BPM, a youth section was formed named the Black Students' Movement (BSM) made up predominantly of attendees of local supplementary schools, or children of BPM members including Victor Sylvester, as well as Keith and Michael La Rose. On 23 April 1975 the founding meeting of the BSM took place with '20 young people and students' in attendance alongside two members of the BPM.[16] Most students were in their final year of secondary school, or attending college, with little experience of being 'involved in organised political activity'.[17] However, the students had some awareness of the political activity of groups like the BPM, the Race Today Collective (RTC) and the Black Liberation Front (BLF). Although the BSM could be misconstrued as the youth wing of the BPM, it wanted to retain its autonomy and thus sought guidance not only from parents but also from those other Black collectives too. The RTC was important in the consolidation of student power as its members were often present during the early stages of the development of the BSM. The activity of the BPM and the BSM was closely followed and publicised in the magazine. Evidently, the McDaniel incident was the springboard that birthed two autonomous organisations reliant upon methods of self-help, political education and collaboration.

THE CLIFF MCDANIEL CAMPAIGN

A defence campaign began to grow soon after Cliff McDaniel's arrest and was formally launched in preparation for his trial in June. In the May 1975 issue of *Race Today* the BPM released a statement on the incident and to:

> … invite Black Parents who share our anxieties to contact us … we urge the teachers and the schools to take a stand against police brutality … We also call on the Haringey Education Authority … to take action on this matter.[18]

The BPM's Steering Committee organised a meeting with the Chairman of the Haringey Education Committee (HEC), and Chief Education Officer. According to BPM member and teacher Rex Dunn, the 'meeting … led to no action and turned sour when the latter discovered that these black parents were not middle-class "uncle toms" such as those who serve on the community relations councils'.[19] The BPM had put forward four topics of concern prior to the meeting including the reconsideration of police presence in schools, a pressing concern at the heart of the Cliff McDaniel campaign. While the HEC had put an end to banding in 1970 in the Labour-led borough, Black parents' concerns regarding the treatment of children by teachers and police went unresolved. Dunn's critique of community relations councils underpinned the consensus of politically active Black members of the working class, that neither the Labour nor the Conservative Parties were willing to respond to their community effectively. Thus, the BPM launched a campaign fund, picketed HEC meetings, gathered witness statements and organised political defence for McDaniel in preparation for his trial.

THE CLIFF MCDANIEL TRIAL AND APPEAL

Outside Highgate Magistrates Court on 26 June 1975, 30 people carried out a silent picket, with a further 50 students and parents inside.[20] McDaniel had received legal support from Darcus Howe and from Scottish barrister Ian Macdonald, who had famously defended members of the Mangrove Nine in 1971. However, McDaniel was convicted of insulting behaviour and assault, despite the substantial evidence gathered by the BPM to prove his innocence. As stated in the July issue of *Race Today*: 'It was a political trial in that Cliff ... represented the black community who in turn felt represented by him.'[21]

Over the summer months, the movement banded together to prepare for the appeal of this unjust verdict. The BPM organised a press conference at the Keskidee Arts Centre on 1 July, published a document of demands insisting for an investigation to be carried out on Hornsey police and for an appeal to be granted.[22] After the appeal was formally presented in September, a hearing was confirmed for 2 October at Middlesex Crown Court, where the verdict was quashed. There simply was not enough evidence against McDaniel to find him guilty. The victory was reported by many publications, including *West Indian World*, *Morning Star* and *Race Today* and praised by many allies, including David Coetzee of the Communist Party.[23]

While a two-year unsuccessful investigation was launched by the appeal hearing judge into Hornsey police for misconduct and for the expulsion of PC Ryan David, this did not mire the victory for the BPM. Within the first six months of its existence, the movement was able to successfully fight against the oppressive courts system and abusive policing. Their adoption of collaborative tactics such as pickets, crowdfunding, demonstrations and public conferences played an integral part in the final decision, while the entire case was further evidence of the state's criminalisation of Black youth.

PRINCIPLES AND METHODS OF ORGANISATION: LONDON SECTIONS AND EXPANSION

It was the McDaniel campaign that had spurred discussions about what type of organisation the BPM wanted to be and how it might expand. Its members dedicated much of their time to the drafting of its 'Principles and Methods of Organisation' document, outlining the initial basic principles of membership, the responsibility of members, finance and fundraising, security, suspension, or expulsion of members and changing the principles and rules of the organisation. While the document was a work in progress, the need to establish further sections was a necessity. The second section of the BPM was formed in Hackney in 1975, after an incident at Clapton Comprehensive School. Four Black schoolgirls, including sisters Glenda and Joyce Caesar, were detained by their teachers in their classroom. The teachers physically assaulted them and called the police who 'showered' them 'with racist insults' and arrested them for no lawful reason.[24] When the sisters were charged with assault, the BPM was quickly able to build membership in the area, to establish a fact-finding team and to compile their own set of evidence independent of the school and police.

In 1976 the Ealing Concerned Black Parents and Youth Movement (ECBPYM) was founded by Guyanese activists, Jessica and Eric Huntley. The outbreak of violence in Ealing at the hands of the police was reported as commonplace in a study published in 1973 by the Runnymede Trust. It concluded that 'the probability of conflict between West Indian youth and the police is high but a demand for independent black organising was absent'.[25] Thus, in 1976, the ECBPYM published a handbill in 1976 entitled *Police, Schools and the Black Community in Ealing* after a 17-year-old Black teenager was beaten and arrested by plain-clothes police officers when he and his friends were catching a bus. The bill asserted that 'SUS is the most frequent and notorious charge laid against black youth'[26] and declared that 'concerned parents and young people in the borough of Ealing must take action now and oppose the increased police harassment'.[27] Like the McDaniel campaign, the production of statements and supplementary material was an essential method in lobbying support, and the ECBPYM were formally absorbed into the BPM as a section in 1977.

In September 1979 the BPM, RTC, the Black Youth Movement (BYM – formerly The Black Students' Movement) and the Bradford Black Collective (BBC) – became known as the 'Alliance'. Members of the 'Alliance' came together to support political and social campaigns unique to the advancement of Black community interest. As stated in the final draft of 'Principles', the BPM sought to 'take all the organisational steps to maintain a policy of close coordination and alliance with the Black Youth Movement' to perpetuate the shared notion of self-reliance adopted by the adult members of the 'Alliance'.[28] The following month, the BPM held its first annual conference and announced the official adoption of its principles.

THE MANCHESTER BLACK PARENTS' ORGANISATION

The BPM had secured monumental victories in London, and its presence was beginning to stretch across the country too with one of its largest sections forming in Bradford in 1976. By 1978, Manchester Black Parents' Organisation (MBPO) was founded by Gus John, a Grenadian youth and community organiser who had settled in the city in 1971. John had set up the first Black supplementary school in Handsworth, Birmingham, by 1968, and became an active member in BPM's initial organisation in London.[29] The MBPO 'was formed against the background of struggles in education waged by the North London West Indian Association, the Caribbean Education and Community Workers Organisation, and The Black Parents' Movement'.[30] Clearly, the success of the BPM in London informed the practices of the MBPO. Ten members of the Black working-class communities in Moss Side, Whalley Rage and Hulme founded the movement, and all had deep connections with Manchester's history of Black independent organisation.

Early collaborators of the MBPO included the Manchester Black Women's Cooperative (MBWC), later renamed the Abasindi Cooperative in 1980. The organisation itself sought to 'retrain unsupported and unqualified black mothers in the office skills needed to re-enter the workplace in Manchester'.[31] Often Black women's labour went underpaid in the city, and these women either had children or extended family to provide for, alongside organising against the racism of the state. The MBWC thus carried out a lot of work to ensure that Black women were trained to undertake better employment opportunities, to afford housing and afford to reside in the city. The MBWC was founded in Moss Side by sisters Ada Phillips, Coca Clarke and Kathleen Locke in 1975 whose father was a Nigerian-born seaman and their mother a white woman from Lancaster, who had lost her job as a college teacher in Blackpool as her employers had discovered she was married to an African.[32] As a young woman, Locke was a contemporary of Nkrumah and involved in the 1945 Pan-African Congress in Manchester, making her a part of the Black political fabric of the city.[33]

THE STEPHEN LOCKE ACTION COMMITTEE

One of the MBPO's first campaigns was in November 1979 in defence of Kath Locke's son Stephen, a student at Wilbraham school near Moss Side. An unnamed student from St. Bede's College, a school in Whalley Range, was 'allegedly attacked' at a bus stop by students from Wilbraham and Chorlton High.[34] There had been a long-standing history of contempt from the predominantly middle-class student body of St. Bede towards those attending schools in Moss Side, signifying a significant class divide. Stephen was among five young Black boys aged 12–14 that were identified by plain-clothes police and their school deputies as the attackers, and they were charged with assault and actual bodily harm.

The Stephen Locke Action Committee was formed by his family and the MBPO. A letter from Gus John detailing the incident was circulated in April 1980 and a public meeting was called. The committee gathered statements from student witness Anesta Guishard, accused students Stephen, Richard Thomsett, Leslie Caine and Raymond Oloma, as well as Kath Locke and Raymond's mother. From the statements it was deduced that those charged were not arrested or even seen at the incident location, nor were their parents made aware of the incident by the schools. The collaboration of school deputies and police was abundantly clear. On 10 April, a meeting of 25 was held to discuss the proceedings of Stephen's case including members of the Abasindi Coop, Gus John and John La Rose. The minutes, recorded by Kath, outlined how integral it was that 'Stephen is playing a role on the committee'.[35] Much like McDaniel's case, with the help of solicitors Ian Macdonald and Rhys Vashu, Stephen was an active participant in the discussion of his case and encouraging support for the other boys accused.

Seven months after the incident, Locke was to appear at Manchester Juvenile Court for trial. Outside the court, a picket had been organised by members of the MBPO and various London BPM members who had travelled to support Locke. During the proceedings, the two St. Bede's students that were assaulted were called to the stand but fortunately, neither one of them identified Locke as their attacker. Furthermore, while the police had alleged that Locke voluntarily stated that he had stood on the hand of one of the St. Bede's students, that very student contested this information. This evidenced the fabrication of Stephen's first statement given to the police, an obvious tactic utilised by officers in their attempts to frame innocent Black youth. Upon his arrest, Constable Pugh had tricked both Stephen and his mother into signing a statement with false facts, and yet Pugh contended he put 'no pressure'[36] on them to do so. After a short prosecution, the counsel concluded that the evidence was insufficient, and the charges were dropped. The Stephen Locke campaign was supported by the established London sections of the BPM, so much so that they invited the MBPO to establish themselves as the Manchester Section of the movement in 1980. The Manchester BPM went on to continue to support young Black students, immigrants and women who were threatened by violent policing, volatile educational environments and hostile immigration legislation, and even formed a local branch for the Black Youth and Student Movement (BYSM) in September 1985.

BOOKSHOP JOINT ACTION COMMITTEE, 1977–83

One of the BPM's longest-lasting campaigns was the Bookshop Joint Action Committee (BJAC), formed in response to several violent, racist attacks upon Black-owned and socialist bookshops across the country. As stated by John La Rose, New Beacon's founder, 'colonial policy was based on the withholding of information ... Publishing, therefore, was a vehicle to give an independent validation of one's own culture, history, politics – a sense of self.'[37] The presence of Black bookshops and publishers ensured that cultural institutions existed for Black youths, workers, parents and professionals during a time which saw the drastic rise of fascist organisations. The BJAC was active from 1977 until 1983, and saw the BPM become part of one of the organisation's most significant joint actions.

New Beacon was founded in 1966 by John La Rose and his partner Sarah White; its premises were first located in Hornsey but were moved to Finsbury Park the following year. According to Gus John, 'New Beacon is one of the most important and influential institutions in post-war Britain.'[38] It was named after Trinidadian journal *Beacon*, which 'carried short stories ... [and] novels based on the struggles of workers and peasants that were framed within the politics ... of race and class in colonial Trinidad'.[39] Informed by the literary scene and political landscape of Trinidad and Tobago, La Rose's Black-owned bookstore and publishing house became the first one of its kind in Britain.

Following suit was Jessica and Eric Huntley's publishing company Bogle L'Ouverture, founded in 1968. The premise of its founding rested upon the global 'protest against the banning of the political activist and scholar, Walter Rodney, from re-entering Jamaica' and its impact upon the growing radicalised diaspora.[40] In 1974, the Huntleys opened up the Bogle L'Ouverture Bookshop in West Ealing and renamed the premise after Walter Rodney following his assassination in 1980.[41] The Huntleys and La Rose shared a collective goal, their activism in Britain perpetuated the need for global recognition of a socialist and Black revolutionary tendency and education as a key promoter. In an interview with Harry Goulbourne, Jessica Huntley stated that 'that bookshop was very important ... because I communicated with people ... teachers would drop in, just ordinary parents, kids would come in ... and they wanted to know about history, African history'.[42] These bookshops, alongside others across London, Manchester and Bradford served as cultural hubs in cities with rapidly growing political alliances.

On 15 March 1973, the fascist National Front (NF) had 'firebombed' a Black bookshop in Brixton named Unity Books.[43] The news of this tragedy was widely circulated in publications such as *Race Today* and *Black Scholar* but was barely mentioned in the mainstream media. The NF was founded in 1967 by Arthur Kenneth Chesterton, a far-right journalist. Following Conservative MP Enoch Powell's 'Rivers of Blood' speech on 20 April 1968, the NF saw an opportunity to expand and by the October 1974 General Election, the NF had secured 113,843 votes averaging to 3.1 per cent of the total vote.[44] Much like the persistence of brutal policing, the NF's presence sought to cause physical harm and intimidation towards Black communities. Both the NF and police targeted Black people, and their cultural institutions such as clubs, supplementary schools and bookstores.

By 1977, numerous Black-owned bookshops across Britain had been attacked by the NF. On 19 and 20 February, the first attack of Bogle L'Ouverture was carried out, with 'racist signs … smeared on windows and doors … [and] literature of [the] National Party … left behind'.[45] Following the attack, Jessica Huntley wrote to Home Secretary, Merlyn Rees, in March requesting a meeting to address the lack of police or state investigation into the attack on Bogle L'Ouverture. As expected, she received no response and mainstream media too had failed to address the further disabling of Black educational initiatives.

THE BPM AND THE BOOKSHOP JOINT ACTION COMMITTEE

By September 1977 several bookshops that had fallen victim to these attacks sent an urgent telegram to the Home Secretary to notify him of numerous threatening phone calls. Later that month, ten bookshops wrote to the Home Secretary 'outlining the escalation of fascist terror' that had been unleashed with free reign against Black community spaces, receiving merely a card of acknowledgement in return.[46] Meanwhile, the Greater Manchester Police were granted £250,000 of state money to protect the National Front March which took place in Hyde on 8 October. It was abundantly clear that the British state was continuing to dismiss the danger that fascist groups posed to not solely Black, but also South Asian and migrant communities and their independent spaces. After holding a meeting between bookshops and delegates of the BPM on 17 October, Bogle L'Ouverture, New Beacon, Grassroots, Unity Books, Soma Books, Headstart Books & Crafts and Sabarr Books formed the Bookshop Joint Action Committee (BJAC). The BJAC penned a press statement outlining the horrendous attacks that had taken place thus far, and their attempts to contact the Home Office and the Metropolitan Police. With the BJAC underway, Bogle suffered two more blows to their store in October and December of 1977, with paint splattered everywhere and white supremacist literature left behind. By the year's end, 22 attacks had been carried out, but the BJAC were then ready to collaborate with the BPM and the RTC to launch their joint campaign.[47]

In January 1978, the BJAC held a successful picket outside the Home Office to protest against their dismissive attitudes towards the rise of fascist attacks on bookshops. Jessica Huntley sent another letter to Merlyn Rees criticising his position as a Labour Party representative. She stated, 'How can a Labour Home Secretary ... whose party ... warns ... about the dangers to this society of the National Front and other fascist organisations, so conspicuously fail in his duty to meet those, who are asking to meet him to discuss this matter?'[48] Huntley's letter outlines the severity of the risk of the far-right and emphasised that the Labour Party, the party of the people, the workers, were yet to respond. The Labour Party's track record of police and community relations, particularly with Black Britons and migrants, was poor. The party had set up the Police Complaints Board under the Police Act of 1976, which sought to oversee complaints against police, but rarely were Black people taken seriously when they reported the brutality they faced. On the same day this letter was sent, Huntley led a successful picket outside the Home Office which saw 'some 60 people' in attendance.[49] In a letter addressed to 'Friends' of the BJAC, Huntley went on to state how many people wrote to the committee offering solidarity, including 'schools, libraries, bookshops, trade union branches, publishers, journals, lawyers, writers, artists and readers'.[50] After the turnout at this picket in January, more and more institutions came together to support the BJAC including W.H. Smith, the *Guardian*, *The Times*, Sangster's Book Store, Grassroots Books and the National Association for Multi-racial Education.[51]

THE BPM AND THE INTERNATIONAL BOOK FAIR OF RADICAL BLACK AND THIRD WORLD BOOKS

Although the activities of the BJAC had quietened after the attacks of 1979, the committee had evidently highlighted the necessity of Black radical literature and independent cultural spaces. Subsequently, numerous members of the movement became involved in 1981 in the organising of the first International Book Fair of Radical Black and Third World Books, or the Black Book Fair. According to Gus John, 'New Beacon, Bogle-L'Ouverture Publications and Race Today Collective ran an international book fair and book fair festival that spanned all five continents and was located in Bradford/Leeds, Manchester and London.'[52] Such activities would continue until 1995.

By 1983, the BJAC were back in action after the first successful year of the book fair. On 13 January, Jessica Huntley arrived at the Walter Rodney bookshop and was confronted with graffiti reading 'We are coming reds ... Wogs out' amongst many more horrifying racialised slurs. The store was also attacked just a few days later on 16 January, 'the third attack' since the store was renamed. The Huntleys reinvigorated the BJAC and called for a public meeting to be held on 22 February at the Ealing Town Hall. Speakers included those from New Beacon, Bogle L'Ouverture Publishers, the National Union of Teachers (NUT) and the Black Parents' Movement. While very little headway was made in terms of arrests, the BJAC and BPM contributed significantly to the opposition the National Front came up against. With the growth of anti-fascist organisations across Britain, 'the sheer quantity of violence meted out to the NF contributed to a high turnover in NF membership and the demoralisation of those who stuck with it'. As a result of the militant action taken against the NF, it was considerably weakened.

This chapter reflects just a snippet of the history of the Black Parents' Movement and the place it occupies in Britain's Black radical tradition. The strength of community organisation, self-help and reliance was key to its success, and the victories of the BPM were victories for the Black community. By uniting the efforts of parents and youth and its push for the advancement of community interest through education, the BPM concretised a legacy in the wider social and political history of Britain. While the BPM has remained in the shadows of global Black Power and the Black Supplementary School Movement, its activity has shaped current discourse on the ever-lasting struggle against violent policing and the racism of British schooling. The BPM is survived by some of its key participants, Gus John, Akua Rugg, Roxy Harris, Leila Hassan and others, their oral testimony and the ephemeral materials of the movement are stored at the London-based, Black-led archives, the George Padmore Institute and the Black Cultural Archives.

NOTES

1. Michael and Trevor Philips, *Windrush: The Irresistible Rise of Multi-Racial Britain* (London: HarperCollins, 1999), p. 257.
2. George Padmore Institute (GPI), 'The Black Education Movement 1965–1988', *Our Collection*, www.georgepadmoreinstitute.org/collections/the-black-education-movement-1965–1988 (accessed 1 May 2021).
3. Sarah Garrod, Nicole-Rachelle Moore and Sarah White, *Dream to Change the World: The Life and Legacy of John La Rose (the Book of the Exhibition)* (London: George Padmore Institute, 2018), p. 14.
4. Bernard Coard, *How the West Indian Child Is Made Educationally Subnormal in the British School System* (Kingston: McDermott Publishing, 2021), p. 4.
5. Diane Reay and Heidi Safia Mirza, 'Uncovering Genealogies of the Margins: Black Supplementary Schooling', *British Journal of Sociology of Education*, 18/4 (1997), p. 477.
6. Ellis Cashmore and Eugene McLaughlin, *Out of Order? Policing Black People* (London: Routledge, 1991), p. 154.
7. Beverly Bryan, Stella Dazie and Suzanne Scafe, *The Heart of the Race: Black Women's Lives in Britain* (London: Virago Press, 1985), p. 160.
8. Garrod et al,. *Dream to Change the World*, p. 19.
9. 'Parents against Police Harassment', *Race Today*, 7/5 (May 1975), p. 101.
10. Ibid., p. 101.
11. 'Police Attacks on School Students', 16 June 1975, GPI, BPM/1/3/1/3, p. 1.
12. Overview of the BPM, 1976–1977, GPI, BPM/1/1/4.
13. *Black Supplementary Schools and the George Padmore Institute Archives*, 2 June 2021, GPI, www.youtube.com/watch?v=JBzrz8-s6ks (accessed 9 June 2021).

14. Ibid.
15. Foundation of the George Padmore and Albertina Sylvester Black Supplementary Schools, 15 August 1972–14 June 1974, GPI, BEM/3/1/2/1.
16. BSM Report, 19 February 1978, GPI, BPM/1/1/2, p. 1.
17. BSM Discussion Paper, 9 October 1975, GPI, BPM/1/1/3, p. 2.
18. 'Parents against Police Harassment', *Race Today*, p. 101.
19. 'Police Attacks on Black School Students' Draft Report, 16 June 1975, GPI, BPM/1/3/1/3.
20. 'The Verdict Is Unacceptable', *Race Today*, 7/7 (July 1975) p. 148.
21. Ibid., p. 148.
22. Parents Movement Against Police Harassment, 'Hornsey Police and Black Students: Time to Call a Halt' leaflet, July 1975, GPI, BPM/2/6/1/1, p. 5.
23. Newspaper articles on Cliff McDaniel Campaign, May–October 1975, GPI, BPM/5/1/1/10.
24. BPM Clapton School Girls Statement, July 1975, GPI, BPM/2/6/1/1.
25. Dr Stanislaus Pullé, *Police Immigrant Relations in Ealing* (Runnymede Trust, 1 November 1973), p. 88.
26. Ealing Concerned Black Parents and Youth Movement, 'Police, Schools and the Black Community in Ealing', 1976, GPI, BPM/2/6/1/2.
27. Ibid.
28. BPM Alliance: Working File: Principles and Methods of Organisation (annotated), 5 March 1981–26 March 1985, GPI, BPM/1/2/1, p. 5.
29. Gus John, personal comment via email, 26 March 2021.
30. The Black Parents' Movement and the Black Youth Movement, Manchester, 26 September 1985, GPI, BPM/3/2/1/1.
31. Jessica White, 'Black Women's Groups, Life Narratives, and the Construction of the Self in Late Twentieth-Century Britain', *The Historical Journal* (2021), p. 1.
32. Francesca Nottola, 'The Legacy of Black Power in Moss Side: Activist Coca Clarke Tells Her story', *The Meteor*, 2 September 2018; George Bankes, 'Exploring Africa in Manchester', *Journal of Museum Ethnography*, 13 (2001), p. 24.
33. Bankes, 'Exploring Africa in Manchester', p. 24.
34. Stephen Locke Action Committee, 'Schools Join Police in Terrorising School Students: No Bogus Charges against Stephen Locke' Press Statement, 9 May 1980, GPI, BPM/3/2/3/9, p. 1.
35. Report on Stephen Locke Action Committee, 10 April 1980, GPI, BPM/3/2/3/9.
36. Draft Report of the Stephen Locke Action Committee, July 1980, GPI, BPM/3/2/3/10, p. 7.
37. Garrod et al., *Dream to Change the World*, p. 6.
38. Gus John, A Public Lecture at the British Library to mark 50 Years of New Beacon Books, 3 December 2016, Gus John (via email), p. 1.

39. Ibid., p. 2.
40. Philippa Ireland, 'Laying the Foundations: New Beacon, Bogle L'Ouverture Press and the Politics of Black British Publishing', *E-rea*, 11/1 (2013), p. 25.
41. Alison Donnell, *Companion to Contemporary Black British Culture* (London: Routledge, September 2002), p. 53.
42. Jessica and Eric Huntley interviewed by Harry Goulbourne, 20 May 1992, LMA/4463/F/07/01/001/F.
43. *The Black Scholar*, 9/10 (July/August 1979), p. 45.
44. Michael Higgs, 'From the Street to the State: Making Anti-fascism Anti-racist in 1970s Britain', *Race and Class*, 58/1 (2016), p. 69.
45. Bookshop Joint Action Committee Press Statement, January 1978, LMA/4462/J/01/002/001, p. 1.
46. Ibid., p. 4.
47. *Race Today*, 10/3 (March 1978), p. 51.
48. Letter to Mr Merlyn Rees, 17 January 1978, LMA/4462/J/01/002/001.
49. Ibid.
50. Ibid.
51. Various letters, January–February 1978, LMA/4462/J/01/002/001; Various letters, March–July 1978, LMA/4463/J/01/006.
52. John, 50 Years of New Beacon Books, p. 10.

14

Mollie Hunte – Educational Psychologist, Educator and Activist: What Archival Collections Can Tell Us

Rebecca Adams

Archives can be a key source in gaining a better insight into societies of the past. The role of archive services and the archivist is to collect, appraise and preserve societal memory and provide access to collections for all sections of society. In the UK there are a wide array of archives: the national archives of the government, county record offices, university archives, specialist archive services and business archives. The vast majority of these are open to the public for free access. Where there was once a lack of diverse voices within the archive there is now a growing awareness of the value of archives to highlight marginalised voices.

Despite there being gaps in mainstream archive collections especially around under-represented groups, there has been a determined effort to create institutions that cater to marginalised people. One of the earliest relating to Black British history is the Black Cultural Archives co-founded by Len Garrison and others in 1981 to provide a structure where Black children could have representation of their own histories in Britain and beyond.[1] Today the archive has a permanent building in Brixton's Windrush Square, housing over 3,500 records and 41 collections.[2] What was once an archive of the community is now an institution which represents Black British history in the UK. The George Padmore Institute (GPI) was set up in 1991 and was created by its founder John La Rose, publisher and cultural and political activist.[3] The archive holds materials on 'the political and cultural history of people of Caribbean, African and Asian descent in Britain and Continental Europe'.[4]

While these archives were born out of early grassroots and political activist movements, there are some archives which are embedded within larger archival, state-run/mainstream institutions. For example, the Huntley Archives focuses on the work and lives of Jessica and Eric Huntley. They were Black political activists and radical publishers from Guyana who deposited their archives with London Metropolitan Archives (LMA) in 2005.[5] LMA is the principal archive for the City of London and Greater London area. The LMA consist of the records of local government, businesses, religious organisations, charities, hospitals and health authorities, schools, court records as well as the papers of families and individuals.[6]

The Huntley collection features both a personal and business collection of audio recordings, letters, leaflets, posters and original publishing material.[7] The LMA also works closely with the Friends of the Huntley Archive at LMA (FHALMA) which was established with a remit:

> to ensure that the Huntley's passion for writing the wrongs and inequalities in society, their decades of collaborative initiatives in community, their desire to achieve social justice, to advocate for educational interventions, to start up and support grassroots activist campaigns, their radical Black publishing ventures – all provide irrefutable evidence of the Black contributions to British life – and that Archives are an independent witness, one of the strong, comprehensively spoken, Black voices of the story of the 21st century.

FHALMA is a collaboration with the LMA, facilitating regular events created around the collection. By allowing communities to have regular collaborations, consultations and engagement with their own archives, the relationship between mainstream archives and communities are strengthened. LMA also houses the Cy Grant collection. Grant was a Guyanese actor, writer, musician and poet, and as one of the first West Indians to be regularly featured on British television, his collection contains Grant's writing, scripts and cast lists and campaigning material.[8]

I shall be exploring the significance of the Mollie Hunte Collection which was gifted to LMA in 2016 by Mollie's family and records the life of Mollie Angelia Hunte, an educational psychologist, educator and community activist. As the archivist for the Mollie Hunte Collection, I worked closely on Mollie's records to make them available to be accessed by the public. During the 1970s and 1980s it was unheard of that educational psychologists were available for parents and families to seek out. Those who knew Mollie regularly emphasised the importance of Mollie's presence in the education system, as a professional Black woman whose training and expertise were both greatly valued.

There are very few archival collections in London which focus specifically on the work and personal papers of Black women. Collections at LMA, the Black Cultural Archives and the British Library include the archives of author Andrea Levy, the business archives of Lorna Holder, which focus on Black women including Lorna Holder, a fashion designer and producer.[9] Furthermore, the Black Cultural Archives also holds the archives of Stella Dadzie, writer, historian and education activist, Melba Wilson, a journalist, activist and champion for mental health, and Suzanne Scafe, a lecturer and writer.[10]

Despite these archives being available to the public, this is still a small sample size and therefore the addition of Mollie Hunte's archives is unique in presenting the documents of a Black female educational psychologist, community activist and businesswoman. Mollie's collection explores her journey from arriving in Britain in 1961 until her passing in 2015 through research notes, diaries, event recordings and letters evidencing how people were impacted by her constant work. The significance lies with her name being relatively unknown and her archives allow historians to be able to understand who she was and why her work was vital to Black people's development through the education system in Britain, despite the racism and prejudice they faced.

EDUCATOR, PSYCHOLOGIST AND ADVOCATE

Mollie Hunte (1932–2015) was an educational psychologist from British Guiana, now Guyana. She was a significant part of the Black

Education Movement which spanned several decades beginning in the 1960s.[11] The Black Education Movement operated alongside the Black Supplementary Schools Movement and was created to aid Black children and their families against a racist education system.[12] The Black Supplementary School Movement arose as a response to an education system that perceived Caribbean culture and communities as being unable to raise intelligent children.[13] To counteract these racist ideas the Black community set up supplementary schools sometimes in private homes, for Black children who wanted assistance with their learning.[14] Much like other activists and educators of her time period, such as John La Rose, Mollie founded and co-founded a variety of community organisations in London, which advocated for Black children during a time when they faced racism and prejudice within the education system.

Mollie began her work as an assistant teacher in Georgetown, Guyana, from 1956 until 1961 when she decided to migrate to Britain to continue her higher education. She didn't have the financial means to be able to further her studies and see herself through university full time. Therefore, for twelve years, from 1961 to 1973, she taught in infant, junior and three types of special schools while she completed her part-time studies. During this period, she attended university to become an educational psychologist and attended Birkbeck College, the Institute of Education, the University of Birmingham and the Northeast London Polytechnic between 1964 and 1972.

In 1973 she joined the London Borough of Ealing as a Senior Officer in the Education Department. Due to her extensive training and knowledge, she was perfect for the position of Education Assessor, researching the educational needs of Black and Asian children.[15] In 1982 Mollie moved on from Ealing and became an Educational Psychologist for the London Borough of Brent where she expanded on her previous role in Ealing, producing reviews and assessments of children, liaising with teachers, schools and health authorities as well as aftercare services within the borough.[16]

Throughout her employment in Brent and Ealing, Mollie founded and co-founded various community organisations designed to aid Caribbean families in education, health and employment, as she felt the education system was failing young Black children due to racism. These organisations included the Caribbean Parents Group (CPG), The Caribbean Parents Group Credit Union (CPGCU), Westphi Academy and PEV Consultancy. The Caribbean Parents Group was formed in July 1975 and was created in reaction to Ealing Council's policy of moving children of African, Caribbean and Asian heritage outside their local catchment area to special schools or, as they were called at the time, 'Educationally Subnormal Schools'.[17] Parents and teachers in Ealing came together to oppose this action which they viewed as racist and an interference in their children's education.[18]

The CPG was a pressure group which offered support for Caribbean parents and children in a mixture of services, such as career advice and helping parents with their children's learning. The group also organised several events such as regular member meetings and annual conferences on many topics such as 'Black youngsters in the educational system' and care for the elderly.[19] The CPG also organised regular outings, including theatre visits, Christmas parties and travelling to different parts of England. In 1978 the CPG also set up two supplementary schools, to supplement Black children's education. They offered classes in a variety of subjects such as English and Mathematics.

The CPG allowed Mollie and other founders to focus on specific issues that affected the Black community. This meant using professional educators to work directly with young people and adults who needed guidance in different areas of their education, mental health and career development. This can be seen in the events programmes created for the community. For example, the CPG conference programme entitled 'Black Youth, Community and Employment' in 1981 features meeting minutes, financial reports and discussions on how the issue of Black youth unemployment can be rectified.[20] Mollie and members of the CPG brought the community together to discuss current and key issues which affected many, further emphasising Mollie's importance as a community facilitator and educator.

The Westphi Academy was also formed to support the Black community. Set up in July 1988, the organisation was formed initially from the surnames of the founding members of the consultancy in West London. The academy provided a wide array of services including in-service training, interviewing techniques and workshops explaining reform acts such as *The Education Reform Act 1988* which was passed and set up a National Curriculum for state schools and assessments with a structure of key stages for different age groups.[21]

Each founding member of Westphi was a consultant and had separate job roles which they held within the academy.[22] For example, Mollie's main area of expertise related to the special educational needs of children, as well as parental involvement in their children's education.[23] Westphi aimed to place the abilities of Black people at the forefront of training and education programmes and to counter the negative stereotypes of the Black community in higher education and beyond.[24]

In 1989 the PEV Consultancy was formed by Mollie to assist in creating psychological and educational services such as therapy sessions, counselling and assessments for neurodivergent children and adults.[25] Mollie was a consultant within the PEV and there are many examples within the archival collection, correspondence for instance, which demonstrate that Mollie's expertise was vital to the consultancy's success. She provided assessments of children and adults who were neurodivergent and felt that they were being neglected by the education system, and for individuals who had struggled with mental health issues, which had not been identified previously. Her work with children to assess their behavioural difficulties led to liaison with schools and racial equality departments across several boroughs.

Therefore, Mollie's expertise in the field of education was essential in being able to counter the racism against Black children and their families. She was able to provide services which many could access and advocate and support her community against a system that wanted to undermine them.

IMPACT AND LEGACY

The Mollie Hunte Collection is an example of a community archive, including large amounts of ephemera such as leaflets, posters and tickets for events.[26] These ephemera add value to the collection and allow us to see Mollie's wider interests, while also demonstrating the activities of a larger community of educators and activists. These records further enable us to understand Mollie's impact on her community, and the environment in which she combated and addressed the issue of anti-Black racism in education.

Within the collection there are examples of Mollie's kindness and supportive nature, not only towards her friends and family but also the people she worked with and helped. While living and employed in the London Borough of Ealing and Brent, Mollie worked with teachers, social workers and community workers, gaining a better understanding of her profession, and sharing her knowledge. In the 1970s, Mollie was part of a forum where she spoke with fellow educators. In a recording of the event Mollie can be heard stating her personal goals, and her desire to ensure that teachers are viewed as individuals who can continue to learn and grow within their profession.[27] Mollie also explains how she helped give parents and children a 'second life', by listening to them and aiding them through the educational struggles they faced.[28] The main objective of Mollie's work was to ensure that parents and children were treated with respect and empathy within the education system. This goal aligned with her role as a community leader.

Mollie's presence as a Black female educational psychologist, during a time when Black children were being disproportionally sent to 'Educationally Subnormal Schools', meant that she offered a wide breadth of desperately needed expertise to her community. Mollie was as a supportive figure who took the time to work with families, helping them to gain a better understanding of the education system, and teaching them how to best advocate for themselves and their children.

Mollie knew many influential individuals who were part of the Black Education Movement in the UK and who also advocated for the health of Black children and families. Mollie was a good friend of Dame Elizabeth Anionwu, Britain's first sickle cell and thalassemia nurse specialist and professor and dean of the nursing school at the University of West London.[29] Elizabeth also established the Mary Seacole Centre for Nursing Practice in 1998, to address racial inequalities in the nursing profession.[30] Elizabeth and Mollie first met during Mollie's time in the London Borough of Brent. In describing Mollie, Elizabeth expresses that she was a wonderful and incredibly intelligent individual, who in her unique role as a Black female educational psychologist in the 1980s was key to enacting great change.[31]

Additionally, Mollie's role within the London Borough of Brent meant that she was able to provide greater support for Black families dealing with health-related issues. Mollie's understanding and experience of working within the UK education system meant that she was well equipped when dealing with families, enabling her to provide advice to the parents of children who had sickle cell anaemia.

Furthermore, Mollie was a member of many organisations such as the Caribbean Communications Project (CCP), the Primary Curriculum Development Project (for Pupils of Caribbean Origin) and the Thomas Coram Research Institute. Within Mollie's papers there are minutes and correspondence which provide information on her roles and responsibilities in each organisation, where she advised, supported and collaborated with members of her community. The Caribbean Communications Project in particular was an organisation which aimed to 'promote literacy and other communications skills among adults of Caribbean origin and other people with similar needs'. This was created during the 1970s, with group members including Len Garrison, co-founder of the Black Cultural Archives. Within the organisation Mollie was a trainer for adult members providing advice and guidance.

Mollie was also a member of the Thomas Coram Research Unit, and on the University College, London, Advisory Committee during the 1980s. Along with Barbara Tizard, a British Psychologist who co-founded the Thomas Coram Research Unit in 1973, Mollie would consult on publications such as *Young Children at School in the Inner City* published in 1988 which studied the progress of British children in infant schools.[32] Through correspondence from the research unit, it's established that Mollie would consult around language and terminology used in these publications and on the psychology of Black children.[33]

Mollie has left us with a collection of her records which allows us to understand her significance as a Black woman living and working in late twentieth-century Britain. She gave many people the tools they needed to help themselves and their communities. Mollie Hunte was an extraordinary woman, who put her community first and had an impeccable drive to make a difference in people's lives. Fortunately, her legacy can continue within the archives and the public will be able to understand the impact she had on those around her through her records. Her decision to create and sustain several organisations tells us that Mollie saw problems which needed to be addressed and, alongside other activists, friends and community leaders, she made sure families were not left to fend for themselves. While Mollie was relatively unknown as an historical figure, her archives can grant her the recognition she deserves. During the period in which Mollie lived and worked it was unheard of for individuals to be able to seek out qualified Black female educational psychologists, who were available for the Black community. Therefore, Mollie's presence was incredibly valued, hence her archives are significant for the development of Black British history and understanding society through the eyes of a Black female professional woman who was embedded in the education system in Britain.

The archive can therefore grant us a new outlook on history, providing us with a greater understanding of how individual and collective contributions have shaped and shifted Britain's cultural landscape. Furthermore, seeing Black people and their experiences in the archive offers representation and a greater understanding of the crucial work done by previous generations. Collections such as Mollie's hold a tangible record of the history of Black communities and can be resources to positively reflect the contributions of those of Caribbean and African heritage. Through this tangible history of written communications and ephemera we can develop a greater understanding of the past and learn from this history.

NOTES

1. A. Flinn, M. Stevens and E. Shepherd, 'Whose Memories, Whose Archives? Independent Community Archives, Autonomy and the Mainstream', *Archival Science*, 9/71 (2009), pp. 71–86.
2. The Black Cultural Archives, 'About the Black Cultural Archives', https://blackculturalarchives.org/collections (accessed 14 August 2021).
3. The George Padmore Institute, www.georgepadmoreinstitute.org/about (accessed 12 August 2021).

4. A. Flinn, 'Community Histories, Community Archives: Some Opportunities and Challenges', *Journal of the Society of Archivists*, 28/2 (2007), pp. 151–76.
5. M. Roberts, 'The Huntley Archives at London Metropolitan Archives', in A. Livingstone (Author) and D. Sutton (ed.), *The Future of Literary Archives: Diasporic and Dispersed Collections at Risk* (Amsterdam: Amsterdam University Press, 2018), pp. 33–40.
6. Ibid.
7. Ibid.
8. The Cy Grant Trust, 'About Cy Grant', https://cygrant.com//about-cy-grant (accessed 15 July 2021).
9. Nottingham Trent University, 'Lorna Holder: Member of the Board of Governors', www.ntu.ac.uk/staff-profiles/board-of-governors/lorna-holder (accessed 29 April 2022).
10. Black Cultural Archives, Collections Overview, https://blackcultural archives.org/collections/overview (accessed 20 April 2022).
11. L.K. Johnson, 'In Memoriam: John La Rose (1927–2006)', *The Black Scholar*, 37/2 (2007), pp. 61–2.
12. Ibid.
13. K. Andrews, *Resisting Racism: Race, Inequality, and the Black Supplementary School Movement* (London: Institute of Education Press, 2013), pp. 60–1.
14. Ibid., pp. 17–18.
15. Ibid.
16. London Borough of Brent Notes, 1973–1978, LMA/4774/B/01/05, Mollie Hunte [Educational Psychologist] fonds, LMA.
17. Caribbean Parents Group Annual Reports, 1979–1994, LMA/4774/C/01/03/001.
18. Ibid.
19. Caribbean Parents Group Promotional Material, 1986–2000, LMA/4774/C/01/08/001.
20. Caribbean Parents Group Minutes, 1975–2000, LMA/4774/C/01/01.
21. T. Fisher, 'The Era of Centralisation: The 1988 Education Reform Act and Its Consequences', *FORUM*, 50/2 (2008), pp. 255–61.
22. Westphi Academy Conferences and Training, 1991–1998, LMA/4774/D/01/05/001, Mollie Hunte [Educational Psychologist] fonds LMA.
23. Ibid.
24. Ibid.
25. PEV Consultancy Notes, 1989–1991, LMA/4774/B/04/06/001, Mollie Hunte [Educational Psychologist] fonds, LMA.
26. Flinn et al., 'Whose Memories, Whose Archives?' pp. 71–86.
27. Mollie Hunte Pathway 1, 1975–1976, LMA/4774/B/02/07/001, Mollie Hunte Collection [Educational Psychologist] fonds, LMA.

28. Ibid.
29. Alex Mistlin, 'Elizabeth Anionwu: The "Cool, Black and Exceptional" Woman Who Fought to Make the NHS Fairer' (2020), www.theguardian.com/society/2020/dec/10/elizabeth-anionwu-the-cool-black-and-exceptional-nurse-who-fought-to-make-the-nhs-fairer (accessed 6 May 2022).
30. Ibid.
31. Adams Rebecca 'Londoners Archived', Mollie Hunte: Health Advocacy, May 2020, Spotify (No longer broadcast).
32. B. Tizard, P. Blatchford, J. Burke, C. Farquhar and I. Plewis, *Young Children at School in the Inner City* (1st edn) (London: Routledge, 1988), https://doi.org/10.4324/9781315210216.
33. Ibid.

15

'Black Footprints': A Trio of Experiences[1]

Zainab Abbas, Tony Soares and Ansel Wong

It is important for us to remember the history of how we got to where we are today and to be aware of the struggles that have been waged by our predecessors to get us here. It is too easy and convenient to act as if this is year zero in our struggles for justice and to mainstream our presence on the national landscape.

As three community activists we recount our experiences over the last 50 years as we confronted and challenged the barriers that hindered progress in our daily lives and developed strategies and projects to establish and defend our presence on the social, cultural and political landscapes of Britain. Our mantra was, come what may, we are here to stay. For each of us, different factors led to our parents and ourselves settling in, or migrating to Britain, that included opportunities for upward mobility, employment and tertiary education.

The three of us are former members of the Black Liberation Front (BLF), an organisation of activists that the Home Office described as an 'extremist organisation' and we will draw on our roles in that organisation plus other personal experiences, before and after BLF, to acknowledge the history of Black people in Britain and capture the contributions made by many activists and community champions so that we do not have to revisit battles waged and won or deny contemporary leaders and activists the importance of these historical linkages, if only to maintain continuity of practice. There have been too few opportunities for those of us directly involved in community politics and activism to reflect on the past: an absence of a Sankofa moment. And as memories fade, ill health intervenes and death occurs, these moments become more challenging to recall and verify and are thus lost as important memories and lessons to inform contemporary struggles.

This is our Sankofa moment – coming together to record our experiences in selected areas of our activism that we hope will lever more detailed research and evaluations by future scholars.

Each of us has different historical, cultural and political antecedents but, together, they underpinned our commitment to robustly challenge the structural inequalities and systemic injustices we all faced.

In this final chapter, the three of us have chosen to report on the different journeys we each had and continue to make.

ZAINAB ABBAS

Being born in Britain in 1950 rather than arriving as an immigrant had a profound and long-term impact on my psyche. Where do you belong when you have nowhere else to go? Added to this was my school's insistence that my mother should not speak Arabic to us, claiming it was slowing our grasp of the curriculum. My view of Egyptian culture was limited to conversations with my mother (having lost my father at an early age). I grew up knowing somehow that Elizabeth Taylor's depiction of Cleopatra was not a reflection of my culture, or my country of origin, but rather an attempt to 'whiten' one of the earliest great civilisations and deny its African origins.

However, Middlesbrough, the area I grew up in had its own challenges. One was 'posh' if one even had a job rather than living off state benefits. The poverty of our surroundings did not escape my notice but the racism within it confused me immensely. How can people with so little stake in society still feel the need to oppress others based on the colour of their skin? As soon as I was physically able, I moved south, first to Hull and then to Birmingham only to discover that experiences there were the same. The difference was in numbers.

To be a part of a Black community gave me both a sense of purpose and a sense of belonging. I joined the Birmingham Panthers and Beenie Brown, the founder of the Afro-Caribbean

Self-Help Organisation (ACSHO) who has archived the history of both organisations, not only proposed me as a member but took me to my first meeting. Black Power made sense to me then as it defined our narrative in an overwhelmingly white and racist country. I became active in teaching basic skills, particularly Maths and Black Studies at the Saturday school run by the ACSHO, a political and educational response to decolonise the curriculum, mitigate the negative impact of students' poor educational experiences and support their cognitive development to achieve academic success. We could but try.

As part of the Birmingham Panthers, I attended the first National Black Power Conference at Alexander Palace in May 1971 and heard Altheia Jones-LeCointe speak. She was and is a powerful orator. It was at this conference that I met many of the London-based Black Power activists.

After moving down to London in 1972, I met Olive Morris at the Gresham Project in Brixton, a youth development project with Gerlin Bean as its Principal Youth Worker. Olive invited me to move in with her and Liz Obi in a squat on Railton Road. She initiated me into the squatters' movement where our job was to break into empty properties, change the locks and then invite homeless Black families to move into them. It is interesting to note that the then head of housing for the London Borough of Lambeth was a white South African – even to this day this amazes me given the size of the Black population in Lambeth and the housing chief's apartheid background.

By the time I joined the BLF my politics were well defined. I wasn't interested in a narrow definition of Black nationalism as I was inspired not only by the Vietnamese war of independence but also the Pan-African movement and the Palestinian struggle. The attitude to our identity in the BLF was to encourage a holistic approach towards the concept of Blackness and all those people who were suffering. The concept of Blackness was based upon ideology as opposed to skin colour and so anybody who suffered from discrimination and was not white was Black. That encompassed not just people of African origin but the people of Caribbean, Chinese, Latin American, Asian and Indian origin too. That was the deliberate ideological approach that we took.

There were one or two people who argued the case of whether the Irish were Black or not and whether they should be included under that banner. The Irish was not recognised as Black but we acknowledged that the Irish occupied a similar position to our own people in Africa. Their struggle was an anticolonial one. We saw the Irish as very much part and parcel of the struggle for liberation but not as part of the Black community. We knew our struggle as Black people in this country was about justice and anticolonialism and anti-imperialism, the Irish struggle fitted well into that definition.

The BLF represented what I understood about liberation from my earliest consciousness and seemed focused on the need to prioritise engagement with comrades from all over the world. Hence, we became part of the International Panther network established by Eldridge and Kathleen Cleaver while they were exiled in Algeria. I believe it was in 1973 that Ansel Wong and myself went to interview Eldridge in Paris and after a hilarious interview session, during which I began crying with laughter at some of Eldridge's remarks, I established what has become a life-long friendship with Kathleen Cleaver.

In 1974 the BLF was invited to attend the 6th Pan-African Congress (PAC) in Dar es Salaam, Tanzania. It is important to note that of the three comrades representing the BLF within the British delegation in Dar, two were women, myself and Gerlin Bean, with Ansel Wong being the third representative. It was at this time that through my then partner, Emil Appolus, the former South West African Peoples' Organisation (SWAPO) UN representative, I was given personal letters of introduction to the Tanzanian representatives of the southern African liberation movements. I was fortunate enough to meet Herbert Chitepo, then ZANU leader and Marcelino dos Santos of FRELIMO (Mozambique) alongside many others. They completely understood the poverty of our situation as a Black community in the UK and asked only that we inform our people about their struggle and highlight their fight for liberation.

On my return I published a book on the 6th PAC for which I wrote the introduction and then wrote extensively, almost continuously, in *Grassroots Newspaper* about the international struggle for liberation. *Grassroots'* contributors often wrote articles under a pseudonym; for women it was Sister Yemi but I also wrote under my own name, most notably about Palestine.

Directly after the 6th PAC the three of us BLF representatives were invited both to Idi Amin's Uganda and to Somalia. We declined the invitation to Uganda as Idi Amin's politics did not align with ours and instead accepted the invitation to Somalia. It was for us an enriching experience and we were treated like visiting representatives of a state, rather than representatives of a Black organisation, the BLF.

Our Pan-African commitments later put us in touch with the Palestine Liberation Organisation (PLO) under Yasser Arafat and in 1977/8 I wrote a paper explaining to the PLO how diaspora Black people are their natural allies and should be approached to take on the Palestinian cause in European and North American capitals. I know these ideas were taken up and I am proud of our involvement in that struggle then and to this day.

One of the interesting things we are only now discovering is how much of a threat we appeared to the state. It is almost farcical to discover that annotations on Home Office documents recently released to the public indicate that they were particularly interested in the use of state funds to finance 'subversive' activities. They powers-that-be were worried that 'extremist organisations' like the BLF were using Operation Headstart and Ujima Housing Association for recruitment efforts and to send state funds to liberation movements like the New Jewel Movement in Grenada.

It would also appear that, as always, the state relied on informants in the Black community. For instance, a Home Office note stated: 'The inference from this would appear to be that the Ujima Housing Association is yet another front organisation for the Black Liberation Front (BLF) and exists solely to encourage and further the aims of its progenitor, and enquiries among more moderate leaders of the Black community in London have confirmed this inference.'[2]

Neither the Home Office nor 'moderate leaders' of the Black community understood the nature of our strategic intervention in developing infrastructure and independent agencies and survival platforms – the power of the community working in unity for the benefit for all. The BLF was committed to developing what Ansel

Wong coined as Central Communal Combative Centres (CCCC) and this is what we did with our bookshops, housing association, prisoner welfare scheme, legal aid advice, Saturday school, etc.

In early 1973 Gerlin invited Olive Morris, Liz Obi and myself to a meeting to discuss feminism and any problems we as women were having in our various Black organisations. We met at a sister's house (Marcia) in Brixton. She had a small child, so it was more convenient for us to meet there. At our first meeting, we named ourselves the Black Women's Group later to be renamed the Brixton Black Women's Group (BBWG). There is a lot of controversy around the founding of this Group as many people claim credit for its creation. I find this saddening as those of us who attended those early meetings know Gerlin Bean as the only founder. Gerlin was that much older, ten or eleven years, than the rest of us. However, her engagement with the radical feminist movement had been long-standing. She wanted us to focus on feminism within the Black Power movement and create a support network across the various groups we belonged to. It was an exciting time and interesting as all the women were powerful in themselves. None of us faced blatant misogyny and if we did come across it, had the strength and background to challenge it. However, within our community there were major issues which it was essential for us to address. This we did and as our discussions developed, so did our membership.

Barbara Beese of the Brixton Black Panthers later joined as did Leila Hassan of the Black Unity and Freedom Party. I recall they wanted to discuss 'Wages for Housework', a concept developed by Selma James, the wife of C.L.R. James. We had a heated debate about this because I felt that wages for housework was a concept our community could not relate to nor empathise with. It felt to me like a very white, middle-class concept, as many of the discussions in the white feminist movement were at that time. However, it was an important debate since we needed to define the parameters of feminism in our community. The BBWG should be remembered as part of the Black radical tradition that crossed organisational boundaries.

My groundings in Black activism and a physical presence in the heart of a major metropole provided ideal stepping stones for the setting up of my own public affairs and public relations agency, working with countries in Africa including Nigeria, Libya and South Africa. Reconnecting with activists, many of whom were then in government, added a dimension to my experience that has enhanced my understanding of struggle. I fully embrace the continuity of struggle, *aluta continua*, and bask in the actions of our young activists who are informing themselves about our past and not accepting the narratives written either by the state or those with a Eurocentric perspective who deny our history.

ANSEL WONG

Tony Soares and I were two of the early instigators who developed the BLF over its formative years. The organisation did not have a constitution or membership. Like most Black community organisations at the time, the development and management of activities coalesced around a dynamic individual. Tony Soares was the BLF's dynamo. As a teacher, I became the acceptable face of the organisation and being in full-time employment was able to sign contracts and leases where the governance of the BLF could not provide the necessary legal or regulatory requirements.

I am the offspring of a father from China and maternal concubinage of Caribbean, Spanish and African descent. In Trinidad where skin colour is prized, I was able to straddle all the various ethnicities of the country, taking pride in my diversity and championing the liquidity of my cultural and ethnic heritages. However, schooled in the verses of Wordsworth, Blake and Milton, proficient in British constitutional practice, taught about the Tudors and Stuarts and forced to memorise the annual tonnage of coal extracted from English coal fields, I was not prepared for what confronted me on arrival to the UK in 1965. Interestingly, not the weather but Hull University Fresher's Week. First item of induction for 'Overseas' students, courtesy of the British Council – How to flush the toilet. Laughable as this was, I do not count this as my epiphany or Road to Damascus revelation that led to my awareness of myself as an 'other'. Instead, like Nelson Mandela, my Black awareness grew as I was exposed to a 'steady accumulation of indignities' – several instances of individuals and institutions being explicit and implicit with their prejudices.

I learnt to manage these indignities without rancour, aggression or defeat. Instead, my accumulation was of lessons learnt from steeling myself reading and researching, curating projects and devoting time and energy to various community initiatives – Central Communal Combative Centres (CCCC) that became the frontlines of battle and resistance. Two milestones in my journey of activism were in 1971, the year I joined the BLF and the year I decided to learn but not return to my native Trinidad by accepting a full-time job teaching English at Sydenham Girls School. I decided to make London my home.

I immersed myself in several initiatives – fundraising to send ambulances to Haiphong, in North Vietnam; supported Caribbean students confronting racism at the Sir George Williams University in Canada; flirted with the liberation theology of the Catholic Church in Latin America; implemented a radical agenda for the West Indian Students' Centre in Earls Court; established the Black Arts Workshop showcasing performance poetry, agit prop plays and modern dance; read Pablo Freire's *Pedagogy of the Oppressed*; set up the C.L.R. James Supplementary School; ran the Shalom Project in East Harlem, New York, during my summer breaks from university; provided financial support from other UK activists for the families of soldiers who mutinied in Trinidad; and occupied the University of Hull as a member of the Radical Students Alliance and, being the only Black student, was nominated for a place, one of five, on the alternative university Senate. Radical associations were frowned upon and still having my Trinidad nationality, my government made it clear to two Trinidadians, Tony Martin, the Garvey scholar, and I, that a visit to Cuba to attend a student conference as the respective Chairs of the global body, Union of West Indian Students, and the UK branch, West Indian Students' Union UK would result in the loss of our nationality.

However, all of these activities strengthened my commitment to a radical agenda for change. I remain unmoved by the small individual indignities that I experienced in Hull and London. Being chased along the streets of Britain's smallest village in Hull, Yorkshire, Cottingham, by children asking to see my tail; contemptuous spitting from old codgers upset with me walking the streets of Hull with my white girlfriend; waiting for ages to be served at the Earl of

Granby pub in Hull; and having to cope with a novel experience of being nonchalantly given loaves of bread with no wrapping.

I was ready then to channel my frustrations and determination to initiate change into any meaningful opportunities. The BLF provided that opportunity for me. A political home where I could continue my activism after Hull University and the West Indian Students' Centre.

After 1971 there were two pathways for my growing awareness – the overtly political in the BLF and the radical educational in projects. I benefited from my role as secondary school teacher, learning from my students and participating in several educational projects and organisations that tackled the major issues – self-identity, under-achievement, expulsions, curriculum development and racism among teachers. I continued to take a special interest in issues and projects with an educational and cultural bias. I was active in the Caribbean Teachers' Association and helped to set up the Caribbean Club and the Fourth World Club (Women as the Fourth World) at Sydenham School and I joined several other groups championing Black Studies and Multicultural Education.

With this track record, I was invited to establish the Ahfiwe School in Brixton in 1973, funded by the Inner London Education Authority (ILEA) and managed by the Council for Community Relations in Lambeth (CCRL). Housed in the Gresham Project run by Gerlin Bean and the Reverand Tony Ottey, Ahfiwe was the first publicly funded supplementary school providing out of school learning seven days a week for all ages – school trips to France, workshops, festivals, supervised homework sessions, lectures, films, etc.

My activism was like two concentric circles: the BLF in one orbit and my professional career in another with some overlapping. The development of the Ahfiwe School in Brixton and the Elimu Community Education Centre in Westminster grew out of my goal to create and curate community alternatives to state education not as supplements but as revolutionary, liberation centres that can become a *Comuniversity*, a multi-level learning platform for the whole community. Not supplementary education but centres of learning to celebrate, educate and commemorate us as a people and a community. Our motto: Each One Teach One.

I was able to navigate between these two circles, using my contacts and experiences to help develop and manage projects for the BLF as a form of voluntary activism – not a full-time position but a full-time commitment, sworn to at each meeting, to its revolutionary principles.

Like the calypsonian, there were two sobriquets we used – Sister Yemi for the sisters of the BLF and Ade Kimathi for the male members. It is as Ade Kimathi that I edited the *Grassroots Newspaper.* We thought we were clever using this tactic but at my cross-examination at the trial of Tony Soares, the prosecuting attorney boldly displayed a file that had an annotation that Ansel Wong is Ade Kimathi.

Two projects that deserve special mention for the impact they had on the Black community – Ujima Housing Association that Tony Soares writes of below and the Prisoner Welfare Scheme ran by Pauline Wilson. Pauline ran a prison visitor service to support prisoners on remand or serving a sentence. One of the students that I taught at Bulmer College was a major recipient of our services. Pauline arranged prison visits, legal aid and a letter writing scheme involving BLF members. I was one of many who used their homes to support released prisoners with resettlement licences to prepare for their independent living.

TONY SOARES

Many housing associations were set up to complement the housing work of local authorities by housing people from their waiting list as well as people who were made involuntarily homeless.

Nestled among them were a few associations promoting good 'race relations', the expression used at the time to refer to efforts aiming to tackle racism. For example, the Inter-Racial Housing Association promoted 'integration' by specifying each property would be split into two flats, one let to a white family and the other to a 'coloured' family. The Metropolitan Coloured Peoples' Housing Association was set up by the wife of the Governor-General of Jamaica, Lady Molly Huggins. She had returned to the UK when Jamaica achieved independence with numerous servants. She wanted somewhere to house them and created the Metropolitan Coloured Peoples' Housing Association that later became the Metropolitan Housing Trust.

In the main, these associations housed very few Black people, most being housed under nomination agreements with local authorities. Most of the people on the local authorities' date order waiting lists had been white people who had to spend years on these lists. Enter the Black Liberation Front. In 1977 a group of Black housing workers, Leo Clouden, Tina McLeod, Basil Williams and myself, got together and were advised by the Commission for Racial Equality (CRE) to set up a Housing Association to meet the needs of the mainly single people and couples without children. For these people, even if they were homeless there was no statutory responsibility to provide housing.

We established Ujima which, although it was not the first Black and minority housing association, quickly emerged as the major one. There were some Black and minority housing associations in the North of England but not in London. By the time Ujima was founded, frustration had long simmered in the London streets particularly among Black youths. Many young people, particularly girls, had to negotiate the hard edge of conflict between their growing independence and their parents' imposition of strict regimes of behaviour. Failure to comply resulted in being thrown out of their parental home. Among the Asian communities, there were complaints of being barred from the best jobs and council housing despite the 1968 Race Relations Act. The CRE had been established to tackle racial discrimination and promote racial equality. Housing, however, was outside its remit despite various reports of inequality in housing and the entrenched racism in many housing policies.

The Home Office was not far off the mark by defining as 'extremist organisations' the Black Liberation Front and allied organisations like the Afro-Caribbean Self-Help Organisation in Birmingham. Released Home Office files show that there were internal Home Office investigations into what they saw as 'BLF initiatives like Ujima Housing Association and Operation Headstart'. The latter was indeed a BLF project that wanted to shed its housing project (Ujima) which was becoming difficult to manage and run with only voluntary help. Operation Headstart asked the newly formed Ujima Housing Association to take the six short life properties it managed. It also offered a start-up fund of £200 as an added inducement.

We accepted and I became the first unpaid coordinator and Leo Clouden, a social worker in Hackney, became the chairman of the management committee. We opened a drop-in housing aid centre at 773 Harrow Road in London, premises taken over from the BLF's Unity Books, a Black bookshop that had been firebombed. We made no attempt to hide the relationships and synergies between the BLF and these various projects. These community projects relied heavily on the voluntary activism of several individuals willing to use their expertise and employment status to drive our agenda for change. You didn't have to be a member of the BLF to get involved.

Together with Leo Clouden's expertise with Black youths in London and my knowledge gained as an employee of the Threshold Advice Centre and Housing Association, we managed Ujima for its first three years as volunteers. An Urban Aid grant application to the Greater London Council was successful. Ujima was able to appoint me as a paid coordinator and Terry Rocque as Ujima's first paid housing officer responsible for collecting rent from 70 short life properties, housing mainly young Black people sharing kitchens and costs for utilities. Because housing development took as long as 12–18 months to get formal approval, empty properties were targeted for occupation and squatting. Ujima was able to reach an agreement to occupy these properties rent free and used them to build its portfolio.

Ujima secured registration with the Housing Corporation in 1980 and was able to access government capital finance for its own projects but there remained many obstacles as there was a marked reluctance to give us a Housing Association Grant (HAG), capital funding of housing associations. Ujima tried to become as independent as possible and exercised tight control of standards, but it was not until 1982 that it was allowed to undertake its own development. Notwithstanding these obstacles, Ujima's rate of general development was phenomenal but we still struggled to acquire sufficient permanent self-contained housing. In no time, Ujima branched into new areas, a single parent's project, a youth unemployment project (Finsbury Park Project), a housing advice centre and 28 Manpower Services Commission (MSC)-funded building and training projects and hostels. Managing housing for young Black people who were increasingly being marginalised, ready to resist and uncompromising in their demands was a major challenge for agencies. Ujima turned out to be the only Black organisation that could deliver and address the housing needs of these young Black people. We established several small special housing schemes, including hostels for young mothers and for single people, some developed in partnership with other housing associations under development agreements.

Eventually, Ujima was allowed to redevelop its own properties and its first scheme was in Islington at Hornsey Rise, a project that was considered as an exemplar of community development. Soon there were 800 young people living in shared housing in short life properties made habitable by funding from the MSC. There were two major hostels – a 13-room hostel for young girls in Colville Terrace, Notting Hill, that Ansel Wong and his wife managed and in the London Borough of Haringey, the Philip Lane hostel. This was the golden period of Ujima that saw committed individuals getting involved and giving of their expertise and time to make the organisation better. Staff numbers grew under my leadership. I decentralised Ujima's housing management operations with seven area offices and localised staff. Liverpool's celebrated activist and pioneer, Dorothy Kuya, took on the governance as Chair of Ujima and its offices occupied two floors in Kilburn High Road with over 50 staff. Herman Ouseley, now Lord Ouseley, succeeded Dorothy Kuya as Chair and Ujima's progress continued apace.

Ujima had a good relationship with London's local authorities, many of which were Labour controlled. It proved that there was scope for genuine community-based housing associations catering for the housing and other needs of the nation's Black communities that were largely housed in the insecure private rented sector in areas with multiple disadvantages. We understood the pressures of managing a housing association without the rental income to employ experienced staff. However, Ujima was in a different boat, it had healthy cash reserves from the short life housing it provided on a large scale and its MSC-funded schemes made the houses temporarily habitable until the properties were required for redevelopment or clearance. Soon the Association had a cash reserve of £1,000,000 which allowed it to invest in projects relevant to Black people. However, May 1987 was a significant watershed. Disappointed with the bickering at the management committee, I announced my resignation with November 1987 as my last month of service.

CONCLUSION

The organisational framework and governance of the BLF were just buttresses for the activities of individual projects. It is not surprising that the BLF, as the framework, gradually lost its importance due to volunteers' time and income streams being expended in managing these projects. In time, these projects required total engagement and participation and the role of the BLF as the mothership became less and less important for us.

During the 16 years of our involvement, over 50 activists participated in the work of the BLF. We initiated several projects that included *Grassroots Newspaper*, Operation Head Start, Unity Books, Grassroots Storefront, Ujima Housing Association, the Prisoner Welfare Scheme, Saturday school, Legal Aid Centre, international relations, publications, Head Start Books & Crafts, youth hostels and defence campaigns, among others. This work was extensive, ambitious and timely. Framed within our ideology of Revolutionary Black Nationalism and informed by the liquidity of Blackness that reflected the multiplicity of ethnicities, skin colour, nationality and heritages that define us, the three of us spent a major part of our lives finding solutions to mitigate and eradicate the systemic and structural inequalities that affected every part of our lives. And, in our retirement, the struggle continues.

NOTES

1. In Memory of Ken Braithwaite, 1935–2021.
2. 'Disaffected Young West Indians', Special Branch report, 15 November 1982, p. 4 in The National Archives (TNA) HO 376/222.

Notes on Contributors

Zainab Abbas is the former international Secretary of the Black Liberation Front. After attending the 6th Pan African Congress in 1974 she published and produced a book of major conference speeches entitled *The Resurgence of Pan Africanism* (Kalahari Publications, 1974). She is also the co-author (with Nicholas Hyman) of *Responsible Reporting? Libya in the Western Press* [4 vols.] (Highclere, 1981). Zainab was a founding member of the Brixton Black Women's Group along with Olive Morris, Girlin Bean and Liz Obi. In 1980 she founded the first black owned PR and Public Affairs Agency in the U.K., working mainly with African and Middle Eastern countries.

Rebecca Adams is currently working at London Metropolitan Archives (LMA) as an Archivist of the Africa Centre Collection. She was previously the archivist for the Mollie Hunte Collection also available at LMA. Her research interests include decolonising archives, community archives and archival representation. She is currently part of the International Council on Archives, New Professionals Programme for 2023.

Kate Bernstock is a researcher and educator of Black British History, specialising in historiographical reconstructions which counter history's tendency to continue the violent archive's abuse of its subjects. She finds inspiration in the work of Saidiya Hartman, Zakkiyah Iman Jackson, Stephanie Smallwood and Christienna Fryar.

Perry Blankson is a columnist at *Tribune* magazine and has a historical interest in the 'British Black Power' movements of the post-war period and beyond, with a particular historical focus in the response of the state to such organising. He is a project coordinator at the Young Historians Project, a collective encouraging the development of young historians of African and Caribbean heritage in Britain. He is a member of the editorial working group for the *History Matters Journal*.

Rey Bowen is a PhD student at the University of Chichester researching for a thesis entitled 'Dusé Mohamed Ali's Pan-Africanism 1912–1945: His influence Across the African Diaspora'. He has over 25 years of experience working in further, higher and private education and is currently a member of the editorial working group of the *History Matters* journal.

A.S. Francis is a PhD student at the University of Chichester, researching women's involvements in Britain's Black radical organisations during the 1960s–1980s, and the development of a Black women's movement. Francis' book celebrating the longstanding and far-reaching activism of Gerlin Bean, is to be published by Lawrence & Wishart in 2023 as part of a series of publications about Black Radical women. Francis is also a consultant to the Young Historians Project, member of the History Matters collective and co-founder of the *History Matters Journal*.

Hannah Francis is currently a Trainee at the Runnymede Trust, the UK's leading race equality thinktank, working across two major work-strands: research and policy. After completing an MRes in the History of Africa and the African Diaspora at the University of Chichester in 2021, they joined the Young Historians Project as a volunteer researcher and is currently a member of editorial working group for the *History Matters Journal*.

Annabelle Gilmore is a PhD student at the University of Birmingham funded by AHRC Midlands4Cities. Her thesis is in collaboration with the National Trust and is analysing the hidden connections between slavery and imperialism and the country house of Charlecote Park in Warwickshire. She is also working on how to bring these histories to the public.

Aleema Gray is completing a PhD on a history of the Rastafari movement in Britain at Warwick University. Aleema's work focuses on documenting Black history in Britain through the perspective of lived experiences. Her research is driven by a concern for more historically contingent ways of understanding the present, especially in relation to notions of belonging, memory, and contested heritage. She was previously the Community History Curator at the Museum of London and a founding member of the Young Historians Project.

Christian Høgsbjerg is a Senior Lecturer in the School of Humanities and Social Science at the University of Brighton, and the author of *C.L.R. James in Imperial Britain* (Duke University Press, 2014) and co-author of *Toussaint Louverture: A Black Jacobin in the Age of Revolutions* (Pluto, 2017). He has recently co-edited *The Red and the Black: The Russian Revolution and the Black Atlantic* (Manchester University Press, 2021) and *Revolutionary Lives of the Red and Black Atlantic since 1917* (Manchester University Press, 2022).

Elanor Kramer-Taylor is a Ph.D. student at King's College London. Her research explores the relationship between the Caribbean diaspora in Britain and independence movements in the British West Indies after 1945. Her thesis aims to recentralise Caribbean decolonisation in the politics of West Indians in Britain and is particularly concerned with figures on the political left.

Montaz Marche is a historian, writer and PhD researcher at the University of Birmingham, currently focusing on black women in eighteenth-century London. She is part of the editorial working group of the *History Matters Journal*, is the Artistic Director of the Ruckus Theatre Company and works regularly in historical public engagement, historical consultancy, media and television. Her recent publications include: 'Centring Blackness: A Focus on Gender and Critical Approaches Through Black Women's Lives,' for the *European History Quarterly*.

Tony Soares was a founder member of the Black Liberation Front.

Claudia Tomlinson is currently a PhD researcher at the University of Chichester, completing a thesis titled: 'Biography of Jessica Huntley: A Political History of Radical Black Activism'. Her research is due to be published by Bloomsbury Academic (2024) as part of its Black Literary and Cultural Expressions Series. She is also the author of a chapter in the forthcoming *Handbook of Contemporary British History* (Routledge, 2025). Claudia is also a member of the editorial working group of *History Matters Journal*.

Theo Williams is a historian of modern Britain and its connections with the wider world. His research focuses in particular on the politics of race and empire. He is the author of *Making the Revolution Global: Black Radicalism and the British Socialist Movement before Decolonisation* (Verso, 2022).

Ansel Wong is a cultural and community activist campaigning for creative diversity and against discriminatory practices and a former member of the Black Liberation Front. He received a CBE in the Queen's birthday honours in 2022 for the promotion of the arts and culture. He has written extensively on Carnival arts, his publications include: with David Sutcliffe, *The Language of the Black Experience*, (Blackwells, 1986) and, with Akyaaba Addai-Sebo, *Our Story: A Handbook of African History and Contemporary Issues* (London Policy Studies Unit, 1988).

Olivia Wyatt is a PhD student at Queen Mary University of London whose research concentrates on the politics of complexion within Black British communities during the twentieth century. She has written for *History Matters Journal*, BBC Radio 4 and *History Today*, she also writes for Harewood House about the estate's imperial relationship with the Caribbean.

Index

PLUTONIAN PLUTO PRESS PATREON SUPPORTER | SOLIDARITY LEVEL 4

The Pluto Press Newsletter

Hello friend of Pluto!

Want to stay on top of the best radical books we publish?

Then sign up to be the first to hear about our new books, as well as special events, podcasts and videos.

You'll also get 50% off your first order with us when you sign up.

Come and join us!

Go to bit.ly/PlutoNewsletter